D1473969

Itinerant
Ambassador

Itinerant Ambassador

The Life of Sir Thomas Roe

by Michael J. Brown

THE UNIVERSITY PRESS OF KENTUCKY

Lexington : 1970

CONTENTS

FOREWORD

THERE is a certain charm that lies upon many of the figures, as of their writings, of the early seventeenth century—those halcyon years of internal peace before the Civil War, of which Clarendon wrote so movingly in his Autobiography. It is partly a question of style, both of life and manner, as expressed in their letters no less than in their poetry and painting. The long peace at home, ensured by the wise rule of Elizabeth I, enabled characters to grow up well rounded and civilized, to develop their own idiosyncrasy and tastes.

Of such was Sir Thomas Roe, of whom this biography gives us a faithful and reliable account. His career touched the life of the time at several significant points; indeed he made a marked contribution to it, was a part of it, a well known and much esteemed figure. For, after youthfully spending his inheritance in exploring the Amazon, doing his bit to open up South America, he became one of the best and most relied-on diplomats of the day.

"Of a pregnant understanding, well spoken, learned, industrious, and of a comely personage," he was first sent to the Court of the Mogul Emperor at Delhi to establish English trade on a sure footing. In this he was successful and made history— from this ultimately flowered the astounding British Raj in India. It is evident that Shah Jehangir had a personal respect for the portly, genial, dignified Englishman, who, a man of taste, presented the Mogul with a choice miniature by Isaac Oliver. And Roe's vivid Journal is the best record of Indian history in those years, events at the Mogul Court, its personalities and scenes.

Next, Roe spent seven years as ambassador at Constantinople, with similar good results for English trade and a comparable account of Turkey in his racy descriptive letters. A scholarly man, he found this a good post for collecting Greek manuscripts and coins, most of which came to the Bodleian at Oxford. His religious discussions with the Greek Orthodox Church bore fruit later in good relations with the English church, and are of ecumenical interest today. He was caught up in the diplomatic complexities of the Thirty Years' War on the Continent, partly through his constant devotion to the interests of James I's daughter, Elizabeth, the Winter Queen of Bohemia, whose husband had brought about the war by accepting that crown. Elizabeth took refuge in Holland: it was from her daughter's son, George I, that the British royal family of today descends, who were given priority over the senior lines of descent from Elizabeth's brother, Charles I, because they were Protestants.

In his correspondence with Elizabeth we see "honest Thom Roe," or "honest fat Thom Roe," as she sometimes called him, at his best, for he was not only exceptionally intelligent and kindly, but, what was rarer among politicians, honest. It was just this combination that made him so successful a diplomat. On this opponents agreed: the Emperor Ferdinand said that as an ambassador he was irresistible, while the great Gustavus Adolphus allowed politely that it was Roe who impelled him to take the plunge into the Thirty Years' War—and that settled the issue.

Roe, who had begun life as an Esquire in attendance on Queen Elizabeth, knew exactly the right tone to take with Court ladies, with princesses and queens in good or ill fortune. Coming back from the Orinoco he presented the young Princess with a parrot, a great rarity. When she grew up to become a queen without a throne and sent Roe her portrait, he replies with courtly gallantry that the gift made "my house a Court, my chamber a Presence [chamber] . . . . No adversity hath power to banish those smiles which yet smile upon us." And he subscribes himself, "your Majesty's unfruitful, humble, honest, east, west, north, and south servant." And this he faithfully was.

It will be seen that Professor Michael Brown has a charming no less than a significant subject. There are many such rewarding themes in the rich field of our past, in which Americans and British share alike, and it is a pleasure to welcome younger American scholars into exploring it and giving us the fruits of their research, as this book admirably does.

A. L. Rowse

PREFACE

THOMAS ROE was born near London in 1580 or 1581. His family was a prominent one in the city and produced three lord mayors within the space of a generation. Young Thomas made the most of his family's influence and embarked upon the life of a courtier. He served the aging Elizabeth and later developed intimate and lasting friendships with the children of King James I. The patronage of Prince Henry (and the support of men like Sir Walter Raleigh and the earl of Southampton) gave Roe an opportunity to lead an English expedition to the Amazon and to make a modest contribution to the record of English exploration.

The voyage to Guiana formed a dramatic prologue to Roe's career, but a more substantial phase began in 1615 when he was sent by King James as ambassador to the court of the Great Mogul at Ajmere. Chosen for this important and delicate work by the East India Company, Roe spent three years in India and succeeded in winning valuable concessions for English merchants. On the basis of his experience he offered the company a good deal of sound advice and, in fact, laid down the policy that guided their actions for more than a century. Roe has a strong claim to be regarded as the first of the long line of Englishmen who constructed, over many years, the British dominion in India.

Upon his return to England Roe became active in the affairs of the Virginia Company, but before long he was off on his travels again. In 1621 he sailed for Constantinople to continue the double role he had played in India: this time he was both ambassador and the representative of the Levant Company. During the seven years he spent at the Ottoman Porte he was instrumental in bringing about a material improvement in the fortunes of the company and at the same time was busily engaged in intricate negotiations that were part and parcel of the complex diplomacy of the Thirty Years War.

His service in Constantinople added fresh laurels to the fine record Roe had made in India; so it was not surprising that, upon his return to England, he was almost immediately chosen for yet another overseas mission. This time his instructions were to help to negotiate a peace treaty between Sweden and Poland that would pave the way for Swedish intervention in Germany. The treaty was made and Gustavus Adolphus embarked upon his remarkable career of conquest with the acknowledgment that the work of Sir Thomas Roe had been instrumental in making his great enterprise possible.

Roe's mission to the North was followed by an enforced retirement of almost eight years. Although he was without any official post he did everything he could to aid the unfortunate queen of Bohemia, a friend from childhood days with whom Roe carried on across the years a correspondence full of interest and charm. On two occasions he was sent by Charles I to negotiate on behalf of the queen, but all efforts were made ineffectual by the king's inability to commit sufficient resources to influence continental affairs in his sister's favor. Roe, for his part, was impatient with half measures and expressed himself fearlessly. He was dedicated to the view that England should be actively involved in Europe. He poured out a deluge of letters to the leading figures of his time pleading for the creation of a strong Protestant alliance against the Hapsburgs. He worked untiringly for any cause that promised to help to bring about the restoration of Elizabeth and her family in the Palatinate. His persistence did not make him popular at the court of King Charles. Accordingly he was disqualified from the high political posts which, on grounds of sheer knowledge and ability, he was eminently qualified to hold. But for all that, he was elected to parliament on three different occasions, was sent on half a dozen diplomatic missions, and late in life was appointed a privy councillor. Along the way he found time to dabble in efforts to establish a West Indies Company and for several years was the principal supporter of an organized attempt to promote unity among the major Protestant churches of Europe. Whether in office or out he carried on a marvelously comprehensive correspondence that demonstrated a keen grasp of contemporary affairs.

When civil war came to England Roe was a convinced advocate of the middle way. Although he was critical of royal policy he could not sever the ties of service and affection that bound him to the House of Stuart. Ill health and advancing age made it possible to avoid taking sides, and he died in 1644 while the issue between Charles I and his subjects was still in the balance.

Even this sketchy outline of Roe's activities suggests the unusual range of his experiences and hints at the importance of his career. Yet in the works of modern historians Sir Thomas Roe has been a dimly viewed figure, lurking in the wings, but never brought to the center of the stage. His name is mentioned quite regularly—and always with some admiring comment—in books that deal with the diplomatic and commercial history of the first half of the seventeenth century. Occasionally in the past some particular phase of his eventful career has attracted concentrated attention; but, despite the urgings of prominent contemporary scholars—C. V. Wedgwood, A. L. Rowse, G. E. Aylmer, and David Mathew among them—no full biography has ever been attempted.

This must be regarded as a regrettable oversight. By any standards, Roe was one of the most capable diplomats of his time and his career was intertwined with developments of capital importance: colonial and commercial expansion, the beginnings of empire, foreign relations, religious movements, domestic dissent. His dealings brought him into contact with a broad array of seventeenth-century luminaries ranging all the way from Sir Walter Raleigh to Archbishop William Laud and from Queen Elizabeth of Bohemia to the Great Mogul Emperor of Hindustan. Moreover, the materials for a study of his life are plentiful and of easy access. He was a prolific letterwriter, a diligent author of official dispatches, and an entertaining reporter of the exotic sights to which his peripatetic career exposed him. The Public Record Office, the British Museum, and the published collections of state papers are rich in the raw materials of his story. The lack of a biography is not attributable to any scarcity of evidence. But it may, perhaps, be explained on other grounds.

Although Roe was a most attractive figure, worthy of the respect of any biographer, there is something both elusive and frustrating in his story. His activities were so varied and ranged over such a wide area that anyone who presumes to describe his career must become involved in territories that lie at the fringes of conventional English history. To skip from Guiana to India, to Constantinople, to Sweden and Germany, with any number of intermediate stops along the way, necessitates a good deal of "scene-setting" and an inevitable lack of penetration that specialists will find irritating. Certainly I am all too keenly aware of my own lack of expertise in some of the areas where the itinerant Sir Thomas has led. But a strong conviction of the importance and the intrinsic interest of Roe's career has persuaded me to launch out, albeit with the hope that those readers who see their areas of special interest being treated with less authority than they could wish, will deal charitably with the intruder.

It is a pleasure publicly to acknowledge my gratitude to a number of people who, in one way or another and over a long span of time, have helped me in writing this book. At Emory University, Professors Ross H. McLean and Walter D. Love guided me in the early stages. More recently, Professor A. L. Rowse has twice read my manuscript, talked with me about it, and made many helpful suggestions. I hasten to add that he must not be held responsible for any of the opinions that now appear; the material that has survived successive rounds of editing is attributable to me alone. I am especially grateful to Professor Rowse for having written the Foreword. The trustees of Agnes Scott College generously made possible my research in England where, at every turn, I benefited from the courteous assistance of librarians, archivists, and curators.

My wife, Lee Hale Brown, has been a source of constant encouragement and help; while Julie, Colin, and Kathryn with good humor have accepted Sir Thomas as being sufficient excuse for tales untold and games unplayed.

CHAPTER 1
The First Adventure

In Elizabethan days London enjoyed an ascendancy over the rest of England even greater than it exercises today. It was a colossus whose actions were felt in every corner of the island. More than ten times as populous as the next largest city, it aroused both wonder and resentment in the people of other towns who often complained that London was taking away their trade and attracting their ambitious young men. By 1600 London handled seven-eighths of England's trade; it provided most of the country's industrial capital, and it constituted by far the biggest single market in the land.

London belonged to its merchants. Governed by its mayor and aldermen, the city was a bourgeois island in an otherwise aristocratic and monarchical state. On both sides it was flanked by symbols of royal power: Westminster and Whitehall to the west and the Tower to the east. But between these markers was the domain of the merchants who operated through their venerable companies and guilds to regulate the life of their city and push their influence far afield into distant lands they had never seen. They were an advancing class in an aggressive state and were fully aware that, no matter what appearances might suggest to the contrary, they and their city represented the true foundation of England's strength.

For all its great importance London in the days of Elizabeth was not the sprawling confusion that it is today. It scarcely spilled beyond the limits set by Westminster and the Tower, and even in the busiest city street the influence of the country-side was not wholly absent. For those who could afford them, comfortable homes in peaceful hamlets were within leisurely distance of the centers of commerce. London was expanding rapidly beyond her walls, but quiet footpaths linked the city to a cluster of villages around its northern rim, where lived many of the merchants who by day made the decisions that regulated the economic affairs of the kingdom.

Among the earliest of the villages to become popular as residential areas for the wealthy merchants of London were Hackney, Walthamstow, Leyton, and Woodford. By the time of Elizabeth each of these places had residents who belonged to a family that spelled its name variously "Roe," "Rowe," and "Row."[1] They seem to have had their roots in Kent, but, as so often happened, London had exerted its attraction and, by the beginning of the sixteenth century, a member of the family named Reynard Roe had moved from country to town. It is not known how he fared, but his son Robert must have prospered, for he was recognized as a full-fledged citizen of London and became a member of the influential Merchant Tailors.[2] The family fortunes leaped forward in the hands of the next generation. By 1560 Robert's son Thomas had been chosen an alderman of the city. Soon afterwards he was knighted, and then, in 1568, he was elected lord mayor of London.

Like many other men of his day who had accumulated wealth in the world of commerce, Sir Thomas Rowe was eager to provide his family with the status and stability that only the ownership of land could give. Even before he achieved any real prominence in the city he purchased some property in the Isle of Ely.[3] He did not keep this for long, but a few years later he paid almost £800 for the manor of Slapton in Buckinghamshire.[4] This had been monastic land, but it was granted to

---

[1] A. P. Wire, "An Essex Worthy: Sir Thomas Roe," *Essex Review* 20 (1911): 135.

[2] William Herbert, *The History of the Twelve Great Livery Companies of London* (London, 1836), 2:427.

[3] R. B. Pugh, ed., *The Victoria History of the County of Cambridge and the Isle of Ely* (London, 1938–1960), 4:105.

[4] *Calendar of the Patent Rolls* (London, 1939), II Elizabeth, 25 January 1560, 1:311; William Page, ed., *The Victoria History of the County of Buckingham* (London, n.d.–1928), 3:412.

Rowe by the Crown and it was retained by his descendants for several generations.[5] In the years that followed, Sir Thomas added steadily to his possessions: a number of dwelling houses and shops in London;[6] two manors in Bedfordshire with rectory and advowson;[7] more properties in London, and the manor of Shacklewell in Middlesex which had once been the home of Sir Thomas More's youngest daughter Cecilia and her husband, Giles Heron.[8] Finally, in 1568 (the year that he was lord mayor) he bought the place that came to be regarded as the seat of the Rowe family, the manor of Higham Bensted, grandly situated on a hill above the river Ley in Walthamstow, Essex.[9]

During these years Rowe's reputation as a man of substance was enhanced by numerous charitable contributions. He paid to enclose an acre of ground near Bedlam to be used as a burial site for the dead of London parishes that did not have suitable graveyards. He erected a gallery at Paul's Cross for gentlewomen to stand in to hear the sermons. And at his death he gave to the Merchant Tailors a hundred pounds for eight poor men and land to support ten more.[10] For these, and for his more general services to London's mercantile community, Sir

[5] Edward Rowe Mores, "The History and Antiquities of Tunstall in Kent," in *Bibliotheca Topographica Britannica* (London, 1790), 1 (no page numbers).

[6] *Calendar of the Patent Rolls*, II Elizabeth, 22 November 1560, 1:405.

[7] William Page and H. Arthur Doubleday, eds., *The Victoria History of the County of Bedford* (Westminster, 1904–1918), 3:129; *Calendar of the Patent Rolls*, III Elizabeth, 20 October 1561, 2:88.

[8] *Calendar of the Patent Rolls*, VI Elizabeth, 5 June 1564, 3:15; ibid., 24 October 1564, 3:142; *Noble Collection* (Guildhall Library ref. c. 78), "Rowe," p. 22.

[9] *Calendar of the Patent Rolls*, VIII Elizabeth, 20 May 1566, 3:417. It may be noted that there is an apparent discrepancy in the date of this reference—an entry dated 1566 referring to a sale made in 1568. Actually, the letter patent simply gave permission to Thomas Heron, the owner of the manor, to alienate his property, along with other lands in Essex and Middlesex, to Thomas Rowe. See also Mores, "The History and Antiquities of Tunstall in Kent," p. xvii; Philip Morant, *History and Antiquities of Essex* (London, 1768), 1:35; Wire, "An Essex Worthy: Sir Thomas Roe," p. 136.

[10] *Noble Collection*, "Rowe," p. 22; John Stow, *A Survey of London*, ed. Charles L. Kingsford (Oxford, 1908), 1:114; Herbert, *The History of the Twelve Great Livery Companies of London*, 2:485, 504.

Thomas was commemorated by a portrait hung in the great hall of his guild.[11] He had won for himself genuine distinction and for his family a position of influence and esteem. He died in 1570 and was buried in the church at Hackney in Middlesex. There a suitable monument was raised to him. It depicted a knight in armor with his lady at his side and was accompanied by one of the light, tripping verse epitaphs that the age deemed appropriate.[12]

Sir Thomas Rowe's wife for thirty-one years had been Mary, the daughter of Sir John Gresham, who, like Rowe, had once been lord mayor of London. Mary had borne her husband eleven children. Six of them had survived the perils of infancy, grown up, and reared families of their own. Of the four boys—John, Henry, William, and Robert—three achieved considerable stature and added luster to the already distinguished record of their family.

John was the oldest. He inherited his father's Bedfordshire estates and became sheriff of the county. Henry, like his father, became a prominent figure in the world of city government and commerce. In 1597 he served as sheriff of London and Middlesex; in July 1603 he was knighted by the new king, and four years later he became lord mayor of London. When he was able to get away from his obligations in the city Sir Henry lived on the manor of Shacklewell, which he had inherited from his father. He died in 1612, leaving behind him a healthy crop of five children. He was buried alongside his father in the family chapel of the little church in Hackney.[13]

The third son, William, followed a career similar to that of his older brother Henry. Although he inherited the family estate at Higham Hall his principal interests lay in the city, and there he met with the success that seemed naturally to attach

[11] Ibid., 2:476. The portrait was still there when Herbert was writing in 1836.
[12] The *Noble Collection* contains a sketch of the monument, and the epitaph is given on p. 17. See also Mores, "The History and Antiquities of Tunstall in Kent," no page number.
[13] Ibid.

itself to members of his family. On five different occasions he was chosen Master of the Ironmongers' Company and, in 1590, he was made lord mayor of London, thus giving his family the remarkable distinction of providing England's largest city with three lord mayors in less than forty years.[14]

The fourth son made no such distinctive contribution to the advancement of his family's prestige, for he died at an early age. In his will he is described as a "citizen and haberdasher of London." He owned a house at Low Leyton and some land in Kent. His wife, Elinor, was the daughter of a Norfolk squire named Robert Jermy. At her husband's death she was left with two children, a daughter named Mary and a son, born in 1580 or 1581, named Thomas in honor of his grandfather, the founder of the family's fortune.[15]

Thomas's earliest years were spent in Low Leyton, Essex — one of those quiet and comfortable villages that were within easy distance of London. There he must have heard talk of subjects that were as yet beyond his understanding but which were able nevertheless to leave lasting impressions on a young mind: a vague fear that was associated with the name of Spain; an offsetting confidence that came with mention of "the queen"; distrust for papists; a boyish thrill for Sir Francis Drake, and perhaps a precocious familiarity for his elders' repeated talk of ships and trade and the city. It was a secure and sheltered life, but it was rudely changed at about the time the Armada came, for when Thomas was seven years old his father died.[16] Soon afterwards his mother married Sir Richard Berkeley of the renowned Berkeley family who lived at Rendcomb in Gloucestershire.[17] The change from the city-oriented

[14] Wire, "An Essex Worthy: Sir Thomas Roe," p. 136. The ancient procedure by which a lord mayor was chosen is described in George C. Williamson, *Curious Survivals* (London, 1923), pp. 17–20.

[15] The will is at Somerset House.

[16] Wire, "An Essex Worthy: Sir Thomas Roe," p. 136; Stanley Lane-Poole, "Sir Thomas Roe," in *Dictionary of National Biography*, ed. Sir Leslie Stephen and Sir Sidney Lee (London, 1949–1950), 17:89 (hereafter cited as *D.N.B.*).

[17] Sir Richard was subsequently appointed lieutenant of the Tower of

life of Leyton must have been considerable, but Thomas was not long in Gloucestershire, for in 1593, at the age of twelve, he was matriculated as a commoner of Magdalen College, Oxford.[18]

For the next few years his life followed the pattern that was popular for young gentlemen of his time. He stayed at Oxford for about four years, but in 1597 he left without taking a degree and enrolled as a student in the Middle Temple.[19] It seems likely that he spent some time in France during his association with the Inns of Court, but in any case during the last years of the reign of Queen Elizabeth he was appointed esquire of the body to that sovereign.[20]

As he entered manhood and the high circles of London society Roe formed friendships not only at court but also with a number of the most interesting young men of late Elizabethan London. He was a firm friend of John Donne. The two corresponded with each other across the years and across the miles that Roe's career kept putting between them.[21] Another friend was Ben Jonson. Jonson knew other members of the Roe family more intimately than he knew Thomas—no less than seven of his epigrams are addressed to members of the family, and Roe's cousin Sir John Rowe is said to have died of the plague in Jonson's arms.[22] But it is quite clear that Thomas

---

London. The family tie between the Berkeleys and the Roes was made doubly sure when Sir Richard's grandson (from a previous marriage) married Mary Roe. See Sir John MacLean, ed., *The Berkeley Manuscripts . . .* (Gloucester, 1883), 1:264–65.

[18] Joseph Foster, *Alumni Oxonienses* (Oxford, 1892), early series, 3–4:1272. A "commoner" was a student who was not dependent upon a foundation for his support; one who paid for his own living in "commons."

[19] Anthony à Wood, *Athenae Oxonienses*, ed. and continued by Philip Bliss (London, 1813–1820), 3:111. It was not at all unusual to leave the university without graduation. Only about 40 percent of the students stayed long enough to take a degree.

[20] Ibid.

[21] Edmund Gosse, *The Life and Letters of John Donne, Dean of St. Paul's* (New York, 1899), 1:121; 2:66.

[22] C. H. Herford and Percy Simpson, eds., *Ben Jonson* (Oxford, 1925), 1:224–25.

and the poet belonged to the same circle and, in fact, they swapped flattering verses with each other.[23] Yet another friend was the earl of Southampton, patron of Shakespeare and a partner in Roe's first great adventure.[24] In view of all these literary associations the conclusion that Roe was acquainted with Shakespeare himself is all but irresistible; and it is pleasant to think that the style of hundreds of letters and dispatches that Roe was to write in later years might have been fashioned in part by youthful association and friendly hours spent with some of the great literary figures of his day.

But more influential in Roe's life were the connections he made as a result of his introduction to court circles. This must have resulted from the powerful influence he derived both from the family of his stepfather (the Berkeleys) and from the wealthy relatives of his own father. He served the elderly queen as a personal attendant and accumulated a popularity at court that was sufficient to survive the changes that came with her death. Soon after the accession of the new sovereign he was knighted, and his continuing connection with the court led to a genuine friendship with the new royal family.[25] He became especially close to Henry, the king's oldest son, and to his sister Elizabeth, who was later to become electress Palatine and queen of Bohemia. The two royal children seem to have become very attached to the young courtier and their friendship was destined to have no small influence on Roe's subsequent activities.

Soon after his arrival in England Prince Henry had become

[23] Ibid., 8:63, 64. At one point in their account the editors confuse Roe with his cousin, also named Thomas Roe; ibid., 1:52.

[24] A. L. Rowse, *Shakespeare's Southampton, Patron of Virginia* (London, 1965), pp. 242, 288.

[25] There is some confusion as to when Roe was knighted. John Nichols, *The Progresses, Processions and Magnificent Festivities of King James I . . .* (London, 1828), 1:205, 211, says that he was knighted along with some three hundred other gentlemen in the royal gardens at Whitehall on 23 July 1603. Later in the same work (1:496) it is reported that he was knighted at Greenwich on 23 March 1604/5. Foster, *Alumni Oxonienses*, 3–4:1272, gives the former date; Lane-Poole in *D.N.B.*, 17:89, accepts the latter.

the center of a lively and admiring circle of friends. He was a serious-minded young man, but in most other respects he was quite unlike his father. He loved all kinds of sports and was particularly fond of martial entertainment—tossing the pike, shooting, tilting, and riding at the ring.[26] As he grew up his relationship with his father grew rather cool, and James may have been envious of the great popularity his son enjoyed.[27] Henry held a particular attraction for those people who were unhappy with the king's pacifistic policy. Although it may be exaggeration to say that Henry became the center of an anti-Spanish faction at the English court, it is nevertheless true that those people who wished for a more dynamic and Protestant foreign policy looked upon him as the prince who would one day restore to England the prestige and the vigor that seemed to have been lost since the accession of James I.

Of no one was this more true than of Sir Walter Raleigh. The great Elizabethan had fallen afoul of James I in the very year of the king's accession and had been languishing in the Tower, condemned of treason, ever since. Raleigh thought highly of Prince Henry, seeing in him the hope of his own release and the savior of his country's fortunes. He came to know the young prince well and by 1607, or thereabouts, he had won the sympathy and support of both Prince Henry and his mother, Queen Anne. The queen repeatedly begged for Raleigh's release, and Prince Henry is said to have asked, "Who but my father would keep such a bird in a cage!"[28] For his part, Raleigh was flattered and delighted at the opportunity of influencing the young man who was the heir to the English crown. The prince asked his advice about maritime matters and affairs of state, he sought Raleigh's opinion about the marriages proposed for himself and his sister, and he read carefully the papers Raleigh prepared for him about contem-

---

[26] David H. Willson, *King James VI and I* (London, 1956), p. 280.
[27] Ibid., p. 281.
[28] A. L. Rowse, *Sir Walter Ralegh: His Family and Private Life* (New York, 1962), pp. 243, 258, 260.

porary affairs.[29] Increasingly the prince came to share the convictions of the older man: his hatred of Spain, his love of ships and the navy, his view of England as the champion of Protestantism, and his interest in overseas explorations and adventures.

Raleigh's ideas reached a large circle, and his attitudes came to be those of the young men with whom the heir to the throne mixed and mingled. They were certainly the principles that attracted Sir Thomas Roe in the formative years of his life. They had a natural appeal for the sons of a confident and adventurous generation, and in Roe's case they served to reinforce convictions that he had heard spoken since childhood. Raleigh must surely have been one of his boyhood heroes, for Roe was to uphold and to exemplify throughout his life many of the qualities and convictions that had made Raleigh so prominent a figure of the Elizabethan Age and were now making him such an uncomfortable citizen of the England of James I. It is possible to detect early in Roe's life the impact that Raleigh had upon him, for he soon embarked on an adventure that owed much to the urgings and interest of the prisoner in the Tower of London.

In 1595 Raleigh had led an English expedition to Guiana and upon his return had written a book that aroused a great deal of interest in the little known part of the world with which it dealt.[30] Many of Raleigh's accounts were based on nothing more substantial than impressions received during his brief association with the natives, but they were sufficient to develop in England the belief that Guiana was a region that abounded with fabulous riches.[31] There was excited talk about El Do-

[29] Ibid., pp. 259–60, 243; Willard M. Wallace, *Sir Walter Raleigh* (Princeton, N.J., 1959), p. 237.

[30] G. C. Edmundson, "The Relations of Great Britain with Guiana," in *Transactions of the Royal Historical Society* (London, 1923), fourth series, 6:1.

[31] James A. Williamson, *English Colonies in Guiana and on the Amazon, 1604–1688* (Oxford, 1923), pp. 53–54, citing John Stow, *The Annales of England*, 1631 edition. Shakespeare, wishing to convey the

rado, a city whose residents powdered their bodies with gold dust, and of Manoa, the gold-laden home of a mysterious and highly civilized people. These, and other glittering tales, caused a ferment of excitement, and many wealthy Englishmen began to contemplate the gains to be made by investing in expeditions to Guiana and the West Indies.

In the seventeenth century the name "Guiana," like "Virginia," "Florida," and others, applied to an area larger than it represents today. It referred to the vast area between the Amazon and the Orinoco rivers. It included the lower reaches and deltas of both those streams, and it represented the only considerable area of tropical America which, in 1600, had not been extensively explored by European adventurers. It was a land of swamps, jungles, and mountains, unhealthy for Europeans and accessible only by virtue of a large number of nearly parallel rivers which, though not navigable in large ships, could be traveled in canoes or other small vessels.

It is probable that the first Englishman to visit Guiana had gone there before the accession of Elizabeth, but its fabled riches were not impressed upon the English mind until Raleigh's voyage and the subsequent publication of his book. Other adventurers followed his lead, but none of them succeeded in finding the storied gold or the lost empire of the Incas. Gradually the nature of English interest in Guiana underwent a change. No longer was the search for gold the sole objective of the expeditions that went out. Men began to think in terms of settlement and of the development of commercial enterprises. Early in the seventeenth century Charles Leigh had planted a short-lived and ill-fated colony. In 1609 Robert Harcourt, who enjoyed the support and favor of Prince Henry, had taken out a larger party and established little settlements that endured until 1613. There was still no sign of the gold that had first attracted attention to Guiana, but that

idea that Mistress Page is wealthy, has Falstaff say of her: "She bears the purse too; she is a region in Guiana, all gold and bounty" (*The Merry Wives of Windsor*, Act 1, sc. 3).

did not mean that men had lost interest, for other considerations were involved.

To the anti-Spanish faction at the English court, Guiana appeared to be the key to the destruction of the Spanish Empire in South America. This faction felt that Guiana's occupation would drive a wedge between the centers of Spanish power in Mexico and Peru and that its wealth (if found) would add immeasurably to the strength of its conquerors. Moreover, there was a serious weakness in the Spaniards' position in the area, for they were detested by the native population, which they had cruelly mistreated. If England were to adopt a wiser and more humane policy in Guiana her strength there could become almost irresistible. These arguments, and others like them, were advanced by Raleigh as he sought to infect others with his own great desire to bring about the destruction of Spanish power. The project seems to have dominated his mind for the last thirty years of his life, and, because of his genius, it did indeed prove to be infectious.[32]

There were, then, at least two considerations that might impel an Englishman directly or indirectly to support an expedition to Guiana. There was the simple but pleasant prospect of sharing in the division of a cargo of gold—a prospect that was based upon dreams not yet dispelled by numerous unsuccessful searches. There were also the more weighty considerations that stemmed from the deep affairs of state. At any rate, a voyage to Guiana was an adventure in which the emotions of patriotism and greed could combine in happy harmony.

It was also a venture with power to attract a wide variety of people. For all its appeal to the enemies of Spain it was also attractive to James I and his advisers. This arose from the desperate condition of the English treasury. It was probable that, if an English expedition could find some source of great wealth, James would choke back his strong desire for peace with Spain and risk war in order to possess it. In short, the discovery of gold in Guiana could have brought the anti-Span-

[32] V. T. Harlow, *Ralegh's Last Voyage* (London, 1932), p. 1.

ish faction to power in the English court and, in the long run, could easily have changed the course of England's foreign policy.[33]

All these factors made the prospect of an expedition attractive to Raleigh, and his enthusiasm was quickly transmitted to Prince Henry. Henry, in turn, confided in his friend Sir Thomas Roe, and during 1609 the three men talked of plans to send out an expedition under Roe's command.[34] As their talks advanced they were expanded to include other people, among whom was the king's chief adviser, Robert Cecil, the earl of Salisbury, who had been appointed lord treasurer in 1608 and who was now preoccupied with his efforts to place the finances of the Crown on a firm basis. The nature of the king's interest necessitated certain modifications in Roe's program. It was decided that, instead of aiming at settlement (as recent expeditions had done) he should give his best efforts to discovering gold without antagonizing the Spanish. Raleigh and Roe would probably have liked to invade the Orinoco for the very purpose of bringing on war with Spain, but Salisbury insisted on caution, for he was unwilling to become involved in a war unless and until he had convincing proof of the existence, in some specified locality, of great riches that would make the conflict worthwhile.[35]

It seems clear that Prince Henry occupied the key position in the preparation of Roe's voyage. He was the patron who gave Sir Thomas the opportunity to distinguish himself, sending him on an adventure that the prince himself would probably have enjoyed, if his rank had permitted it. But it is clear that the influence of Salisbury and the Crown was also strong, because from the royal point of view Roe was involved in a dangerous enterprise; he was running the risk of provoking a powerful enemy for a prize that, for all anyone knew, might be nonexistent. This was most unlike the usually cautious

[33] Ibid., p. 12.
[34] Ibid., pp. 18–19.
[35] Ibid., pp. 20–21.

foreign policy of the first Stuart, but it surely indicates something of James's eagerness to find new sources of wealth and shows that ultimately every other facet of his policies was secondary to this one major purpose. James's pacifism, and especially his desire for peace with Spain, are well known—and they were real enough. But it is quite clear that Roe's expedition, no matter how cautiously conducted, would jeopardize the peace. The conclusion is unavoidable: in giving their full (but secret) support to Roe's venture, the king and his adviser were taking a calculated risk in trusting that the discovery of gold would precede any possible clash with Spain. For the benefit of the Spanish representatives at the English court, stories were circulated that Roe's fleet was destined for Virginia. This deception, however, cannot have been very effective, for about a month before Roe actually left England, inquisitive John Chamberlain wrote to his friend Dudley Carleton and told him of Roe's true destination.[36]

There was little difficulty in finding people to invest in the expedition. Roe himself joined with a group of men to subscribe some eleven hundred pounds toward the cost of the voyage. Sir Walter Raleigh indicated his particular interest by subscribing six hundred pounds; while the earl of Southampton, famous as the patron of Shakespeare and a supporter of many adventurous expeditions, also made a sizable contribution.[37]

Two vessels were equipped and they sailed from Dartmouth on 24 February 1610. Sir Thomas Roe was only about

[36] Norman E. McClure, ed., *The Letters of John Chamberlain* (Philadelphia, 1939) 1:292; Chamberlain to Dudley Carleton, 30 December 1609.

[37] On the question of financial contributions there is a discrepancy between the accounts of V. T. Harlow, ed., *Colonizing Expeditions to the West Indies and Guiana, 1623–1627* (London, 1925), and that of Williamson, *English Colonies in Guiana and on the Amazon, 1604–1688*. Both men rely for their information upon Tanner MSS, 168, f. 2; but, while Harlow says that the earl of Southampton contributed £800, Williamson reports that there is a blot over the first digit of the item, making it read ()oo. Williamson accordingly reports Southampton's contribution as being at least one hundred pounds.

twenty-nine years old, but the expedition he controlled had the power to change substantially the whole course of his country's foreign policy. His instructions, which had been sanctioned by the principal adviser of the Crown, ordered him to proceed cautiously. His mission was to search for gold without antagonizing the Spaniards. A clash with them must be avoided, but the implication was clear that, if Roe should succeed in finding gold in substantial quantities, the English government was willing to risk war in order to get it.

The expedition arrived at the mouth of the Amazon two months after its departure from England. Sir Thomas was able to sail some two hundred miles up the river in his ships, but at that point he found it necessary to change over to smaller boats. This was done where the Amazon is joined by the river Tapajos, a tributary that early travelers sometimes thought of as being the main stream. It is possible, therefore, that when Roe transferred to his small boats, he continued his journey up the smaller river which runs almost due north. Be that as it may, Sir Thomas continued his journey for at least a hundred miles, finding the country unusually attractive, but noting that the natives could not be relied upon to provide his company with the necessary food supplies. Having reached a point at least three hundred miles from the mouth of the Amazon, Roe and his party turned back and made their way to the coast.[38]

The northeastern part of the South American continent is watered by a large number of nearly parallel rivers whose cataracts and rapids render navigation into the interior very difficult. Nevertheless, Roe continued his voyage of discovery by exploring some of the numerous rivers that come to the coast between the Amazon and the Orinoco. He made a determined effort to reach the fabled city of Manoa, about which Raleigh had written, by following the course of the river Wiapoco. No less than thirty-two rapids were successfully negotiated, and the party entered "a level and uniform country

[38] Ibid., pp. 53–54; Harlow, ed., *Colonizing Expeditions to the West Indies and Guiana, 1623–1627*, p. lxx.

without any more rapids, and afterwards a very deep and broad river, and they would have voyaged onwards by it," but their provisions failed and they were obliged once again to turn back toward the coast.[39]

This disappointment apparently convinced Roe that neither Manoa nor El Dorado existed, so the little expedition took its leave of the main coast and made its way to Trinidad, but "not finding all the West Indies to be full of Gold as some suppose," they continued homeward and arrived at the Isle of Wight in July 1611.[40]

Information regarding Roe's voyage is meager, but it is nevertheless of great interest not only to Roe's biographer but also to the student of England's foreign policy. He had failed in his primary objective but could claim to have spent a longer time on the coast than any previous explorer had done and to have seen "more of this coast, rivers, and inland from the Great River of the Amazons under the line to Orenoque in 8 degrees, than any Englishman now alive."[41] He had tasted of the adventure that seems to have strengthened the spirit of so many of his contemporaries and had met face to face some of the Spaniards whom he regarded as his country's most dangerous enemies. The voyage taught him to despise them for their weakness and duplicity and he returned home with information that he hoped would be used to obstruct the implementation of Spanish plans in South America.[42]

The journey to Guiana seems to have given Roe the beginning of a lifelong interest in England's commercial policies and overseas relationships. Soon he would become involved in enterprises concerning the colonial settlements in North America and embark on a career intimately involved with England's interests in Asia, the Middle East, and on the European conti-

[39] Harlow, *Ralegh's Last Voyage*, p. 13; Williamson, *English Colonies in Guiana and on the Amazon, 1604–1688*, p. 54n.

[40] Wallace, *Sir Walter Raleigh*, p. 255.

[41] *Calendar of State Papers, Colonial Series, 1574–1660* (London, 1860), p. 11; Roe to the earl of Salisbury, from Trinidad, 28 February 1611 (hereafter referred to as *C.S.P. Colonial* with the appropriate dates).

[42] Wallace, *Sir Walter Raleigh*, pp. 56–57.

nent. His whole life was to have an outward orientation, even though the age in which he lived was preoccupied with domestic affairs. Perhaps the voyage did not initiate these interests, but it may well have reinforced in him a latent Elizabethan tendency to dream of an imperial destiny for his country. He sensed that in the days of his youth there were empires to be won, and he was impatient of any delay in entering the race. It may be that he would have been happier if he had been born early enough to have sailed with Sir Francis Drake or late enough to have marched with Robert Clive. As it was he was destined to live in an England that gave more attention to constitutions than colonies and more energy to domestic disturbance than to international competition. For much of his life he would be out of step with the course of events, a persistent voice trying, without the advantages of high dignity or position, to remind his countrymen of the role that awaited them on the broad stage of world affairs. His course was suggested to him by the great events that took place in his youth, by the interests of the family into which he had been born, and by his association with men like Sir Walter Raleigh and Prince Henry. Now it was confirmed by firsthand experience of the fertile fields that awaited exploration overseas.

It would be foolish to suggest that Sir Thomas Roe's voyage to Guiana deserves an important place in the annals of England's foreign policy, but the fact remains that his adventure was surrounded by implications that so seasoned a scholar as V. T. Harlow has called "startling."[43] This comment arises from the simple fact that although friendship with Spain was the principal feature of James I's foreign policy, he nevertheless associated himself (in ineffective secrecy) with a venture that originated with and was commanded by persons whom he must have known to belong to the "war party." Raleigh and his friends believed that England should retain her Elizabethan role as the Protestant champion and persevere in war until

---

[43] Harlow, *Ralegh's Last Voyage*, pp. 104–106.

declining Spain collapsed from sheer exhaustion.[44] Much of Roe's life was a testimony to the fact that he shared in this view, and there can be no doubt that while he was exploring the South American coast he was on the alert for pieces of evidence that could be used to persuade the earl of Salisbury of the wisdom of a war policy and the likelihood of military success. He reported that the Spaniards planned to settle colonies on the Orinoco and was careful to point out that the river had much wealth along its banks and flowed into the heart of the Main.[45] He wrote of seething discontent between Spaniards and natives and between rival Spanish factions. He told Cecil that he intended to bring back with him to England a disaffected Spaniard who knew the country intimately and who would thus be useful either to future expeditions or to the military in the event of war.[46]

His hopes were destined for frustration. No gold had been discovered and his travels did not serve to involve England in a war with Spain. But this does not mean that Roe's voyage was without value or significance and it did not cause him to abandon his interest in South America. We cannot be sure that he ever returned to Guiana, but it is certain that he was intimately associated with two further expeditions to the coast. The relevant quotation from Stow's account (on which all other secondary works are based) is somewhat ambiguous: "Since which time hee hath twice sent thither to make further discoveries, and maintained 20 men in the river of Amazones for the good of his Countrey, who are yet remaining there and

[44] Ibid., p. 1.

[45] *C.S.P. Colonial, 1574–1660*, p. 11; Roe to the earl of Salisbury, from Trinidad, 28 February 1611.

[46] Ibid. Some historians, drawing on their knowledge of Raleigh's ventures, have suspected that James's policy was bolder than has usually been thought. D. H. Willson, for example (*King James VI and I*, p. 371), says that James "considered the Orinoco a highly desirable possession and was prepared to take some risk in order to acquire it." The facts surrounding Roe's voyage prove conclusively not only that James knowingly risked war with Spain for the mere possibility of American gold, but that he did so long before he sanctioned the fateful voyage that cost Raleigh his head.

supplied."[47] Some authorities have taken this to mean that Roe returned to Guiana,[48] but it is more probable that he did not actually go with these later expeditions but merely assisted in their organization and watched them with interest. Whatever the facts may be, Stow's passage does serve to prove Roe's continuing interest and involvement and to make it clear that on either the second or the third voyage some attempt at settlement was made. But the little colony planted on the Amazon was destined to be short-lived. By 1614 the men were complaining of neglect and they gladly took the opportunity to throw in their lot with a fresh band of adventurers that had gone out from England under Robert Harcourt.[49] Under his leadership their fortunes apparently revived, for some years later Roe learned that four or five of the settlers had made handsome fortunes and intended to stay in Guiana.[50]

In England, meanwhile, Roe, who was now about thirty years old, was experiencing sweeping changes in the conditions of life. He had depended much on and benefited substantially from his friendship with the children of the royal family, but now his two friends were taken from him. In November 1612 Henry, the young and lively prince who had already exerted such an important influence upon Roe, died of typhoid fever. All England was stricken with a grief that Sir Thomas must have felt in a pressing and personal way. Then, with almost unseemly haste after her brother's death, Princess Elizabeth was married to Frederick of the Palatinate, a young man on whom her own affections and her father's diplomacy combined in happy harmony.

The wedding was celebrated in February with a lavish ostentation that King James could ill afford. On 25 April the

[47] Harlow, ed., *Colonizing Expeditions to the West Indies and Guiana*, p. lxxi, quoting Stow, *Annales*, 1631 edition.
[48] Lane-Poole, "Sir Thomas Roe," in *D.N.B.*, 17:89.
[49] Harlow, *Colonizing Expeditions to the West Indies and Guiana*, p. lxxi.
[50] *C.S.P. Colonial, 1574–1660*, p. 18; George Lord Carew to Roe, March 1617.

young couple sailed from England; Sir Thomas Roe was a member of the party that accompanied them to Germany.[51] While he was on the Continent Roe took part in a theological discussion at Flushing in the Netherlands,[52] but we may assume that he did not tarry long, for at home a new bride awaited his return. Some time before the end of 1613 Roe had married Eleanor, the daughter of Sir Thomas Cave of Stamford in Northamptonshire. It seems that she had been married before, to Sir George Beeston of Beeston Hall in Cheshire, but there is no reason to believe that the new match was anything but an affair of the heart. Sir Thomas and his wife were to be happily married for some thirty years.[53] This did not change the fact, however, that Lady Roe brought with her some useful political connections. Her grandmother had been Margaret Cecil, sister of Lord Burghley and the niece of Oliver St. John, the master of the ordnance in Ireland who shortly afterwards was appointed lord deputy of Ireland and created Viscount Grandison.[54]

Soon after his wedding Sir Thomas Roe resolved to enter public life and in 1614 he was elected member of Parliament for Tamworth in Staffordshire. In that capacity he served in the famous "Addled Parliament" and probably came to know some of the men who, in later years, would earn fame as leaders of the parliamentary opposition to the Crown.[55] All the

[51] Mary Anne Everett Green, *Elizabeth, Electress Palatine and Queen of Bohemia*, rev. S. C. Lomas (London, 1909), p. 151 (hereafter referred to as Green, *Elizabeth of Bohemia*).

[52] Wire, "An Essex Worthy: Sir Thomas Roe," p. 135; Lane-Poole, "Sir Thomas Roe," in *D.N.B.*, 17:90; Rowse, *Shakespeare's Southampton*, p. 242, says that in 1613 Roe "went soldiering in the Netherlands." The source of this information is not given.

[53] Peter Whalley, *The History and Antiquities of Northamptonshire, Compiled from the Manuscript Collection of the Late Learned Antiquary John Bridges, Esq.* (Oxford, 1791), 1:579; Arthur Oswald, "Stanford Hall, Leicestershire," in *Country Life*, 18 December 1958, p. 1473.

[54] Whalley, *History and Antiquities of Northamptonshire*, 1:579; A. F. Pollard, "Oliver St. John, Viscount Grandison and Baron Tregoz," in *D.N.B.*, 17:637-39.

[55] W. M. Mitchell, *The Rise of the Revolutionary Party in the English House of Commons, 1603-1629* (New York, 1957), p. xv.

signs pointed to a settled, domestic, and possibly uneventful career for the young courtier and traveler. But the signs were misleading, for the year 1614 proved to be one of great moment and had far-reaching significance in his life.[56]

[56] The assertion that Roe did not participate in the second and third voyages to Guiana is not made with any certainty and is based simply on the chronology of his known activities. He returned from the first voyage in July 1611, after an absence of some seventeen months. From early in 1613 his movements can be traced in some detail, so the only time available for travel was from about August 1611 to the end of 1612. This seems hardly sufficient time in which to plan, finance, equip, and execute two expeditions to the New World, especially when it is remembered that the first voyage alone took that long. However, the possibility that this was done cannot be excluded; and it must be confessed that his absence in Guiana would provide a plausible explanation of the lack of any other evidence as to his whereabouts during those months.

CHAPTER 2

John Company's Man

WHEN Thomas Roe was an impressionable boy less than ten years old, one of the epic battles of history took place. The defeat of the Spanish Armada had ended King Philip's hope of invading England and had given to the English sailor a new confidence that he would win the struggle for supremacy at sea. The victory of 1588 had the effect of making it appear to English merchants that the seas of the world now lay open to receive their commerce. Accordingly, in October 1589, less than a year after the defeat of the Armada, a number of London merchants approached the queen for permission to send ships to trade in India and on the coasts that surrounded the India and China seas. It was small wonder that their attention was attracted by the prospects of Eastern trade, for in India and the islands to the east were the sources of those commodities like silk, spices, and cotton goods that could always be relied upon to bring handsome profits in the markets of western Europe.[1]

The demand for silk and spices was not new, and the European connection with India went back to the days of the Greeks, although direct contact had lapsed after the fall of the Roman Empire. Occasional travelers, like Marco Polo, continued to reach India but in the Middle Ages trade with the East was carried on through a complex series of middlemen who moved the goods by various routes and through many jurisdictions to the distribution centers of Alexandria and Constantinople. In the thirteenth century some of the trade routes were closed as a result of the invasions of Genghis Khan;

others disappeared with the fall of Constantinople to the Turks in 1453. The trade continued, but under increasing difficulties and at higher cost.

> Spices were brought from the East Indies to Calicut in south India and there sold to Arab merchants. They were carried to Jidda in the Red Sea where an ad valorem duty of one-third was paid to Egypt. Thence they went in smaller boats to Suez, then by camel to Cairo, by boats down the Nile, and by camel again to Alexandria. At each place an ad valorem duty was charged, with a special one at Cairo of one-third. A parting shot was a 5 per cent duty for permission to move the cargo oversea. After this must be added the Italian charges and the cost of distribution beyond the Alps. On top of this came the bribes and other inducements needed to clear each customs barrier.[2]

It was not surprising that the maritime nations of Europe, lured by the joint prospects of financial gain and an increase in the enjoyments of daily living, and unwilling to leave the monopoly of such a trade in alien and infidel hands, turned their eyes eastward.

The Portuguese led the way. Under the leadership of Prince Henry "the Navigator" they made their way down the west coast of Africa until, in 1486, Diaz rounded the Cape of Good Hope and, in 1498, Vasco da Gama landed at Calicut. Soon the Portuguese began to supplant Arabian merchants in the Far East, and by the middle of the sixteenth century Lisbon was established as the leading port for the redistribution of far-eastern products throughout Europe.[3]

The Portuguese Empire relied upon sea power and fortresses. Its center was at Goa, an Indian port captured in 1510. From there the spice trade of the Malabar coast and commercial activity with Egypt and the Persian Gulf could be con-

---

[1] The general background material for this discussion is derived from two principal sources: T. G. P. Spear, *India: A Modern History* (Ann Arbor, Mich., 1961), pp. 160–67; Vincent A. Smith, *The Oxford History of India*, 3d ed., rev. (Oxford, 1958), pp. 327–36.

[2] Spear, *India: A Modern History*, p. 161.

[3] Marguerite Eyer Wilbur, *The East India Company and the British Empire in the Far East* (New York, 1945), pp. 54–55.

trolled. Malacca in the Malayan Peninsula controlled the trade routes of the East Indies and it was taken in 1511. In 1515 another strategic location was brought under Portuguese control—Ormuz, an island city that overlooked the entrance to the Persian Gulf. This was a farflung empire, but it was given additional strength by a policy of intermarriage that produced a "Portuguese" population, and by an aggressive Catholicism that was represented by such diverse forces as St. Francis Xavier, the Inquisition, monasteries, and Jesuits.

The Portuguese Empire in the East was a remarkable achievement, but it was always plagued by a number of serious weaknesses. The Portuguese were cordially disliked by the native peoples, with whom they felt no obligation to deal honestly. The support received from home was inadequate, for it was too much to expect that a kingdom of less than a million people could properly maintain itself among the growing nation states of Europe and, at the same time, support colonies in both the new and old worlds. In 1580 Portugal itself was absorbed by Spain and this was a serious blow to the continued well-being of her eastern empire, since the dominant power naturally gave primacy to her own colonial interests in the West.[4]

These and other weaknesses inevitably invited competition, and soon the energetic Dutch, who were even then in revolt against Philip II, came to contest Portugal's eastern supremacy. They focused their attention on the East Indies, driving straight for the center of the spice trade in hope of controlling the sources of supply. But they traded in other commodities throughout the East in order to secure the goods needed to buy the spices and to meet the overhead costs of the trade as a whole. These extended operations brought them into direct conflict with the Portuguese. They drove them out of Malaya and contested their hold on Ceylon and the Malabar Coast.

[4] K. M. Panikkar, *Malabar and the Portuguese, Being a History of the Relations of the Portuguese with Malabar from 1500 to 1663* (Bombay, 1929), pp. 147–52.

They established fortified posts at the Cape of Good Hope and St. Helena and set up scattered factories on the Indian peninsula. India, however, was for them a secondary theater of activity; their operations were directed from Java, and India played only a supporting role in the grand design of monopolizing the spice trade of the world.

This was the situation in the East as the sixteenth century and the reign of England's great queen drew to a close. The Dutch and Portuguese were locked in bitter struggle and, although the fight was by no means ended, the dynamic Dutch seemed to be gaining the upper hand. England had had a longstanding alliance with the Portuguese, but her strongly Protestant merchants, long nurtured in an anti-Spanish faith, felt that any obligations had terminated with the Spanish conquest of Portugal. Thus, when they contemplated the situation in the East, they were inclined to regard the Portuguese, rather than the Dutch, as their natural enemies. To join in wresting the lucrative trade from them would be a process consistent with their faith and conducive to their prosperity. For neither the first nor the last time the pleasing harmony of principles and profits beckoned them and they looked eastward and approached their queen for permission to trade with the Indies.

Elizabeth, who was "ever alive to the interest of commerce, and ready to give the weight of her authority, if not at all times of her purse, to . . . any project calculated to add to the power of England," gave her permission and in 1591 three ships under the command of a Captain Raymond set sail for the East.[5] Only one ship survived the voyage, but the knowledge that was acquired and the prospects that were unfolded encouraged the sending of another fleet. The results of this expedition, combined with the knowledge that the Dutch were in the process of establishing formal associations for eastern trade, spurred a number of English merchants to band together

---

[5] W. Noel Sainsbury, *Calendar of State Papers, Colonial Series, East Indies, China and Japan, 1513–1616* (London, 1862), pp. xxxiv–lv (hereafter referred to as *C.S.P.C.*, with the appropriate dates).

for a similar purpose. They subscribed more than thirty thousand pounds and petitioned the queen to give her assent. After some delay they were given a certificate "as an earnest of a further warrant to be afterwards granted to them." On the basis of this assurance they began to equip a fleet to sail under the command of Captain James Lancaster, an experienced mariner who had already led an expedition to the East. Before the fleet left England the permanent charter Elizabeth had promised was drawn up and delivered. "The Charter of Incorporation of the East India Company by the name of the Governor and Company of Merchants trading into the East Indies" was granted on 31 December 1600. Lancaster's fleet left England in February 1601 on the first voyage officially sponsored by the East India Company. It was highly successful. The ships made straight for the East Indies where spices were to be had. They did not go to India itself, but the mission established factories at Acheen and Bantam and won favorable privileges for English merchants to trade there. On the basis of these promising accomplishments a second voyage was soon sent out, this time under the command of Henry Middleton. Like its predecessor, it was highly successful although it too was concerned solely with the trade in spices. By the time preparations were being made for a third voyage, plans were afoot to broaden the scope of the venture. The English felt that if factories could be established at Cambay and Surat in India they might be able to get into their hands the very lucrative trade in cloths and calicoes that was carried on between India and the islands.[6]

Accordingly, the fleet that sailed from England in March 1607 had a double objective. The "general" of the fleet, William Keeling, was to sail for Java while William Hawkins, in command of the "Hector," was to visit Surat on India's west coast. This plan was carried out successfully with the result that on 24 August 1608 the first ship to fly the English flag off

[6] S. R. Gardiner, *History of England from the Accession of James I to the Outbreak of the Civil War, 1603–1642* (New York, 1883–1884), 2:310–11.

the coast of India dropped anchor in the river Tapti near Surat.[7]

Hawkins's overtures for trading rights met with a general apathy, for the local officials were much more interested in his gifts. In reply to his request for permission to establish a factory at Surat he was told that only the emperor could give such permission. Undaunted, Hawkins undertook a journey of two months' duration in order to present his plans to the Mogul emperor, whose court was then situated at Agra. The difficult journey was successfully made. Hawkins, who could speak Turkish, was warmly received by the emperor, who took an immediate liking to the Englishman and invited him to stay at the court as a resident ambassador. Hawkins, ever hopeful of establishing a profitable trading agreement, accepted the invitation and stayed at the court for over two years. However, Portuguese influence at the Mogul court was still strong enough to persuade the emperor to reject the Englishman's petitions for trade, and in spite of his long stay Hawkins was not able to achieve his primary objective.[8] He retired from the court in disgust on 22 November 1611. The first diplomatic mission of an Englishman in India had ended.

From one point of view Hawkins's mission appeared to have been a failure. He had not obtained any formal assurances of future trade between England and India, and his experiences had served to demonstrate the continuing influence of the Portuguese at the Mogul's court. But the venture of which his journey was a part had been a huge success, paying its sponsors a profit of more than 230 percent.[9] It was not surprising, then, that the merchants of the East India Company were disinclined to draw any gloomy conclusions from Hawkins's experience. On the contrary; the prize had been shown to be

[7] Philip Woodruff, *The Men Who Ruled India: The Founders of Modern India* (New York, 1954), pp. 21–29.

[8] Sir George Dunbar, *India and the Passing of Empire* (New York, 1952), p. 63; Woodruff, *The Men Who Ruled India: The Founders of Modern India*, p. 28.

[9] *C.S.P.C., 1513–1616*, pp. xxxvi–lv.

every bit as attractive as anticipatated, and they now prepared to press forward and contest the issue with their European rivals. Soon English ships were going everywhere there was a chance of trade. Permission was received to settle factories at numerous key locations within the empire of the Great Mogul. As a result of all this activity the rivalry with the Portuguese and Dutch was intensified as the three European powers competed for the favor of the emperor and the merchants of his dominions.

The English found the Indian attitude toward them to be strangely mixed. They were often regarded with indifference and even contempt, but these sentiments were punctuated by an avaricious curiosity about the gifts that were an indispensable part of the traders' equipment.[10] At the factory stations there were periods of friendship and hostility. These moods sometimes grew out of the personal caprice of the individuals involved, but more often they reflected apprehension that English activities might interfere with the trade of the local merchants and even with the commercial ventures engaged in by high officials of the province or of the royal court.

Gradually, however, because of the widespread dislike of the Portuguese and the growing conviction on the part of Indian merchants that the English trader was generally dependable and honest, the attitude began to soften and the British began to win the upper hand.[11] On more than one occasion the Portuguese themselves aided this development. In 1613, for example, they foolishly seized a ship in which the Mogul's mother was a principal investor. This led to much ill-feeling and the offense was never entirely forgotten or forgiven.[12] In 1612, and again in 1615, English captains defeated superior Portuguese naval forces in clear view of the Indian coast. These reverses greatly weakened the Portuguese

[10] B. G. Gokhale, "Indians and the British: A Study in Attitudes," *History Today* 13 (1963): 231–32.

[11] Ibid., p. 232.

[12] *C.S.P.C., 1513–1616*, pp. xxxvii–lv.

image. The natives were impressed now with the power of the English and extended them permission to establish a factory at Surat (a city with an excellent harbor) and to trade throughout the province of Gujarat, a fertile and prosperous district that included many fine towns rich with commercial promise.

Englishmen who visited India in these early years quickly learned that they were not dealing with an economically primitive people. On the contrary, they discovered a mature, sophisticated commercial system. Indian merchants were experienced and expert; they controlled large supplies of capital and were quite familiar with such things as bills of exchange and marine insurance.[13]

The policy followed by the East India Company in establishing trade in new lands was a simple one. The ruler of the region would be given gifts and letters from responsible English officials (frequently these letters were written by the sovereign) and by this means his consent would be secured for vessels to trade with the native merchants. If conditions seemed promising, young men who had gone out with the expedition would be left ashore to collect cargoes in readiness for the visit of the next fleet. These men were known as "factors" or "agents," and the houses in which they lived were called "factories." One of the great advantages of this system grew out of the fact—noticed by all Europeans trading with the East—that when a trading ship came in, prices invariably went up. The factors, however, since they resided abroad the year around, could buy the goods they wanted when prices were at their lowest, and then store their purchases until a ship arrived from the home country.[14]

There were, however, a number of disadvantages inherent in the factor system. The factories were quite separate from each

[13] Wilbur, *The East India Company and the British Empire in the Far East*, p. 58; Sir William Foster, "The East India Company, 1600–1740," in *The Cambridge History of the British Empire*, ed. H. H. Dodwell (Cambridge, Eng., 1929), 4:91.

[14] Woodruff, *The Men Who Ruled India: The Founders of Modern India*, p. 43.

other and each regarded itself as an autonomous unit. Their activities were uncoordinated and their policies adhered to no consistent pattern. There was no centralized control of any kind; indeed, any assertion of primacy from one factory would bring quick denials from the others. Under these circumstances there was frequent competition and considerable acrimony among the little settlements. Their residents were far from home and visited only infrequently by the company's ships. Freed from the supervision of higher authority, some of the more ambitious among them engaged in unwarranted pretensions that aggravated their comrades and created bad impressions among the natives. Homesickness and the restrictiveness of their tiny communities frayed the nerves and undermined the efficiency of all.

A second weakness of the factor system grew out of the first. The company's representatives in India, far from the watchful eyes of their superiors, were constantly tempted to feather their own nests and to engage in personal trade whenever an attractive opportunity presented itself. Why should all the profits of India be sent home to the already wealthy merchants of London? Wasn't a man who had left home and friends to live in a strange and alien land entitled to some recompense? There is no evidence that thoughts such as these led to any serious inroads in company profits, but there is ample evidence that the members were jealous of any enterprise undertaken by the factors that was not designed to increase the return on their investment. Some sort of regulatory agency was needed to curb and control these practices and prevent them from reaching dangerous proportions.

The third, and perhaps the most serious, deficiency of the system was related to the impression it created in the minds of the Indians among whom the factors lived and worked. The East India Company's agents were usually, at best, middle-class men and they constituted England's main contact with the countries with which she traded. They were frequently persons without dignity or bearing, and the natives tended to have little real respect for them or for the country they represented. The factors were often scorned and ridiculed and were generally regarded as being inferior to the native merchants with whom they carried on their business.

The governor of the East India Company, Sir Thomas Smythe, recognized that this state of affairs was detrimental to the best interests of the company. But he saw too that a remedy was available. In 1612 an East India Company captain named Thomas Best had impressed the Great Mogul by defeating a Portuguese naval force near Surat. He had been rewarded by a promise that an English representative would be made welcome and permitted to reside at the Mogul's court. Such a representative could presumably do a great deal to further the company's interests. He would be able to negotiate for dependable and binding commercial agreements, supervise and coordinate the activities of the English factories, enforce the company's prohibition against private trading by the factors, and, most important, seek to overcome the low opinion of England that had been planted in the Indian mind as a result of long association with the generally mediocre men who served as factors.

In the mind of Sir Thomas Smythe these were persuasive arguments and they must have been reinforced by a letter that had recently come to his attention. It was from Thomas Aldworth, who was in charge of the company's factory at Surat. Aldworth had expressed the opinion that it would be most beneficial to the company if "a suffitient man be sent in your first shippes that may bee Resident in Agra withe the Kinge, and sutch a one whose person may breade regarde, for they here looke mutch after greate men."[15] This opinion from the

---

[15] William Foster, ed., *The Embassy of Sir Thomas Roe to the Court of the Great Mogul, 1615–1619, as Narrated in His Journal and Correspondence* (London, 1899), p. iii. This work is the main source of information about Roe's mission to India, and the references to it call for some explanation. The heart of the work is the journal that Roe kept during his embassy. This will be referred to in subsequent notes as Roe, *Journal.* However, the editor has written an introduction, added some

company's representative in India confirmed Smythe's own conviction: the East India Company should be represented in India by somebody of real stature—by a man who could command the respect of the natives and perhaps persuade them to enter into formal commitments with respect to future trading activities.

On the basis of this conviction Smythe suggested that "an ambassador of extraordinary countenance and respect" should be sent to India; he offered the name of Sir Thomas Roe as a man who could meet the demanding requirements of the position. He described Roe as "a gentleman of pregnant understanding, well spoken, learned, industrious, of a comely personage," and one who offered promise of doing much good for the company.[16] The governor's proposal was discussed in subsequent meetings and there was never any serious opposition. The names of Sir John Brooke and a Mr. Bailie were put forward, but Roe's supporters spoke up, described him as being a gentleman of "civil behaviour, good breeding, personage and very good parts, able to answer any matters whatsoever and of understanding to settle any privileges for the good of the Company."[17] Their confidence and their oratory carried the day and on 7 October 1614, it was concluded that "none [was] esteemed so fitting as Sir Thos. Roe if he may bee had."[18] The governor was requested to contact Roe and to discover on what terms he would accept the appointment.

The seventeenth century had rather definite ideas about the qualities necessary in a good ambassador. This was entirely to be expected, for in an age when intercourse among widely separated states was infrequent and spasmodic the impression

---

valuable notes and appendixes and interpolated some materials into the body of the work. Since these cannot properly be credited to Roe, they will be cited in subsequent notes as Foster, *Embassy*.

[16] Court Minutes of the East India Company for 7 September 1614, in *C.S.P.C.*, *1513–1616*, p. 318. The Court Minutes of the East India Company will hereafter be cited as Court Minutes.

[17] Court Minutes for 4 October 1614 in ibid., p. 324.

[18] Court Minutes for 7 October 1614 in ibid., p. 326.

made by an ambassador was vitally important. People would often formulate their total conception of a country by the impression made upon them by that state's official representative. If he were dignified and confident, he would probably make a good impression and generate respect for the king and the country he represented. If, on the other hand, he were a person of low quality and little bearing, then his country would likely be despised and its offers spurned. It was generally felt that the ideal ambassador should be rich, well born, and handsome. He should be well educated and preferably of middle age, that is, between thirty and fifty. He should be well-schooled in all the moral virtues and be absolutely brave, loyal, and temperate.[19]

These were rigorous requirements, yet there is every reason to believe that the directors of the East India Company made a wise choice in selecting Sir Thomas Roe as their ambassador to India. His experience at court and his friendship with royalty, in the persons of Prince Henry and Princess Elizabeth, had given him the suave bearing of a courtier. His voyage to Guiana had given him breadth of experience, his family background identified him with the commercial community, and his tenure of a parliamentary seat had provided some knowledge of state affairs. There is compelling evidence that he did not meet the requirement of being a wealthy man, but his other qualifications compensated for this deficiency—which was not, in any case, very serious since the East India Company, and not the impoverished Crown of England, would be responsible for the expenses of his embassy. Roe was an imposing man physically and exemplified many of the qualities of a true Elizabethan; in future years he would prove himself to be a genuinely courageous man with a high degree of loyalty and "the great-hearted fanaticism" of the age in which his boyhood had been lived.[20]

[19] Garrett Mattingly, *Renaissance Diplomacy* (London, 1955), pp. 215, 216–17, 219–20.
[20] Stanley Lane-Poole, *Medieval India from the Mohammedan Conquest to the Reign of Akbar the Great* (London, 1906), p. 68.

No difficulty was experienced in arriving at an agreement and Sir Thomas readily accepted the position with the East India Company. He asked to be provided with a chaplain, a physician, an apothecary, a secretary, a cook, and other attendants, and a salary of between five and six hundred pounds a year. These requests were considered to be reasonable. The company undertook to provide the chaplain with a salary of fifty pounds and a "chirurgeon" with twenty-four pounds. They would give him an additional hundred pounds to hire and pay other servants, five hundred marks for the expenses of his outfit, one hundred pounds for the purchase of plate for his table, and a salary of six hundred pounds a year, half of which would be invested annually in the company's stock. In Christian countries the expenses of an ambassador were often borne by the host government, but it was recognized that an embassy to India was a special case and that the Great Mogul might not conform to conventional European practices. It was therefore agreed that Roe would keep an account of all his expenses, noting any allowances that the Mogul himself might provide. On his return to England any such allowances would be deducted from the company's liability to him.[21]

Roe himself was well pleased with these arrangements, for they offered him all the excitement of a highly unusual venture and an opportunity to be of real service to his country. On a more mundane level his employment promised to solve some personal financial difficulties. There is no evidence that his fortune had ever been more than a modest one, but as a young man he had tended toward extravagance and the voyages to Guiana that he had helped to finance had been expensive and unprofitable. His recent marriage had brought fresh responsibilities, so that by the time he made his arrangements with the East India Company he had contracted some pressing debts.[22]

When the contract between Roe and the company had been

[21] Court Minutes for 16 November 1614, in *C.S.P.C., 1513–1616*, p. 338; "The Company's Agreement with Roe," in Foster, *Embassy*, pp. 547–49.
[22] Court Minutes for 11 November 1614 and 17 January 1615 in *C.S.P.C., 1513–1616*, pp. 335, 371.

approved by both parties, all that remained to be done was to secure the royal sanction for the mission, which was readily given; the king approved both the company's choice of an ambassador and the arrangements made for his mission. King James furnished Sir Thomas with a letter to the Great Mogul along with detailed instructions as to how the ambassador should conduct himself. Roe was cautioned "to be Carefull of the preservaccion of our honour and dignity, both as wee are a soveraine Prince and a professed Christian." He was further advised to impress the Mogul with the greatness of the English king and the naval strength that made him "a Terrour to all other Nations and . . . vniversally beloued and admyred of all our People."[23] The instructions were followed by Roe's appointment as "our true and undoubted Attorney, Procurator, Legate and Ambassador."[24]

When all these preliminaries had been completed, the company's directors decided that Roe should sail for Surat with the fleet that was soon to leave England under the command of William Keeling, one of their most trusted and experienced captains. Last-minute arrangements were hurried forward. Roe was supplied with gifts which hopefully would incline the Great Mogul to friendliness. These included a fine coach with all possible accouterments, including a certain William Hemsell, the former coachman of the bishop of Coventry, who had indicated his readiness to leave his Christian master and serve the emperor of India.[25] Attendants were chosen from among the many applicants. The most important of these were John Hall, who was to serve as Roe's preacher, and Joost Smith, a Dutchman who had knowledge of drugs and medicines.[26] It is strange that no mention is made of the employment of an interpreter, but it was presumably felt that one of the compa-

---

[23] The king's instructions, dated Whitehall, 29 December 1614, are given in ibid., pp. 361–62.

[24] The "Royal Commission to Sir Thomas Roe" is printed in Foster, *Embassy*, pp. 549–51.

[25] Court Minutes for 3 January 1615 in *C.S.P.C., 1513–1616*, p. 366.

[26] Court Minutes for 22 November in ibid., p. 341.

ny's servants already in India would be able to serve in that capacity. The language most commonly used at the Mogul court was Persian, although the "learned tongue" was Arabic. Roe was quite a gifted linguist, but neither of these languages was in his repertoire, and in the days ahead he was frequently to complain of the lack of an interpreter.

Soon his group was complete, its ranks expanded to the number of sixteen. Some members of the East India Company thought this excessive, but the directors gave a dinner in honor of their new ambassador. He responded with assurances that he would do his very best in their behalf and that they would never have cause to regret his employment. For their part, the directors professed themselves to be wholly convinced of his sincerity, and they demonstrated their regard by twice honoring his requests for salary advances.[27]

On 2 February 1615 Roe and his followers embarked upon the *Lion* at Tilbury Hope; but, because of the lack of a favorable wind, it was not until 6 March that Sir Thomas could write in his journal: "This day wee lost sight of the Lizard, and begann our Course for the Cape of Good Hope."[28]

The long voyage to India was quite uneventful, and Roe had plenty of time to think about the mission on which he had embarked and to appreciate perhaps more fully than before the extent of the responsibilities he had assumed. He was only thirty-four years old, yet he was now being called upon to represent the full dignity of England. One of his principal tasks was to be the preservation and enhancement of that dignity in the court of an oriental potentate who called himself "The Conqueror of the World." No man was more fully convinced than Sir Thomas Roe of the strength and majesty of England, but how could the impression of those qualities be most effectively conveyed by himself and a little band of retainers? Everything would depend upon his own deport-

[27] Court Minutes for 16 November 1614; 10, 26, and 31 January 1615 in ibid., pp. 338, 368, 374–75.
[28] Roe, *Journal*, p. 3.

ment. It would be necessary to act in every situation with firmness and conviction; to insist, obstinately if need be, upon being treated with the deference and respect due, not to himself, but to the king he represented. From the moment he stepped ashore in India he would have to feign an assurance and self-confidence he would not always feel; there could be no signs of hesitation, indecision, or weakness. It would be a demanding role.

Perhaps as he traveled he sought to pass the hours by reading for his instruction the widely recognized book on diplomatic practices called *El Embajador*—a treatise that reflected and expounded upon the international code of behavior that existed among European embassies.[29] But if he did so he must have reflected that the book had little immediate relevance for his mission. He was a pioneer going into a land where only the unexpected could be anticipated with confidence and where European practices were at best little known and at worst despised. His mission would demand courage and resourcefulness, and the leisurely progress of Captain Keeling's fleet gave him ample time to wonder if he possessed those qualities in sufficient degree.

If the young ambassador experienced misgivings of this kind they found no place in the journal that he began to keep on the day of his departure. He had agreed on his return to England to give his employers a careful account of his embassy, and he intended that his journal should be a part of his report. He thus withheld from his account those personal sentiments that could have made it such a revealing document.

As the *Lion* and her three companion ships made their way across the seas, Roe busied himself with making calculations of latitude and longitude and comparing his results with the data contained in existing charts. He suggested numerous corrections that he thought would be helpful for future navigators. Many of his observations about the stars indicate much more than a layman's knowledge about the heavens and it seems

[29] Mattingly, *Renaissance Diplomacy*, pp. 211–12.

reasonable to assume that Roe had been introduced to the mysteries of navigation during his earlier voyage of discovery. His skill as a navigator was recognized by the East India Company, whose directors indicated on one occasion their willingness for Roe to assume command of one of their ships.[30] Some of the comments in the journal show Roe to have been an effective reporter of novel sights. At Penguin Island he was apparently impressed by the strange birds that had given the island its name. In his journal he wrote: "On Pengwyn there is a foule soe Called that goes vpright, his winges without feathers hanging downe like sleues faced with whyte; they fley not but walk in Pathes and keepe their diuisions and quarters orderly; they are a strange fowle or rather a Miscelanius creator of beast, bird, and Fishe, but most of bird."[31]

After more than ninety days at sea the fleet made its first landfall at Saldana Bay on 5 June. Only four men had died on the voyage and this was considered to be an unusually low casualty rate. Much of the bread had been unfit to eat, but even this did not change the conviction that the voyage so far had been a very fortunate one.[32] In accordance with instructions given by the company before they left home, they put nine condemned men ashore at Saldana and then set sail for the short journey to the Cape of Good Hope.[33] They stopped there only briefly, but Sir Thomas took time to erect a pillar with an inscription about his embassy.[34] From the Cape they sailed north-northeast, staying close to the African coast on their left. They paused briefly at the Comoro Islands in the Mozambique Channel and then pressed on to Socotra, a small

[30] *C.S.P.C., 1617–1621,* Sir Thomas Roe to the East India Company, 14 February 1618, p. 121.
[31] Roe, *Journal,* p. 12. Penguin Island is now called Robben Island. It is situated in the entrance to Table Bay.
[32] *C.S.P.C., 1513–1616,* Robert Gippes to the East India Company, 19 June 1615, p. 413; ibid., Nicholas Banggam to the East India Company, 19 June 1615, p. 412.
[33] Ibid., Robert Gippes to the East India Company, 19 June 1615, p. 413.
[34] Ibid., Richard Baker to the East India Company, 20 June 1615, p. 413.

island situated off the coast of Arabia. From there they sailed eastward across the Arabian Sea, felt their way by frequent soundings into the Gulf of Cambay, and finally, on 18 September, dropped anchor at Swally, the roadstead at which the large, oceangoing merchantmen trading in Surat customarily berthed. Some of the local factors came on board and acquainted the ambassador with the latest news of the area. They gave him a cordial welcome, for they hoped that his presence in India would strengthen their position with respect to their Dutch and Portuguese rivals and give them greater stature in the eyes of local merchants.[35]

Roe did not go ashore at once. He was determined that his landing should be an occasion of dignity and splendor and he knew that these effects would be more readily attained if careful preparations were made. It was clear that a great deal would depend upon the first few days of his mission. No effort or care must be spared to make sure that the ambassador of the king of England would open his embassy with appropriate pomp and be received with due deference by the local native officials. These considerations did not arise from any personal delusions of grandeur on Roe's part but from the simple fact that the success or failure of his mission could well depend upon his ability to develop in the Indians with whom he dealt a genuine respect for the English and for himself. He could not hope to negotiate successfully from a position of weakness, yet at the time of his arrival the title of ambassador was almost meaningless. Many incompetent and unworthy men had assumed the title in the past, but their performance had not been as impressive as their presumption. They had submitted to all sorts of indignities, had pleaded and cajoled with minor native officials, and in general had stripped the title of meaning and respect. Roe commented in his journal on "how meanly an Embassador was esteemed" at the time of his landing.[36] He was

---

[35] Roe, *Journal*, p. 42; Foster, "The East India Company, 1600–1740," p. 80.

[36] Roe, *Journal*, p. 45.

determined to rectify this situation and recognized that the only way to do so was to insist upon being treated with proper respect from the very beginning of his embassy.

On 20 September he wrote a letter notifying the governor of Surat of his arrival. He received a cordial reply, a promise of thirty horsemen to attend him on his landing, and an assurance that, if the English factors could find a house in Surat suitable for the ambassador's use, everything possible would be done to procure it for him.[37] The matter of housing was soon settled and Roe directed his attention to another matter that seemed to be important. On 23 September he wrote again to the governor, seeking assurance that his belongings would not be subjected to the careful examination that the Indian customs officials normally applied to goods coming into their country. In his letter Sir Thomas insisted that submission to such a search would be beneath the dignity of the ambassador of a great king and "that if any such affront were offered" he would promptly return to his ship and report the matter to the Great Mogul.[38] The governor, in his reply, indicated that he would do his best to accommodate Roe in the matter. He pointed out that it was an invariable rule of his country that nothing could be brought in without being examined, but that in this special case he could have the ambassador's goods sealed as they left the ship and then examined formally ("but not in the nature of a search") after they had reached Roe's house. Sir Thomas consented to this after arguing for some time with the messenger and sent word that he would land his baggage the following day and that he himself would come ashore on 26 September "in expectation of the horses and Company offered and the Honorable reception promised by the Gouernor."[39]

All the arrangements had been made and, insofar as it was possible for him to do, Roe had made sure that he would be

[37] Ibid., p. 43.
[38] Ibid., p. 44.
[39] Ibid., p. 44.

appropriately received in Surat. On 26 September all the English ships in the harbor were gaily fitted out with their ensigns aloft and flags flying from their mastheads. A hundred men had been sent ashore to form an honor guard. To the sound of trumpets Roe's boat made its way through the English fleet. As he passed, the ships fired their guns in salute. His boat pulled up on the shore and the ambassador, accompanied by Captain Keeling and the other officers of the fleet, stepped out onto Indian soil.[40]

The chief officials of Surat, with about thirty companions, were sitting under an open tent as the ambassador approached. Drawing nearer, Roe noticed that the men in the tent had not risen, so he stopped and sent a messenger to inform them that he would come no further if they continued to sit still, "whervpon they all rose, and I entered the tent and went streight vp and tooke my place in the middest of them."[41]

At first everything went well. Formal speeches of welcome were made and a spirit of cordiality prevailed. But when Roe indicated that he was ready to go on into the town to reside until he was ready to begin his journey to the Mogul's court, the officials began to insist that the English should prepare to submit themselves to a customs search. Roe blazed in indignation. He asserted that this was contrary to the promise of the governor, on the basis of which he had come ashore. He was the ambassador of a mighty and free prince and would never dishonor his master by submitting to such an indignity. He would give his word that none of his followers had any trading articles, but nothing would induce him to submit to such common and barbarous usage.[42] The officials gave him no satisfaction. They replied only that the inspection was the custom of their country and that they dare not break it. Sir Thomas retorted that ambassadors were above ordinary customs; he would not demean himself by further argument but

[40] Ibid., p. 46.
[41] Ibid.
[42] Ibid., p. 48.

would return to his ship and straightway inform the Mogul of the treatment to which he had been subjected. This brought a concession and an arrangement whereby Roe himself and five of his party would be exempt from search. However, no sooner had Sir Thomas indicated his willingness to accept this compromise than some of his men were seized and subjected to a forcible search. The spirited scene that followed is best described in Roe's own words:

> Master Wallis breaking out came vp after me, and tould me this treachery; wheron I turned my horse, and with all speed rode backe to them, I confess too angry. When I came vp, I layd my hand on my swoord, and my men breake throwgh and came about me. Then I asked what they entended by soe base treachery: I was free landed, and I would die soe, and if any of them durst touch any belonging to me, I bade him speake and shew himselfe. Then they desired me not to take yt in ill part: it was done in friendship. I called for a Case of Pistolls and, hanging them at my saddle, I replyed those were me Frendes, in them I would trust: that they had dealt treacherously with me, and soe I did esteeme them . . . . I was resolued not to returne to my Cuntry with shame; I would rather dye there with Honor.[43]

Roe's determination and show of anger carried the day and his servants were released without being searched. But this incident proved to be merely the first in a long series of provocations designed to test the mettle of the new ambassador. There was further wrangling over the matter of the customs inspection and, even before that was settled, Roe and the governor were at odds over which of them should first call upon the other. Sir Thomas insisted that the custom of Europe dictated that the governor should visit the ambassador: to reverse the procedure would be an insult to the honor of the great king he represented. The governor replied that in his country the reverse procedure was followed and that all previous ambassadors had not only called upon him but had also willingly submitted to the customs examination. Sir Thomas replied

---

[43] Ibid., pp. 48–51.

haughtily that these earlier men had been but agents; the precedents they had established had absolutely no bearing upon him, a full ambassador. For several days the arguments went back and forth. Roe stood absolutely firm and eventually won on both points. His chests were released to him without having been searched and, on 30 September the governor, resplendent in cloth of gold, paid a courtesy call.[44]

The feeling of triumph that Roe might have had was short-lived, for in the weeks that followed he was subjected to repeated annoyances and insults. The explanation for this persistent harassment was to be found in circumstances that had developed long before his arrival in India. To mention some of them will serve to show more clearly the deep-rooted and complicated nature of the hostility that stood between Roe and the successful completion of his mission.

The government of Surat in 1615 was under the control of the Mogul's favorite son, Prince Khurram, who had recently been appointed viceroy of the province of Gujarat. Khurram was suspicious of all foreigners, apparently feeling that their activities impinged in some way upon his authority. He knew that the English hoped to get permission to trade with other ports, and he feared that this would result in a decrease in the amount of customs paid at Surat. These considerations would, of course, have applied to any foreigners, but Khurram was particularly wary of the English because he knew that he could be friendly with them only at the cost of alienating the Portuguese, whose enmity he feared.[45] The quality of England's representatives in Surat had done nothing to change his convictions. The most recent, prior to Roe's arrival, had been William Edwards, a well-meaning man, but one who had suffered all sorts of indignities without complaint and who had, in Roe's opinion, "bredd a low reputation of our Nation."[46] The truth of this statement was demonstrated when,

---

[44] Ibid., pp. 52–61.
[45] *C.S.P.C., 1513–1616*, pp. 237, 333; Foster, *Embassy*, p. xxvii.
[46] Roe to Sir Thomas Smythe, 24 January 1616, cited in ibid., p. xiii.

upon the announcement of Roe's own arrival, the natives "laughd one vpon another."[47] It was little wonder the governor of Surat, knowing the attitude of his master the prince and being acquainted with the low reputation of the English, felt free to treat Roe with scorn.

Thus, in the weeks following his arrival Roe was subjected to one provocation after another. Some of his chests were forcibly opened and searched, a servant of one of the English merchants was cruelly whipped for no good reason, and some of the gifts that Roe had brought for the Mogul were temporarily confiscated.[48] The governor required either gifts or a bribe before he would lift a finger to help the English and sought to block them at every turn and make life difficult at every opportunity.

But throughout the length of his stay in Surat, Roe was unshakable in his insistence on being treated in a manner befitting his station. He protested every insult and bombarded the governor with letters that burned with indignation and outrage. His most effective weapon was the threat to report the governor's behavior to the Great Mogul, who had promised to receive an English ambassador with courtesy and respect. Roe made this threat on several occasions and it finally bore fruit. Letters arrived from the court at Ajmere reprimanding the governor for his behavior toward the English representative.[49] Immediately the official humbly desired Roe's friendship and undertook to provide him with anything he wanted. Roe, however, scorned the offer, saying that it was too late. He had learned from experience that the governor's promises were worthless and he suspected that as long as he remained in office the English merchants at Surat would not be kindly treated. This being the case, he must have been gratified to learn that soon after his departure from Surat the governor

---

[47] Roe, *Journal*, p. 45.
[48] Roe to the governor of Surat, 15 October 1615 in Foster, *Embassy*, pp. 73–74; Roe, *Journal*, p. 68.
[49] Ibid., pp. 82–83.

was discharged from his post and replaced by a man who appeared to have been selected because of his demonstrated friendliness with the English. This appointment represented quite an achievement on Roe's part. Surat was the most important of the English factories in India and the harmonious relationships that came to exist between the English community and the new governor were certainly useful to English commercial interests there.[50]

Sir Thomas Roe's sojourn at Surat was only a prelude to his Indian mission, but it nevertheless occupies an important place in the history of his embassy. For Roe himself it was a time of testing and experiment, an opportunity to grow accustomed to the demanding role of ambassador. He had a chance to learn of the duplicity of Indian officials, to become more aware of the difficulties that would attend his efforts to bind the Mogul to long-term commercial agreements. He was able to learn something of the customs and attitudes he could expect to encounter at the court at Ajmere and to draw the conclusion that while the Indians respected strength, they despised weakness and were quick to take advantage of it.[51] Most important of all, it was at Surat that Roe began the long and difficult task of reshaping the image of his country. In the context of the three-way rivalry for Indian trade this was a consideration of paramount importance. Clearly the Indians would be wooed away from their Portuguese and Dutch alliances only if they were convinced that their own interests would be well served by such a move. Roe must somehow learn to project through his character and behavior the image of a mighty king whose offers of friendship could not be lightly ignored. In the weeks he spent at Surat he worked to develop this characterization, and the results of his personal feud with the governor suggest

[50] Foster, *Embassy*, p. 82, *n*.1; Roe, *Journal*, pp. 290, 334; Roe thought highly of the new governor and commented on his value to the English (ibid.).
[51] "These men triumph ouer such as yeeld, and are humble enough when they are held vp" (ibid., p. 46).

that he did so with some success. When, on 30 October, he left the city and began the long journey to Ajmere, the prospects of the English factors at Surat were much brighter than they had been at the time of his arrival.

Ajmere, where the court of the Mogul emperor was temporarily located, was a long and tedious journey from Surat. Although Sir Thomas had received, just prior to his departure, a letter from the Mogul containing a command to all the governors of towns or provinces to allow him safe and free passage, he apparently realized that his journey could easily prove to be a dangerous one. He was therefore accompanied by a heavily armed escort that gave his party the appearance of a military expedition. Water and supplies were carried on clumsy bullocks and each night, when the tents had been pitched, a watch was stationed to look out for the brigands that abounded in the area.[52]

Traveling an average of about 18 miles each day, Roe arrived in mid-November at Burhanpur, an important commercial, governmental, and military center some 230 miles from Surat. On his arrival he learned that the second son of the emperor was in the city so Roe arranged to visit him, thinking that some preliminary experience of an eastern court would stand him in good stead when he arrived at Ajmere.[53] The visit proved to be a memorable one for the Englishman, who was greatly impressed by the "great but barbarous state" that he found at the court. It was unlike anything he had experienced before, but Roe was determined to take it in stride and to treat the prince as an equal. In his colorful and expressive style, but with the mild condescension he reserved for almost anything that was not English, Sir Thomas recorded in his journal the occasion of his first meeting with the prince:

> At the outward Courte wear about 100 horsemen Armed, being gentllmen that attend the Princes sitting out to salute him,

[52] Ibid., pp. 85, 87, 88.
[53] Ibid., p. 91.

making a lane of each side. In the Inward Courte he satte, high in a Gallerie that went round, with a Cannipe over him and a Carpett before him, in great but barbarous state. Comming toward him throwgh a lane of People, an Officer came and brought me woord I must touch the ground with my head, and my hatt off. I answered: I came in honnor to see the Prince and was free from the Customs of seruants. Soe I passed on, till I came to a place rayled in, Right vnder him, with an assent of 3 steepes, wher I made him reverance, and he bowed his bodye; and soe went within yt, wher stood round by the side all the great men of the Towne with their handes before them like slaues . . . . When I was entered I knewe not where to be placed, but went right and stood before him, wher there is an assent of thre steepes, vpon which standes his secretary to deliuer what is sayd or giuen . . . . But standing in that manner belowe, I demanded lycence to Come vp and stand by him. Hee answered: if the King of Persia or the great Turke wher ther, it might not be admitted . . . . Then I demanded a Chaier, but I was answered noe man euer satt in that place . . . . and after some other Questions, he said: to giue me Content, although I might not Come vp wher hee satt, hee would goe into another Place, wher I should Come vnto him.[54]

During this meeting with the prince Sir Thomas sought permission for the establishing of an English factory at Burhanpur. His request was favorably received, but before any positive action was taken Roe was reminded of the indispensable part played by gifts in any diplomatic dealings with Indians. He learned that what had been true of the officials at Surat was also true of the Mogul's son: no satisfaction was to be gained unless and until some English gifts found their way into Indian hands. Accordingly Roe gave some gifts to the prince, one of which was "a Case of bottles." Sir Thomas, perhaps, was deliberately catering to the prince's well-known addiction to liquor, but in any event the gift was well received and promptly enjoyed; after Roe had been in the court a little while he was told the prince was drunk.[55] His incapacity did not, however, cause him to forget or ignore Roe's request for trading privileges in Burhanpur and within a few days Sir

[54] Ibid., pp. 91–93.
[55] Smith, *Oxford History of India*, p. 371; Roe, *Journal*, p. 93.

Thomas had in his pocket the prince's "firman" providing for the establishment of a factory there.[56]

His stay in Burhanpur had been a successful one, but by the time he left there on 27 November, Roe was in anything but a jubilant frame of mind. Nine days earlier he had taken a fever and his condition had gradually worsened. He had to be carried out of the city on a litter and the movement aggravated his condition so that two days later he lost consciousness and some of the members of his company actually thought that he was dead.[57] One of their number, Humphrey Boughton, did in fact die, apparently of the same malady that had attacked the ambassador. Slowly, however, Sir Thomas began to recover, although for more than two weeks his strength was insufficient to allow him to write more than brief notes in the journal that he had kept with such diligence in his embassy.

On 23 December Roe and his party arrived at Ajmere; the ambassador still found it necessary to be carried on a litter by his servants.[58] As they approached the city they were greeted by the English merchants who lived there. For the occasion they had set up tents in the fields outside the town and the ambassador and his party rested there for a time. The merchant delegation was headed by William Edwards and included the irrepressible Thomas Coryate, whom Roe had known in England.[59] Coryate had arrived in Ajmere in July, after his remarkable walk from Aleppo, and since then had been sharing the home of the ten English merchants. Roe must have been pleased to see a familiar face once more, but perhaps

[56] Ibid., p. 100. The factory was not a success. Sales in the first year of operations totaled only £3,000 and, although there were hopes that this amount could be doubled in the second year, the trade was gradually overshadowed by the development of new commercial activity with Persia. By February 1618 Roe was recommending the dissolution of the factory and the removal of its operations to Surat (*C.S.P.C., 1617–1621*, pp. 12, 122).
[57] Roe, *Journal*, pp. 93, 100.
[58] Ibid., p. 105.
[59] Michael Strachan, *The Life and Adventures of Thomas Coryate* (London, 1962), p. 236.

he found a bit trying the long and eloquent oration that Coryate insisted upon delivering in honor of the occasion.[60]

Roe's continuing illness made it necessary for him to send his excuses to the Mogul who, by this time, was growing impatient of the delay and eager to see the gifts he knew the ambassador would have in his train. But it was not until the beginning of January 1616 that Roe began to recover. He, like the emperor, was impatient of the long delay that had been imposed upon him. As soon as he was able to stir he began to make preparations for his first audience with the monarch who is known to history by the impressive title of Jahangir—"Conqueror of the World."

[60] Ibid., p. 238.

CHAPTER 3
At the Court of the Mogul

THE emperor's title, "Conqueror of the World," was something of an exaggeration; but for all that, Sir Thomas Roe's embassy to India did come at a time when that country was near the peak of its power. The Mogul Empire was almost a hundred years old at the time of Roe's arrival and it was still enjoying the golden age made possible by the constructive genius of Akbar the Great, the father of Jahangir. The empire covered a vast area; its territories included what would now be called Afghanistan, much of western Pakistan, and all of northern and central India. These lands had been provided with an efficient centralized government and, although grinding poverty and frequent famine were then as now no strangers to India, the people were able to live in a peace and security they had not known for centuries. There was constant fighting on the frontiers where the emperors sought to extend their lands at the expense of the kings of the Deccan, but in the interior relative tranquillity prevailed.

The Mogul emperors were initially "foreigners" from the Indian point of view. They had invaded the subcontinent at a time when India was turbulent and divided. Their religion was Islam and their culture was Persian. But gradually they had been accepted and the empire had come to represent something more than the domination of one part of the community by the other. The Moguls ceased to be foreigners imposing a foreign rule and an alien religion and became instead the accepted leaders of a joint enterprise in empire-building. The foundations of an Indian empire ruled by Moguls, rather than a Mogul Empire in India, were laid.[1] This new, unified point of view was largely the result of the tolerant spirit of Akbar who, failing to develop a religion to which all his subjects could subscribe, had nevertheless been governed by his generous disposition and his humane temper and treated men equally without reference to their religious principles.

During its relatively brief existence the empire had developed an extensive bureaucracy. The state was divided into fifteen provinces, each under the control of its governor. These officials were, of necessity, given extensive powers, for in an empire so vast there had to be some power of decision at the local level. The governors were grand figures. Some of them (as in the case of the province of Gujarat) were members of the royal family, and all of them were able to live in princely splendor because of the tremendous incomes they were able to make from their offices.[2] From the point of view of the European trader the governors held positions of great importance in that they were empowered to grant or revoke trading privileges. However, they were generally cautious about entering into any binding agreement, for they believed that to do so in some way detracted from their own power and freedom of action. As a matter of fact, even when an agreement could be extracted from one of these men it seldom proved satisfactory, for they were frequently moved from one province to another and the agreements made by one governor were not considered to be binding upon his successor. Thus, even if the man who made the agreement did not himself default (and Roe's experience would suggest that this was a rare occurrence) it was often vitiated by some other means. It was from the faults and uncertainties of this system that one of the principal reasons for Roe's embassy sprang: it was felt that

[1] T. G. P. Spear, *India, a Modern History* (Ann Arbor, Mich., 1961), p. 130.
[2] Sir George Dunbar, *India and the Passing of Empire* (New York, 1952), p. 43, *n.* 12, citing J. Bruce, *Annals of the East India Company* (London, 1810).

he might be able to achieve trading privileges based upon a treaty with the emperor—and that such an agreement would be dependable to a degree that contracts negotiated with lesser officials could never achieve.

Beneath the governors in the imperial hierarchy was a complex and highly developed civil service. Its members were divided into thirty-three grades or ranks and were charged with the detailed administration of the state. To an outsider the structure might have appeared cumbersome and unwieldy, but as a matter of fact it was remarkably responsive to the will of the emperor whose court was the nerve center of seventeenth-century India.[3] The capital was wherever the emperor happened to be, whether in the great palaces of Delhi and Agra or in the "tent-cities" that seemed to spring from the ground at every pause in the itinerant emperor's schedule. The personality of the emperor was the mainspring of the government—and the policies of the government determined to a large extent the economic condition of the empire.

The economy of India was healthier in the seventeenth century than it had been for many hundreds of years.[4] The villages in which most of the people lived formed the base of the economy and were normally self-sufficient. Their populations lived very close to the subsistence level and any surplus that they might have produced was quickly skimmed off for the imperial treasury. A great majority of the people made their living off the land, but India possessed many products and industries that gave the country a worldwide reputation for skillful manufacturing. Most of her industrial production for export was in luxury items, and she was, of course, particularly well known for cotton and silk cloth. Cotton goods were exported in every direction. In Persia they were exchanged for carpets, horses, and luxury goods; while in the East Indies they paid for spices and metals, such as the tin of Malaya. Cotton goods were the staple of India's trade with Europe and it was

[3] Spear, *India, a Modern History*, p. 147.
[4] This paragraph is based on the material in ibid., pp. 153–59.

textiles that purchased India's imports and gave the country as a whole a favorable balance of trade. The chief necessary imports were raw silk, metal, and a number of materials like ivory, coral, and amber that were vital to the handicraft trades of millions of India's people. In addition to these things Indians imported many curiosities and luxury items, but when all had been paid for there was a large balance in India's favor, and this was made up by bullion, chiefly in the form of silver.[5]

This was the dazzling trade that had attracted the mercantile appetites of Europe, and it was the purpose of Sir Thomas Roe to divert what portion of it he could into the ships of the East India Company. If he could persuade the Mogul to enter into a binding agreement, he would liberate English trade from the uncertainties attendant upon agreements made at lower levels and, at the same time, would convince the merchants of the East India Company that the defeat of their European rivals would, in fact, be the prelude to a settled and profitable commercial relationship with India. Those men could hardly be expected to risk their fortunes in competition with the Dutch and Portuguese until there was some assurance that their victory would bring the trade they desired. And that assurance could be provided by only one man: Jahangir, "Conqueror of the World," son of Akbar the Great, and Mogul emperor of Hindustan.

Jahangir had succeeded to his father's throne in 1605 in unusually peaceful circumstances. There was no fratricidal struggle, because his two older brothers had drunk themselves into early graves before their father's death. The new emperor soon proved himself to be a person of contradictory qualities and changeable moods. He inherited something of the religious tolerance of his father though his attitude probably grew more from lethargy than from conviction. To the genuine dismay of the English ambassador he proved very friendly to some Portuguese Jesuits and he admired Christian art to such an extent

---

[5] Ibid., p. 154. The East India Company's original charter guaranteed the right to export a specified amount of bullion.

that his throne at Agra was surrounded by paintings of John the Baptist, Saint Anthony, and Saint Bernardino of Siena. For a time it was popularly believed that the emperor had become a Christian, but the Church's prohibition of polygamy proved to be an insurmountable obstacle to the conversion of a man who had eighteen wives and enjoyed each of them to the full.[6] Soon after his accession Jahangir abandoned the effort to develop a faith to which both Moslem and Hindu could subscribe; but he permitted, and even encouraged, the adulation of the emperor's person and, in doing so, made of himself a semidivine figure. Outwardly he himself conformed to the tenets of Islam, but he was really a free thinker who refused to permit religious scruples of any kind to interfere with his activities. He derived his greatest pleasure from an art school he founded and from some magnificent gardens that he planned; it has even been suggested that he would have been a happier and a better man if, instead of being emperor, he had been the head of a natural history museum.[7] It is certainly true that he was often lax in discharging the affairs of state and that from time to time his authority fell by default into other, more industrious, hands. But this man was capable of exhibiting contrary qualities. In 1606 his eldest son, the popular Prince Khusru, attempted rebellion. On his father's orders more than three hundred of his followers were brutally massacred and the prince himself was partially blinded and imprisoned for life. This aspect of the emperor's character, together with the weakness for alcohol that was such a notable trait of the imperial family, has led one authority to describe Jahangir as a "drunken despot subject to outbursts of fiendish cruelty."[8]

This strange and complex man, whose every word was law, was bound to the strict observance of a daily routine just as surely as his subjects were bound to obey his slightest wish.

[6] Vincent A. Smith, *Oxford History of India*, 3d ed., rev. and ed. Percival Spear (Oxford, 1958), pp. 365–66.
[7] Dunbar, *India and the Passing of Empire*, p. 35.
[8] C. C. Davies, "India," in *Encyclopaedia Britannica* (Chicago, 1960), 12:163.

Each morning soon after sunrise, Jahangir would go to a public balcony overlooking a courtyard and show himself to the throngs of people that invariably assembled there to see him. Later in the morning he would return to the balcony to be entertained by a cavalry parade, or perhaps by the spectacle of elephants and wild beasts fighting in the courtyard below. This period of pleasant relaxation was followed usually by a session in the Hall of Public Audience, where the emperor would receive petitions, make appointments, and give audiences. Next, the emperor would proceed to the private hall to discuss confidential business with his principal ministers. Admission to this inner sanctum was one of the most valued privileges at the court, since it carried with it such fine opportunities for catching the royal ear. After these business sessions came a meal and a siesta when the emperor (to use the disapproving words of the very proper English ambassador) retired "to sleepe among his woemen." In the evening, when the emperor was suitably refreshed, there would be a rather informal assembly characterized by a medley of business and gaiety. Matters of state were frequently discussed and, since the king believed a level head was necessary in such situations, each person in the room was carefully examined for signs of recent drinking. The prohibition against alcohol did not, however, extend to the emperor himself and many of the meetings closed with Jahangir soundly asleep on his throne. Sir Thomas Roe quickly learned that the emperor was frequently in a mellow mood during these evening sessions and that consequently they represented an auspicious time for the transaction of his business.

Sir Thomas regarded the activities of the court with a variable blend of exasperation and condescension, but he was occasionally moved to confess admiration for some of the emperor's qualities. In his journal he commented on how each Tuesday the emperor would sit in judgment on cases that had been brought before him, hearing both sides of each case with patience and paying as much attention to the complaints of the lowliest man as he did to those of the highest.[9] On numerous other occasions he was moved to record his appreciation of the emperor's fair treatment and in general to convey the impression that, although he deplored many of the practices and standards of the strange land in which he found himself, he nevertheless looked upon the emperor with some admiration and no little respect.

As he recuperated from his long illness and awaited his first audience, it was difficult for Roe to know what kind of reception to expect from this complex man. He knew that for much of his reign Jahangir had been friendly to the Portuguese and correspondingly cool to the English, whose distant and little-known homeland made no impression on the self-assured Mogul court. But he knew too that in recent years English envoys had been kindly received and that his countrymen had made a great impression by defeating superior Portuguese fleets twice within the space of two years. English prestige in India was on the rise and chances of winning imperial favor were improved by the prospect that England's strength could be used as a counterpoise to the Portuguese, who often appeared to Indian eyes as intolerant and overbearing.[10] The time seemed ripe for a major step forward.

By 6 January Roe was largely recovered from his illness and he began to make preparations for his first audience. Because of the unfamiliar intricacies of the protocol of the Mogul court he sought permission to use the customs of his own country. His request was readily granted by an emperor who was eager to see the gifts the ambassador had brought. The audience was arranged for 10 January, and Sir Thomas presented himself at the court late in the afternoon when the Mogul was sitting out "to entertayne strangers, to receiue petitions and presents, to giue Commandes, to see, and to bee seene."[11] As he approached the court the Englishman was immediately reminded of a

[9] Roe, *Journal*, pp. 106–108.
[10] Smith, *Oxford History of India*, pp. 367–68.
[11] Roe, *Journal*, p. 106.

theater, for the king was seated in a raised gallery so that all the people might see him clearly. The main floor of the place was divided by a number of rails. Within the first rail, and closest to the emperor, were the great men of the kingdom; the second rail enclosed the people of lesser rank whom Roe called the "gentry," and beyond that barrier stood the ordinary people. Each of the three groups stood on a different level, so that the leading men of the kingdom were raised above those of lesser rank and the gentry were higher than the common people. Roe was led through the crush of people by two slaves until he came to stand within the innermost rail. His interpreter began to make a formal statement, but the emperor silenced him and spoke first, welcoming the ambassador, inquiring about his health and offering the services of his own physicians.[12] Sir Thomas, in return, presented his commission and a letter from King James and then produced the gifts he had brought from England. These were apparently well received and Roe took his leave of the court well pleased with the results of his first audience. He wrote in his journal that the emperor had used him "with more fauour and outward grace . . . then euer was showed to any Ambassador, eyther of the Turke or Persian, or other whatsoeuer."[13]

Encouraged by his initial experience at the court, Sir Thomas decided to come to grips at once with what promised to be a crucial and difficult part of his embassy. The favorite son of the emperor was named Prince Khurram. His friendship was vitally important to the English because he had been appointed by his father governor of the province in which Surat was situated—and England's most important Indian factory was in Surat. Unfortunately, the prince had the reputation of being an enemy to all foreigners, especially Christians.[14] Roe had indirectly experienced some of his ill will in the exasperating behavior of the governor of Surat, the prince's

    [12] Ibid., pp. 108–109; Roe to Lord Carew, 17 January 1616, in Foster, *Embassy*, p. 112.
    [13] Roe, *Journal*, p. 109.
    [14] Ibid.

subordinate, and he had been able to see how difficult the transaction of business could become when the governor opposed it. He knew that the well-being of the factors and the health of the company's business demanded the establishment of a more satisfactory relationship with the prince. These considerations in themselves would have been sufficient to necessitate action on Roe's part, but they were given a fresh urgency by the arrival of news from Surat that the governor was inflicting new provocations on the English there.

Soon after Roe's departure the governor, who claimed to be acting on the orders of the prince, had forced the general of the English fleet, Captain Keeling, to sign a statement to the effect that the English would agree to leave India within a year. They would be permitted to continue their trading activities, but were not to maintain any residences ashore.[15] These restrictions, if enforced, would have ended the factor system upon which English trading practices were built and would have delivered a most serious blow to the prospects of the East India Company. The whole relationship between England and India, still young but so carefully and expensively built, would have been jeopardized; and nothing could have shown more clearly the precarious position of the English in India at the beginning of Roe's embassy than this threat of expulsion. It was clearly the ambassador's responsibility to do what he could to prevent this.

With some trepidation he requested an audience with the prince, but he had to wait impatiently for a whole week while Khurram went on a hunting trip with his father. It was not until 22 January that he was granted an audience. He was received kindly, and, with almost visible relief, he broached the question of the ill-treatment suffered by the English at the hands of the prince's officials. Perhaps unwisely he hinted that he would appeal directly to the Mogul if speedy satisfaction were not given. The prince's reply was that he had been quite ignorant of any ill-treatment of the English and especially of

[15] Ibid., p. 74; Foster, *Embassy*, p. 115, *n.* 2.

any command to dismiss them from their factory. The governor, he said, had acted falsely and would be called to account for his actions. He asked Sir Thomas to provide him with a list of the specific injuries suffered by the English and promised that he would act quickly to provide a written statement confirming them in their rights and privileges.[16]

Roe was gratified by the results of his audience, but he soon learned that victory was not to be had so easily or so quickly. When he received the promised statement, he found that it made the continuation of English privileges at Surat contingent upon an agreement whereby the Portuguese would be free to trade there without molestation. Roe absolutely refused to agree to this; first, because he believed that any concession to the Portuguese at Surat should be accompanied by a similar concession to the English at Goa, and second, because he feared that a treacherous attack by "boates laden with fire woorkes" might take place if Portuguese ships were allowed to move freely among the English in the harbor of Surat.[17]

The prince met Roe's refusal by saying simply that no firman guaranteeing English rights would be issued. In exasperation and disgust Roe took his case to a highly placed official named Asaph Khan. He did this, presumably, because he feared that a direct appeal to the emperor, over the head of Khurram, would create an irreparable breach with the prince, and because he believed that Asaph Khan exercised great authority over the prince and at court. He was a brother of the emperor's favorite wife, a son of the prime minister, the father-in-law of Prince Khurram, and an extremely influential person whom Roe depicts as a cool and calculating character, the epitome of Oriental duplicity, and a man unalterably opposed to any extension of English influence at the Mogul court. This last attitude was, as yet, unknown to Roe, who hoped to achieve redress from this powerful individual. Instead, he got for his pains the disturbing revelation that Asaph Khan, far from being

[16] Roe, *Journal,* pp. 114–15, 117.
[17] Ibid., p. 117.

disposed to help, was in fact the author of the hostile action and the effectual leader of a powerful group within the court that took advantage of the emperor's well-known antipathy to the affairs of state and asserted its own authority. Sir Thomas had been deceived and, in thinking that he needed only to win over the emperor to achieve his ends, had greatly underestimated the difficulties of his mission. He was going to have to deal with an influential and hostile clique, and it was unlikely that he would achieve anything unless he could contrive to win the support of the people who constituted this formidable power behind the throne.

The principal figure of the group was the emperor's favorite wife, a forceful and able woman named Nur Jahan. She had been in the service of Akbar and had caught the eye of his son, who married her in 1611. She had made use of his devotion to her to advance the interests of her family. Her father and brother (who was ennobled as Asaph Khan) soon became the leading figures at court, and the power of the family increased still more when Prince Khurram married Asaph Khan's daughter. From that time on the group devoted itself to advancing the claims of Khurram to be recognized as the heir to his father's throne. These claims were advanced in opposition to those of the popular Prince Khusru who, though the oldest of the Mogul's children, was out of favor because of his involvement in an ill-advised rebellion. The English ambassador was inclined to agree with the great majority of the Indian people who were convinced of Khusru's virtues and hoped that he would succeed to his father's throne. Needless to say, Roe kept his opinion to himself, but it must have been difficult for him to conceal his strong dislike of Khurram and his friends. It is quite possible that his true sentiments were suspected and that they contributed to the chilly relationship that came to exist between Roe and the court faction.[18] But there were other

[18] Smith, *Oxford History of India,* pp. 365, 369. Roe said of Khusru: "Sultan Khusru, the eldest brother, is both extremely beloved, and honoured of all men (almost adored) and very justly for his noble parts.

than personal considerations involved. The empress had rather extensive commercial interests. She would frequently invest in some promising trading expedition, and she had grown accustomed to reaping handsome profits. These enterprises, however, appeared to be threatened by the European powers whose purpose was to lure the trade of India into their own ships. It was little wonder that the lady used her influence against the foreign representatives in her husband's court.[19]

This, then, was the true nature of Roe's opposition—a powerful faction that periodically controlled the emperor and continually argued against the very thing that Roe had come to secure, namely, the extension of England's trading privileges in India and a definite, binding, long-term commitment to future trade between the two countries. It is to Roe's credit that he discerned this opposition at an early date and with remarkable clarity. Less than a month after the start of his active mission, he made the following entry in his journal:

> I saw now the faction, but was irresolute what to doe. Asaph Khan was a broken reede; the Prince gouerned by him; the King was my only refuge, from whom I was sure of Iustice if I Complaynd, but I feard I would draw vpon me the hate of Normall the beloued queene, Ante to Sultan corrons wife, sister of Asaph Chan, whose daughter the Prince married, and all that Powrfull faction, against whom, though I might once preuayle, yet the aduauntage of tyme, language, and opportuni-

. . . If [he] prevail in his right, this kingdom will be a sanctuary for Christians, whom he loves and honours, favouring learning, valour, the discipline of war, and abhorring all covetousness, and discerning the base customs of taking, used by his ancestors and the nobility. If the other [Khurram] win, we shall be losers; for he is most earnest in his superstition, a hater of all Christians, proud, subtile, false, and barbarously tyrannous." On another occasion he said of Khurram: "I never saw so settled a countenance, nor any man keep so constant a gravity, never smiling nor in face showing any respect or difference of men; but mingled with extreme pride and contempt of all."

[19] A significant incident had occurred soon after Roe's first audience with the emperor. The emperor had sent a messenger to Roe asking for his commission, which he wanted to show to the queen in order to satisfy her that the seal was authentic and that Roe was a fully accredited ambassador. The queen had undoubtedly tried to convince the emperor to the contrary (Foster, *Embassy*, p. 109, *n.* 2).

tye, the Power of a wife, a sonne, and fauorite, would produce reuenge.[20]

The recognition of the existence of this strong faction served to clear the air and to demonstrate to Roe the true nature of the obstacles that stood in the way of the successful completion of his mission. The optimism that he had felt after his initial audience must have been tempered now, but nevertheless he set about his negotiations with high hopes. He quickly succeeded in winning the emperor's assurance that some minor annoyances against the English factors at Ahmadabad would be discontinued. Encouraged by this early success, he redirected his attention to the difficult matter of English rights at Surat. He sought to bring pressure to bear upon the prince and his cohorts by threatening to appeal the case directly to the emperor. This threat brought a quick promise of redress from the prince, and Roe was soon presented with a firman that contained all the conditions he sought but was rendered unacceptable in Roe's eyes by the persistent inclusion of a final clause insisting upon Portuguese rights to trade without interference in Surat. Repeating the arguments he had used earlier, Sir Thomas refused to yield any ground and sent the firman back to the prince saying that he would not accept it until the offending clause was removed.[21] The prince's answer was the same as before: either the clause was accepted, or the English would get no firman.

It was clear that a hopeless deadlock had developed. Roe was already aware of the prince's great influence over his father, but he nevertheless resolved that his only chance of success lay in a direct appeal to the emperor. He would just have to hope that he could find the Mogul in an assertive and independent mood. In the meantime he "purposed to prepare the King by Visitations and presents," and then to make his case at the first available opportunity.[22] He appeared at court on a number of

[20] Roe, *Journal*, p. 118.
[21] Ibid., pp. 139, 140-41.
[22] Ibid., p. 142.

occasions during the early days of March and gave the king a gift that was well received. This convinced him that the time to launch his appeal had come, so on the evening of 13 March he made his way to court. The events that occurred there are worth recounting in some detail because they serve to illustrate the obstacles and attitudes against which Roe had to contend and to indicate the determined and tenacious spirit in which Sir Thomas pursued his goal.

It was clear from the start that a lively encounter was going to take place. Asaph Khan, the man who was largely responsible for the dispute, was at court and he contrived to have Roe's interpreter refused admission. Sir Thomas managed to communicate this fact to the emperor who quickly gave instructions for the man to be brought in. But Asaph Khan was not easily cowed. As Sir Thomas stood before the emperor with his interpreter at his side, Asaph Khan drew close to the man and sought "to awe him with wincking and Iogging." Despite this distraction, Roe managed to communicate his complaints to the emperor. He had been at Ajmere, he said, for two months. One of those had been passed in sickness and the other in vain compliments. But nothing had been effected toward the obtaining of a firm and secure trade with residence rights for his countrymen. The Mogul retorted that these things had already been granted. Roe seized the opportunity to assert that all the agreements depended upon a slight thread—temporary and local arrangements that provided no stable or dependable basis for lasting commercial intercourse. What was needed was "an agreement cleare in all poynts, and a more formall and Authentique confirmation then it had by ordinarie firmaens, which were temporarye Commandes and respected accordingly."

Sir Thomas was now pressing toward the central purpose of his entire mission. He was speaking directly to the Mogul and requesting the very thing he had come to India to achieve. But the emperor's reply was to ask what gifts the English would bring. That produced a brief discourse on the possibility that an English horse would survive the sea trip from England to India and it was not until Roe had promised to have six fine stallions shipped to the emperor that he was able to turn again to the matter that was of primary concern to him. With Asaph Khan still trying to intimidate his interpreter, he told the emperor that he had drawn up certain reasonable conditions that would have the effect of confirming the friendship of England and India, settling their trade, and correcting certain wrongs that the English had suffered. At the mention of wrongs Jahangir became furious and demanded to know who had been responsible. Roe was taken aback by the emperor's fury and tried to say that he did not wish to trouble the emperor with his complaints, but would seek justice at the hands of the prince. The emperor misunderstood the reference to Khurram and thought that Roe was accusing his son. He sent for the prince and proceeded to reprimand him, but Roe managed to interrupt and make it clear that he had intended no accusation. The prince, for his part, told his father that he had offered Roe a firman but that it had been rejected. Sir Thomas explained why the firman had been unacceptable and went on again to propound the desirability of one agreement incorporating all the provisions that governed the Anglo-Indian relationship. Then, Roe said, he would not have to trouble the emperor daily with his complaints and in one document would be able to express all the obligations that the king of England and his subjects accepted with respect to their relationship with the Mogul Empire. He proposed that he be permitted to draw up such an agreement, that it be done in triplicate and signed by the emperor, Prince Khurram, and himself, the personal representative of the English king. At this, some of the Jesuits and Portuguese who were present began to protest, but Roe responded by saying that he put a low value upon Portuguese friendship and had only contempt for their hatred and their strength. The emperor expressed his belief that Roe's suggestions were quite just and indicated that Sir Thomas should draw up the agreement he proposed. If its terms were found to be reasonable both he and the prince would sign it and Roe would have the treaty he sought.[23]

This was all Roe could reasonably have expected to gain during his audience, and with high hopes he gave himself to the task of preparing the articles for submission to the Mogul. His purpose was to provide for the security and peace of the English in India and to prevent the recurrence of the kinds of abuse he had experienced since his arrival. He wanted to be sure that the one document would cover every foreseeable contingency so he would not have to go through the tortuous process of making new motions and complaints. He proposed to have many copies of the agreement signed so he could send two to every English factory: one to be kept by the factors, and the other to be exhibited at some prominent point in each place where Englishmen and Indians traded.[24]

For more than a week Sir Thomas labored over his proposals. At last they were compacted into twenty paragraphs, translated into Persian, and made ready for presentation. They provided for the free access of the English to all ports belonging to the Mogul, including those of Bengal and Sind, two areas where the English had not yet penetrated. The English were to be allowed to rent suitable housing at fair prices and to remain peaceably ashore. The goods of the merchants were to pass freely without payment of any duty beyond the normal customs, and the English were to be allowed to buy and sell freely, to rent factories and buy provisions at the usual rates. They were not to be searched when they went ashore, and gifts sent to India for the Mogul were not to be impounded or opened by lesser officials. On the part of the English, Roe was willing to agree that they would not molest the ships of other nations "except the enemyes of the said English, or any other that shall seeke to injure them," and that their factors, while residing ashore, should behave themselves peaceably, do their

[23] Ibid., pp. 145–49.
[24] Ibid., p. 150.

best to procure rarities for the Mogul, provide him (upon payment) with any needed war materials they might have, and assist him against any enemy to the common peace. The Portuguese were to be invited to participate in the agreement, but if they failed to do so within a period of six months, "it shall be lawfull for the said English . . . to Chastice the stubbornes of an obstinat enemie to Peace . . . in taking any of their shippes, boates, or goodes, without any offence to the said great King of India."[25]

On 26 March Roe took his proposals, together with a gift of some pictures, to the royal court. He presented them to the king but was dismayed to see them immediately turned over to Asaph Khan, who was in his usual truculent mood. He criticized the proposals as being too long, and then created an unpleasant scene by complaining that the ambassador was standing closer to the person of the Mogul than he had any right to do. He ordered Roe to step down, but Sir Thomas, with heated and indignant remarks, refused to do any such thing. The incident soon passed, but it did not augur well for the fate of the treaty that now rested in the unfriendly hands of Asaph Khan.

For almost a week Roe waited for an answer, but none came. On 3 April he received word that his demands were considered to be unreasonable and could not be signed. There was no indication as to which articles were deemed offensive. There was simply a blanket rejection of all his proposals. But the rejection was accompanied by strong protestations of friendship toward the English and assertions by Asaph Khan to the effect that he was battling against a court faction that was trying to persuade the emperor to expel Sir Thomas and his countrymen from India.[26]

In the days that followed, Roe received from Asaph Khan many communications designed to convince him that his demands were on the point of being granted. The ambassador's

[25] The articles are printed in Foster, *Embassy*, pp. 152–56.
[26] Roe, *Journal*, pp. 156–57.

excessive confidence in the good will of the emperor made him susceptible to this particular stratagem, and he failed at first to recognize that the cunning minister was making his assurances of friendship as part of an effort to keep the negotiations in his own hands. He had learned that when Roe was openly thwarted he was likely to lay his complaints directly before the emperor. He knew of his sovereign's partiality to the Englishman, but was realistic enough to recognize that it was little more than a passing fancy based upon interest in a new and unusual suitor and upon the expectation of gifts. Asaph Khan knew that if he could delay any direct appeals from Roe to the emperor, there was an excellent chance that Jahangir's attitude would cool and that the Englishman would lose favor.

These tactics were based firmly upon an intimate knowledge of the personality and the attitudes of the Mogul and his court. Asaph Khan knew that an agreement like the one suggested by Roe was repugnant to the Mogul's idea of sovereignty because, by binding him to the performance of certain provisions, it sought to limit his future freedom of action. He knew, too, that the Indians held it to be derogatory for the Mogul to sign a treaty with the representative of an obscure and distant state. Although the emperor had been courteous and considerate to Roe, something of his real indifference to the Englishman is suggested by the fact that his famous personal memoirs make absolutely no direct reference to Sir Thomas or his mission. In the eyes of the Mogul only two other sovereigns had rank approaching his own: the shah of Persia and the ruler of Constantinople. It was presumptuous of the representative of a tiny island kingdom to believe that he could be on equal terms with so great a potentate, and it was little short of impertinent of him to think that he could bind the Mogul to the terms of some written agreement.

Once the Mogul's temporary interest in the Englishman had faded, Asaph Khan could rely upon attitudes like these to prevent him from entering into any binding agreement. In the meantime it was his purpose to keep the articles in his own hands and to act in such a way as to convince Roe that a direct appeal to the emperor was unnecessary.

While his treaty was languishing in the unsympathetic hands of Asaph Khan, Roe had directed his attention once again to the matter of gaining some redress for the hardships inflicted upon the English factors in Surat. His articles, if accepted, would guard against any future difficulties there; but this was insufficient, for Roe was determined that the local officials should be required to compensate the English for the hardships and indignities inflicted upon them in the past. Goods had been confiscated, bribes extorted, and merchandise seized. These things could be paid for, and should be, and Roe was determined to see that accounts were settled. At first he took his complaints to Asaph Khan, and the minister, with the agreeable outward appearance that usually masked his scheming and stubborn mind, promised the ambassador complete satisfaction. But Roe was learning fast, and despite Asaph Khan's repeated promises of satisfaction he determined to take his case directly to Prince Khurram, who had supreme authority over the affairs of Surat. Taking along "some powrfull wyne" as a gift for the prince, he demanded justice against the governor of Surat and was delighted to receive "effectual satisfaction in all my desiers except only some exemplary Iustice vpon his [the governor of Surat's] person."[27] So pleased was Roe with his morning's work that he referred to it in his journal as "the best Morning that euer wee had in India."[28]

Although the negotiations had got off to a promising start, they were inevitably delayed over arguments about the sum that Roe claimed the governor should pay in compensation. After considerable discussion the governor offered 17,000 *mamudis*, an amount that Roe, acting on information supplied by the English at Surat, rejected as being insufficient.[29] Argument

---

[27] Ibid., pp. 159–60.
[28] Ibid., p. 161.
[29] Ibid., pp. 176, 177. Terry estimated the *mamudi* to be worth "about twelve pence sterling."

over the figure went on for over a month, and during that time relations between the ambassador and the prince became even more strained than they had been before. In his persistent way Roe refused to yield any ground, but he was made to feel very foolish by an event of 16 June—an event that was quite beyond his power to control, but one that, nevertheless, put him in a difficult situation. A communication was received from Surat, and from it Roe learned that the governor's original offer had, after all, been a fair one which he could have accepted "with little losse, and finished all long since with good will and . . . avoyeded much trouble and the Princes displeasur."[30] At this point an agreement should have been easily attainable, but once again the intractable mind of Indian officialdom deprived Sir Thomas of a satisfactory settlement when the exasperating governor refused even to pay the amount that he had originally offered. Tedious arguments, innumerable evasions, broken promises, and dashed hopes became the regular order of the day, and it was not until 5 August 1616 that Roe could at last record in his journal: "this long and troublesome business is finished."[31] The full amount demanded had not been obtained, but the difference was almost negligible and, all things considered, the final outcome was a minor triumph for the ambassador, attributable to his determination not to be browbeaten by difficult and persistent opposition. For the first time he had managed to extract a definite settlement, having received not only the monetary compensation but also the prince's firman that the practices Roe had complained of would be discontinued.

Sir Thomas was well pleased with the results of his work, but his primary concern was still with the proposals he had submitted to Asaph Khan in the hope that they would receive the approval of the emperor. His anxiety over the fate of the treaty deepened as the days passed and no satisfactory answer came. His supply of gifts for the emperor had run out and a

---

[30] Ibid., p. 195.
[31] Ibid., p. 224.

new group of Portuguese merchants arrived at the court laden with gifts from the viceroy at Goa. Roe became even more depressed, for he knew only too well that gifts were an effective instrument of diplomacy. It was with more chagrin than surprise that the ambassador noted in his journal that the English "were for a tyme eclipsed" by their rivals.[32] No satisfactory recourse was open to him. Asaph Khan had now been officially appointed to deal with all business between the Mogul court and foreign ambassadors, and when Sir Thomas in desperation tried to take his case directly to the emperor he was curtly referred to Asaph Khan. The minister had achieved his purpose and, sure now of his power, he became more openly hostile than before, actually going so far as to tell Roe that the emperor had given orders that the Englishman was not to present himself at court.[33] This made Roe fairly bristle with indignation. He took a determined stand, saying that the English trade in India was not so valuable that he would buy it at the price of so much injury and dishonor. He decided to wait a few days and then to "resolue of longer residence or to prepare to retyre myselfe."[34] However, his wrath was, in part, unnecessary, for he soon learned that the Mogul had given no such order. The report had been but one more incident in Asaph Khan's campaign to keep inviolate his own and Prince Khurram's control over the trading activities of the empire. When Roe presented himself at court on 25 June, he was "receiued by the King after the ould manner, no difference, without taking any Notice of my absence."[35]

His reinstatement in the good graces of the emperor was undoubtedly gratifying, but Sir Thomas was no nearer to having his proposed treaty accepted than he was before, and the situation was taking on added urgency because of the approach of an English fleet that was due to arrive in Surat in September. Roe was particularly anxious that it should be able

[32] Ibid., p. 183.
[33] Ibid., pp. 181, 218, 183.
[34] Ibid., p. 187.
[35] Ibid., p. 201.

to benefit from the terms embodied in his proposals, and almost every day he approached Asaph Khan and demanded satisfaction. But the maddening calm of the minister remained quite unbroken and his supply of excuses for procrastinating proved inexhaustible. The articles had been carelessly mislaid by a servant;[36] they were ready for the seal but the following day was the king's birthday, when no business could be transacted;[37] the queen was delaying the final confirmation, but the treaty would be sealed as soon as she had seen it.[38] When he could think of no specific excuse, he would lecture Roe on political morality, reminding him that kings could not be hurried, since their "myndes . . . were in Godes handes only."[39]

Roe was infuriated by this kind of treatment, but there was nothing he could do about it, since the king had delegated the transaction of all business to Asaph Khan. As the days passed it became increasingly clear that the treaty was a dead letter and that the most practical course would be for the ambassador to reduce his demands and hope to secure terms that would at least cover the immediate needs of the approaching fleet. Five months of utter frustration had passed since Roe first made his proposals, but it was only with great reluctance that he decided to direct his attention to obtaining a firman that would grant temporarily the concessions needed in the immediate future. This would not involve the abandonment of his original scheme, but it was at least a temporary admission of defeat.

His overtures for a temporary grant were surprisingly well received by Prince Khurram, whom Roe chose to approach because of his authority over the port of Surat. The prince's attitude was undoubtedly mellowed by the realization that the incoming fleet would be carrying fresh supplies of gifts, but more weighty considerations were also involved. A Dutch ship had recently arrived on the coast and there were rumors that

[36] Ibid., p. 222.
[37] Ibid., p. 251.
[38] Ibid., p. 249.
[39] Ibid., p. 219.

others were approaching. Roe recognized an opportunity to use these developments to good purpose. In interviews with the prince and his father, he worked diligently to implant fear and distrust of the newcomers and to portray the English as the potential defenders of the empire against their seaborne assaults. He spoke of how the Dutch, like the Portuguese, invariably sought to dominate the areas in which they traded to the exclusion of the commerce of all other nations and the detriment of the local inhabitants. He contrasted this ambition with the peaceful intentions of the English who wanted not dominion but simply an open and equitable policy that would give all Europeans an equal chance to trade in the ports of the empire.[40] To his journal he confided that his criticism of the Dutch had been overdrawn but that it had served his purpose in a number of ways: it had impressed the prince with his desire to be of service and thus had procured him easier access to that important person; and it had laid serious obstacles in the way of the Dutch, whose admission to the ports of India would, Roe recognized, be a most serious blow to English prospects there.[41]

The immediate fruits of the ambassador's labor came when Khurram granted, fully and without argument, the concessions Roe had requested. The prince's willingness to enter into a temporary agreement demonstrated once again the distinction drawn by the Mogul and his officers between the temporary provisions of a firman and the more binding clauses of a treaty. They were ready and willing to grant the former, but they regarded the latter as somehow inimical to the dignity and grandeur of the Mogul and his court. But the important thing, as far as Roe was concerned, was that the immediate needs of the English were cared for and the incoming fleet could carry on its trade without fear of the hindrances and abuses that had too often been suffered by its predecessors.

His successful dealings with Prince Khurram might have

[40] Ibid., pp. 229–31.
[41] Ibid., pp. 231–32.

encouraged Sir Thomas to believe that his cause in general was making headway, but as a matter of fact a bitter disappointment was in store for him. No sooner had the prince provided him with the firman he wanted than he received an insolent communication from Asaph Khan, who had apparently determined to bring to an end the protracted masquerade over Roe's proposals for a permanent treaty. He sharply objected to many of the articles and expressed his opinion in cutting comments that he wrote in the margins of the document. He criticized the treaty as being badly written and too long; but, what was more to the point, he said that the English would never be given license to trade in other ports, as they had requested, and that they should not seek a treaty at all but content themselves with firmans issued by Prince Khurram who was, after all, the lord of Surat.[42]

It is safe to assume that Roe was dismayed, but not terribly surprised, by this absolute and hostile refusal of his demands. As he himself said, he had "a woolfe by the eares."[43] Although the task seemed hopeless he could not abandon his efforts to win over Asaph Khan, for it was abundantly clear that his power and influence could not be circumvented. There was no other channel by which he could seek to achieve his goal. The minister's purpose was to make Roe wholly dependent upon the prince and the family faction of which he was a member. Indeed, Roe recognized that the principal objection to the articles was that they were drawn up in such a way "that I should nott much neede the Prince, and if wee disliked wee might refuse his Gouerment."[44] It was a point of honor with Khurram and with Asaph Khan that nothing should interfere with their administration of Surat. They were determined to make no grants that would in any way lessen their authority, and their determination stood like a stone wall in the path of the objectives of the English ambassador. Roe was at a loss to

[42] Ibid., p. 260.
[43] Ibid.
[44] Ibid.

know what course to follow. Without any optimism he redrew his demands, putting them this time not in the form of a treaty but in the form of a firman to be granted by the king.[45] But it was all to no avail. Asaph Khan sent word that "hee would procure nothing sealed that any way Concerned the Princes Gouerment: that I should only expect from him what wee desired, whose 'firmaens' were sufficient."[46]

With this refusal it may be supposed that Roe lost heart, but he did nothing of the sort. Determination and persistence were among his most notable characteristics. He was frequently inclined to indulge in the luxury of self-pity, but, in the broader view, Roe must be classified as an optimist, because even when things seemed black he had the courage to press on and to nourish the conviction that things would work out in the end. Now, at the beginning of September 1616 all his efforts appeared to have been frustrated; yet Sir Thomas could think about the diplomatic potential of the gifts that would soon arrive from England and, remembering the firman recently received from Khurram, could write in his journal: "I am resolued to vse the Prince and doubt not to effect . . . by him" my ends.[47]

For the present there was little he could do and, in the absence of any negotiations to report, his journal becomes chiefly concerned with descriptions of the customs and activities of the court. We could wish that the ambassador had permitted himself some more personal reflections and had written some of those things that could have made his account capable of illuminating the personality of its author. It is true, of course, that some of the events that are recorded prove Sir Thomas to have been a man of courage, determination, and patriotism. But there are few glimpses of a more intimate nature. We know, for example, that Roe had been married

[45] "The Copy of my new Demands upon refusall of the former Articles sent this 4th of September, 1616," is printed in Foster, *Embassy*, pp. 261–62.
[46] Roe, *Journal*, p. 262.
[47] Ibid., p. 264.

shortly before leaving England, yet nowhere in his journal is his wife mentioned. There is an obvious explanation for the rather official tone of the journal: that it was intended as an official record of his embassy to be made available to his employers on his return to England. There are several passages that make it abundantly clear that the journal was written with the expectation that it would be read by the officials of the East India Company. Even so, there are places where the man comes through and it is possible for the interested reader of the journal, by means of some well-founded speculation, to arrive at some tentative statements as to the kind of man Sir Thomas Roe must have been.

When his mission to India began he was in his mid-thirties and was beginning to show the first signs of the gouty corpulence that would plague him in later years. He was a big man, an imposing figure, but his face was gentle and sensitive. He had fair hair, which, in the fashion of the time, he wore long. He sported a wide and generous mustache and a modest beard that served to deemphasize his large chin. His eyes were big and soft. He could not have been called a handsome man, but he had an agreeably pleasant face that suggested honesty and sensitivity.[48] His handwriting was neat and easily legible; his signature was written large and firm with an underlining flourish for good measure.

He was a man of large emotions and vivid expression. If he disliked something or somebody he expressed himself heartily; if he was melancholy, he plumbed the depths. He was inclined to be self-centered and was easily hurt by real or imagined wrongs. When his chaplain, John Hall, died in 1616, Sir Thomas devoted two lines of his journal to extolling Hall's virtues and a paragraph bewailing his own sad condition—deprived, by the minister's death, of God's "blessed woord and Sacraments."[49] He passed over the death of other servants with scarcely a word, but devoted whole passages to his own ill-

[48] His portrait, by Van Miereveldt, is in the National Portrait Gallery.
[49] Roe, *Journal*, pp. 245–46.

nesses and discomforts, as though trying to impress the East India Company with the sacrifices he had made on their behalf.

Yet these are minor criticisms and in any event they reflect attitudes that were widespread in earlier times when gentlemen were unaccustomed to mourn at length the death of a cook or manservant. The qualities suggested in the journal that are more likely to impress the reader are positive ones. Roe's courage is attested repeatedly on those occasions when he refused to yield to the studied insults of Asaph Khan. His determination is convincingly demonstrated on nearly every page, and there was never any serious question about his absolute honesty and integrity. His patriotism was profound and his religious faith was apparently rich and real to him. Indeed, his biographer finds himself constantly tempted to conclude that Roe must have been a paragon of virtue and to feel that the discovery of some minor vice would add a welcome tinge of human frailty to a portrait in danger of becoming incredible because of its consistently laudatory tone.

In the search for some corrective criticism it is tempting to dwell upon the wheedling, self-abasing letters that Roe, throughout his life, was to write his superiors, and especially the two kings he served. Pleas for advancement and favor flowed steadily from his pen, and the modern mind finds it distasteful to see a man of great talents meanly seeking favors. "To live in the shadow of a Queen's favor, to strive continually for a King's smile, is not pretty work."[50] But Roe must be judged by the standards of his own time, and in the England of the Stuarts there was only one way for an ambitious man to rise: by royal patronage. In a government that paid even the greatest of its servants a mere nominal sum, yet expected them to live like princes, royal favor was the breath of life; and Roe cannot properly be censured for trying to gain advancement in the only way advancement could be won.

Roe was an ardent patriot whose love of England often

[50] Catherine Drinker Bowen, *Francis Bacon: The Temper of a Man* (Boston, 1963), p. 18.

manifested itself in an intense yearning for the company of his English friends. This was, perhaps, natural for one who was to spend so much of his life away from home, but it led him continually to draw odious comparisons between England and the place where he happened to be at the moment of writing. "This is the dullest, basest place that euer I saw," he wrote to Lord Carew from India.[51] On another occasion, after describing at length the inadequacies of his house in India, he complained about the "fires, smokes, floodes, stormes, heate, dust, flyes," and the lack of any "temperate or quiett season," implying that these were hazards that no civilized English gentleman should be expected to suffer.[52] It is difficult to imagine Roe "roughing it." He was a true forerunner of those Englishmen who, in other centuries, would ignore all the sensible limitations suggested by climate and environment and pursue doggedly the activities they had known in the comfortable and patrician atmosphere of rural England.

Yet he was ready to suffer the things he complained of—and much else besides—in the pursuit of his duty. He knew that his employers were looking to him for some tangible improvements in the volume and the value of their trade with India. The attainment of these improvements was the goal and the purpose of his mission: personal sentiment and personal comfort were assigned second place and he knew that he must stay in India until his work had either been completed or proved impossible. Thus in September 1617, when Sir Thomas received a letter from the company asking him to stay another year, he consented. It is safe for us to assume that, although he longed for "the conuersation and presence of the friends" he loved and honored and looked forward to the end of what he called his "banishment," he agreed to stay simply because he was unwilling to go home without better results than he had then obtained.

[51] The letter is printed in Foster, *Embassy*, pp. 110–14.
[52] Roe, *Journal*, p. 248.

CHAPTER 4
Building Foundations

DURING the first year of his embassy Roe had directed most of his energy toward the negotiation of a binding commercial treaty. But there were many other obligations that demanded his time and attention. His instructions had made it clear that he was expected to do what he could to remedy some of the shortcomings of the factor system by which the East India Company carried on its trade. Although he was not given any power to command the factors, it was anticipated that he would use his influence to give some cohesion and unity to the activities of the scattered settlements and, at the same time, try to improve the relations that existed between the factors and the Indians among whom they lived.

When Roe went to India, there were four English factories in the Mogul's lands: one was at Surat, another at Ajmere, a third at Burhanpur, and the fourth at Ahmadabad. At first the factors welcomed the arrival of the ambassador, for they believed that such an influential person would be able to win concessions for them and improve the conditions of their trade. Almost inevitably, however, this relationship deteriorated, because Roe's instructions required him to put an end to the private trade that many factors found to be so profitable. But Sir Thomas recognized that the resentment caused by a blanket prohibition of trade could be more damaging than the trade itself. Accordingly, he took a very reasonable stand on the matter and wrote to the factors at Surat that their trading would be tolerated as long as it was done with moderation and was not in conflict with the best interests of the company.[1]

This generous attitude did not mean that Sir Thomas was always on good terms with the factors. Occasionally their relationship became troubled and Roe found it necessary from time to time to write conciliatory messages assuring them of his esteem and excusing his occasional sharpness by ascribing it to a weakness in his nature. He sought to convince the factors that they would always find him ready to do them any courtesy and to give to the company good testimony of their services.[2] But even sentiments such as these were often incapable of healing the breach and there was a good deal of grumbling by the factors about Roe's interference in their affairs. Some of them even expressed the opinion that his embassy was an unnecessary expense and that things had been better before his coming.[3]

Some central control was essential. There were constant arguments both within and among the factories. Many of the factors were "young, wanton and riotous lads" whose behavior sometimes caused Roe to marvel at the patience with which the Indians tolerated the strangers within their midst.[4] The ambassador was convinced that the misbehavior of the factors was a basic cause of English difficulties in India, and he sometimes chafed over his lack of authority to make them mend their ways.[5] However, in October 1617 he received from the company a letter that authorized him "to instruct, direct and order" all the factors in the Mogul's country.[6] This would give

---

[1] *C.S.P.C.*, *1617–1621*, Roe to Thomas Kerridge and the factors at Surat, 21 October 1617, p. 67.

[2] *C.S.P.C.*, *1513–1616*, Roe to the factors and their assistants at Surat, 15 October 1616, p. 478: "I esteem you all as my friends, and would merit no other from you. If I am sharp in reprehension, it is my nature. In actions you may find me not only gentle but very ready to do you any courtesy and to give good testimony of your services."

[3] *C.S.P.C.*, *1617–1621*, Mathew Duke to the East India Company, March 1618, p. 138.

[4] Ibid., Roe to the East India Company, 14 February 1618, p. 118; ibid., William Leske to the East India Company, March 1617, p. 23.

[5] Roe, *Journal*, pp. 243, 251. "Want of power saued mee much labor, but disadvantaged much our business."

[6] *C.S.P.C.*, *1617–1621*, "Consultation by Captain Martin Pring and others aboard the James," October 1617, p. 59.

him the power to do the job; but for all his earlier complaints, he was now reluctant to assume these additional obligations and complained that the company was asking him to undertake more business than he knew properly how to handle.[7] It was, perhaps, with the idea of simplifying his complex task that he advocated the dissolution of some of the factories and the concentration of the company's operation at Surat.[8] He supported his suggestion by pointing to the declining sales of the factories at Ahmadabad and Burhanpur, but concentration was the last thing the factors wanted and his recommendations were never acted upon. Indeed, the company was to follow an opposite course and extend its commercial activities by establishing new factories rather than by liquidating old ones.

Thus the factors saw Roe's additional authority as a serious threat to their independence. Moreover, many of them had spent long years in India and deeply resented their subordination to a man whom they regarded as a newcomer. In many particular instances Sir Thomas performed valuable services on their behalf, securing the payment of uncollected debts and winning literally dozens of firmans providing for the settlement of minor annoyances. But these things did not dispel the hostility and disdain with which some of the factors regarded him, and many comments made in letters to the East India Company attested to the strained relations that existed between the ambassador and the factors.[9]

[7] Ibid., Roe to the factors at Agra, 6 October 1617, p. 60.

[8] Ibid., William Leske to the East India Company, March 1617, p. 23; ibid., John Brown to the East India Company, 10 February 1617, p. 16; ibid., Roe to Thomas Kerridge, February 1618, p. 122.

[9] A letter from the factors at Surat implied that they would have been unwilling to entrust a confidential letter to Roe for safe delivery ("The factors at Suratt to the Company," in Foster, *Embassy*, pp. 516–18); *The Court Records of the East India Company*, 25 September 1619, report that some of the factors "haue most baseley and iniuriouslye requited him [Roe] by traducing him in their lettres and wrighting most bitterly and most inuectiuely against him . . . putting vppon him as much as malice can possibly inuent." The members of the company were probably very close to the mark when they suspected the factors of "being ioyned in a confederacy amongst themselues, being ielous that any strange eye should obserue or looke into their accounts."

The instructions that Roe had received from King James before leaving England had enjoined him to do everything possible to advance the trade of the East India Company not only with the Mogul Empire but also with any "bordering nations" where opportunity might arise.[10] Soon after his arrival at Ajmere, Roe had become aware that some of his countrymen in India were extremely optimistic about the possibility of establishing a lucrative trade with Persia. His first impulse was to oppose any such efforts, but his opinion carried little weight with the factors, who went ahead with their plans.

English ships had made several voyages to Persia during the reign of Queen Elizabeth, but these early contacts had not resulted in the establishment of much direct, settled trade. As was the case further east, it was the Portuguese who had been first on the scene. They had used their seapower to win control of the Persian Gulf and the considerable commerce that flowed through it. Initially they had been welcomed by the shah, who was anxious to export silk (which was a royal monopoly) by the Persian Gulf instead of overland, thereby depriving his traditional enemy, the Turks, of a large source of customs revenue. The Portuguese, however, proceeded to seize and fortify the island of Ormuz and demonstrated their determination, in Persia as in India, to establish a monopoly over seaborne trade.

This caused their presence to be deeply resented. It became clear that conditions now favored the appearance on the scene of some third force that could challenge the Portuguese position. The East India Company was quick to see the possibilities and in 1615 (with Portuguese power generally in decline) two factors were ordered to go to Persia to "inform themselves of the condition and hopes of trade . . . and to procure letters from the King of Persia for the peaceable entertainment of the Company's servants, ships, and goods."[11]

---

[10] The king's instructions to Roe are printed in Foster, *Embassy*, pp. 551–53.

[11] W. Noel Sainsbury, "Preface," *C.S.P.C., 1513–1616*, pp. lxv–lxviii.

Roe was not, in principle, opposed to the establishment of a Persian trade, but for a number of reasons he felt that mission to be unwise, and he opposed it. His opposition grew out of his essentially cautious nature. Roe had the capacity for grand enthusiasm. If his interest was thoroughly aroused, or if he was convinced of the rightness of a particular course of action, he could devote himself to a project with persistent effort and magnificent gusto. But if he was doubtful he moved slowly; and he was doubtful now. He was convinced that the development of the Indian trade must have priority over all other considerations, and he feared that worrying about Persia might undermine the position of Surat by diverting too many of the company's ships onto other routes.[12] He felt that it was foolishly optimistic to believe that the Portuguese could be driven from the Persian Gulf and that it was much more important to concentrate upon ending their threat to England's precarious position in India. And in any case, he reflected (in what was for him an unusually pacific mood) the objective of the East India Company was trade and not war. To send a mission to Persia could result in seizure by the Portuguese and the beginning of a struggle that the English were ill-equipped to wage.[13] He would have been delighted to see his countrymen launch a vigorous offensive against the Portuguese in India; indeed, he wrote many letters urging the directors of the East India Company to follow such a course.[14] But war on the coast of India was very different from war in the Persian Gulf. The prize was greater and the conditions were more favorable.

The expression of these fears carried little weight with the factors at Surat. Acting on their own initiative and against the expressed wishes of the ambassador (who, at this early stage of

[12] *C.S.P.C., 1617–1621*, Roe to Connock, Barker, Pley, and Bell, 6 October 1617, p. 61.
[13] Ibid., Roe to William Robbins, 21 August 1617, p. 52.
[14] *C.S.P.C., 1513–1616*, Roe to the Viceroy of Goa, 20 October 1615, pp. 436–37; ibid., Richard Cocks to Richard Wickam, 14 July 1616, p. 470; Samuel Purchas, *Hakluytus Posthumus or Purchas His Pilgrimes* (Glasgow, 1905), 4:445–46 (where a letter from Roe to "unknown persons" is reproduced).

his embassy, had no authority to command them) they dispatched a ship to Jask, one of the principal ports of the Persian Empire.

Roe was angry at the way his advice had been ignored, but he refused to allow his personal pique to interfere with the public service and determined to do what he could to assure the success of the mission. Fearing that its small size and exceedingly modest cargo would cause the shah to assume a contemptuous attitude toward the English, he wrote a letter asking that they not be judged by this small beginning and explaining that the mission had been sent not to trade but merely to determine what kind of reception they could anticipate. He expressed the hope that definite commercial arrangements could be made in the future and that the English would be permitted to establish factories within the dominions of the shah. He solicited information about the kinds of goods "eyther of Europe, India, Chyna, or the South Islands" that the Persians would require, and ended his letter by assuring the shah that "wee ayme not at gnatts and small flyes, but at a Commerce Honorable and Equall to two so mighty Nations."[15]

The apprehension that Roe felt about the mission was made to appear ill-founded, for, although the Portuguese tried to capture the ship, they failed to do so and the mission landed safely. The Englishmen were kindly received and given every indication that English cloth and many kinds of spices would find ready markets in Persia. Five factors were allowed to remain ashore and there were high hopes that they would prove to be the means of developing a lucrative trade.

The measure of success achieved by this first mission was sufficient to open Roe's eyes to the possibilities of the Persian trade. He was now convinced that he should support the efforts being made to develop it. This was not altogether a case of belated conversion to the obvious. Sir Thomas had never

[15] Foster, *Embassy*, Roe to William Robbins at Ispahan, 17 January 1617, pp. 373–74. Robbins was an English jeweler who had found his way to the new Persian capital, where he found employment and became a useful means of getting messages to the shah.

really questioned the potential of the trade. He had simply felt that the factors were too impetuous and that they had acted too soon.[16] But now that was over and done with. The issue had been forced upon him. It was clearly his duty to do what he could to bring to the best possible conclusion a project that he had not initiated but of which in principle he heartily approved.

In London, meanwhile, the East India Company had had the advantages of the Persian trade urged upon them by various travelers. They were also influenced by their knowledge of the activities of the remarkable expatriates, Thomas and Robert Shirley, two Englishmen who were seeking to interest the Spanish government in the Persian trade. After some deliberation the company decided to go forward in the matter. They wrote a detailed set of instructions for Roe and authorized him "to consider of some fitting person or persons . . . whome you may send to treate with the King of Persia . . . for the establishment of such a trade with vs as will aunswer with our meanes. . . ."[17]

These instructions, together with a letter from King James that gave Roe authority to sign a treaty with the shah, clearly put the ambassador in charge of the negotiations. As Sir William Foster points out, Roe, if he wished, could have disavowed the earlier mission that had been sent against his will, but instead of doing so he "acted with his usual moderation and good sense."[18] He sent detailed instructions to the agents in Persia, but told them to feel free to alter them if necessary, because he did not feel that "sober and discreet" men should be tied so strictly that they may not have the use and liberty of

[16] He had considered the mission to be contrived too hastily, "unprovided either of instructions, goods, or means fit for such an enterprise." Before a satisfactory trade could begin "a port must be secured, a mart established, and prices agreed upon as well as the quantities of commodities to be delivered on both sides . . . ; a straggling, peddling uncertain trade will neither profit nor become so great nations" (*C.S.P.C., 1617–1621*, Roe to William Robbins, 21 August 1617, p. 52).

[17] "The Company's Instructions for the Negotiations in Persia" are printed in Foster, *Embassy*, pp. 554–56.

[18] Ibid., p. li.

their own reason and experience. Besides, they were there on the scene and could best judge what needed to be done, for "no man can sit in India and direct punctually business in Persia."[19]

Once associated with the Persian project Sir Thomas supported it with his usual enthusiasm. Perhaps he took a special delight in the work because he could feel that he was helping to forestall the Spanish, whom he always regarded as his country's principal enemy. At all events, he sent a stream of letters to England expressing his optimism about the future of the trade and urging his countrymen's support of it; and there is every reason to believe that his communications were instrumental in keeping the company's interest at a high pitch, even when there was no guarantee that a profitable trade could be developed.

Many difficulties lay ahead. The first group of factors— those who had gone to Persia before Roe gave his support to the project—proved to be a quarrelsome and awkward lot. They did manage to get some useful concessions from the shah, however, and it was a considerable loss when, one by one, they succumbed to the unaccustomed rigors of the climate and died. In February 1618 Roe sent instructions to a new group of envoys and by their efforts further progress was made.

It would be inappropriate to explore in any detail the story of the developing commerce between Persia and the East India Company, for the trade was still in its infancy when Sir Thomas left India. It is relevant to point out though, that it was firmly established by the time he took his leave; that it subsequently developed into a very profitable operation for the company; and that, while Roe cannot be credited with having initiated the trade, he did contribute guidance and encouragement to its early development.

There was another area into which the ships of the East

[19] *C.S.P.C.*, *1617–1621*, Roe to Connock, Baker, Pley, and Bell, 6 October 1617, p. 61.

India Company ventured for the first time during Sir Thomas Roe's embassy to India, and in this instance the ambassador could claim full credit for having initiated a new and profitable commercial connection. In November 1616 (and on other subsequent occasions) Sir Thomas wrote to the East India Company recommending that they give serious thought to establishing a trade in the Red Sea area.[20] Indian merchants already conducted a thriving trade there and Roe was convinced that the English would have no difficulty in getting a share of the traffic. He urged the advantages of this course with special enthusiasm because he had learned that the merchants of the Middle East paid cash for most of the goods they bought.[21] This meant that the Red Sea had the potential of helping to solve one of the most basic difficulties the company faced in its trade with the East—its reliance upon bullion and specie for purchasing the goods it wanted from India.

The market for English goods in India was very limited and the balance of trade was sure to remain unfavorable. English woollen cloth was not suitable for the warm Indian climate and in any case most of the people were much too poor to be able to buy imported goods. The nobles purchased some luxury items like ivory, velvet, and swords; and there was some demand for exotic things like quicksilver and vermilion, Mediterranean laces and gold and silver embroideries; but this could never be sufficient to pay for the great cargoes of indigo and cotton that the company wanted to take out of India to supply the European market. The truth was that England simply did not produce any articles that Indians wanted and could buy in large quantities, and as things stood most Indian goods were being bought with silver and gold which the Indians minted into rupees. From the time of its incorporation the East India Company had been limited in the amount of specie that it could take out of England, and this limitation could be ex-

---

[20] Foster, *Embassy*, Roe to the East India Company, 24 November 1616, pp. 342–52; ibid., "Roe to the Expected Generall which shall arrive this year," 30 August 1617, pp. 407–11.
[21] Ibid., Roe to the East India Company, 24 November 1616, p. 348.

pected to work as a constant check on the growth of the company's trade. But if the Red Sea trade could be developed, it would relieve the pressure by helping to finance the company's ventures not only in India but in Persia as well.[22]

In March 1618 a ship was fitted out and sent to Mokha, a port on the southeastern shore of the Red Sea. Its captain was furnished with instructions from Roe. He was ordered to seek from the governor a safe conduct for English merchants and a firman for the free sale of English goods. If at all possible he was to arrange for an annual visit by an English fleet and to obtain permission for the establishing of a factory. If his overtures were not well received, the captain was instructed to hinder the passage of other ships into the port, thus, hopefully, forcing compliance with the English requests.[23] Roe knew that any ships molested in this way would belong either to the Portuguese or to their allies, and it was clear that he regarded the English incursion into the Red Sea as being an integral part of the project to undermine the Portuguese position in the East.[24]

The voyage was a success. It is true that the cargo it carried was not of good quality and did not find a ready sale, but the governor at Mokha received the English courteously and provided satisfactory firmans for future trade.[25] No fighting appears to have been necessary, and the ship returned safely to Surat in September. This promising beginning was followed up early in 1619 when Sir Thomas, in one of his last official acts before leaving India, dispatched another ship to Mokha. It carried expressions of friendship to the governor and reflected the optimism that Roe felt about the future of the trade he had started.[26]

[22] Ibid., "Roe to the Expected Generall which shall arrive this year," 30 August 1617, p. 409.

[23] Foster, *Embassy*, "A Declaration and Instructions for the shippe entended for the Red Sea . . . ," 14 February 1618, pp. 492–95.

[24] Ibid.

[25] Ibid., p. 495, *n.* 3; Sir Thomas referred to the ship's cargo as "the refuse of India," ibid., Roe to Captain Martin Pring, 10 March 1618, pp. 501–502.

[26] Roe's letter to the governor is printed in ibid., pp. 515–16.

There is no doubt that the establishment of the new trade into the Red Sea area was the result of Roe's personal efforts. He was not led this time; indeed the whole project had been carried through in the face of the hostility and opposition of the Surat factors, who feared repercussions from the company's interference with the trade conducted by the native Indians.[27] Thus Sir Thomas Roe could rightfully claim full credit for starting what was to become an important branch of the East India Company's commerce.[28]

Late in 1616, Roe was somewhat crestfallen over Asaph Khan's recent rejection of his latest set of proposals for a treaty of commerce. His spirits were prevented from sinking too low by the knowledge that an English fleet would soon arrive and that the gifts it was carrying would greatly facilitate his diplomatic efforts.

When in October the ships did in fact appear they brought with them an unexpected bonus. On the way to India they had encountered a Portuguese ship. In the sharp engagement that followed the Portuguese vessel had been forced to run aground where she was abandoned and burned by her crew.[29] Thus at the very time that Roe's hand was strengthened by the arrival of fresh gifts, the prestige of his rivals received a serious setback. Sir Thomas hurried to the court to make sure that news of the Portuguese defeat had reached the emperor. When told of the incident, Jahangir seemed pleased, but he quickly revealed his deeper interests by inquiring about the gifts the English fleet had brought. When Roe described the cargo the emperor said he would grant all the ambassador's desires and Prince Khurram promised to give him "all reasonable content." "This," wrote Sir Thomas in his journal, "is the strength of New Presentes."[30]

[27] Court Minutes of the East India Company, 6 October 1619, ibid., p. 523.
[28] Ibid., p. lv.
[29] Edward Terry, "A Relation of a Voyage to the Easterne Indies," in Purchas, *Purchas His Pilgrimes*, 9:5–12.
[30] Roe, *Journal*, p. 289.

Even with the gifts as inducement, no genuinely satisfactory results were forthcoming. In reply to some of Roe's requests, Prince Khurram supplied a firman written "with such Cunning that it might bee Construed both wayes like the ould Oracles . . . so intricat and doubtfull I could scarse vnderstand the riddle."[31] Time and again the document was returned to the prince for clarification, but the evasions continued, always accompanied by earnest protestations of good faith. Roe's persistence did bring results, but each minor concession had to be bargained and pleaded for and progress was distressingly slow.

The ambassador, however, did not despair. He wrote to the company and assured the directors that he felt confident of success in putting their trade on a firm footing. He hoped that a direct appeal to the emperor might bring results if his request could be presented when Prince Khurram and Asaph Khan were not present. Even if a comprehensive treaty could not be won, Roe thought that the desired results could be gained by means of numerous specific agreements.[32] Although this would be a tiresome and difficult course, he was perfectly willing to pursue it in order to achieve his goal.

In November 1616 the transaction of business was made much more difficult, for in that month the Mogul left Ajmere with his destination unannounced. Hunting as he went, Jahangir followed a route that took him through all kinds of terrain. The English ambassador found that if he wished to keep in touch with the Mogul court he would have to embark on a cross-country journey that was not at all to his liking. His house in Ajmere was a wretched affair ("a poore mudd building," he called it), but he would have infinitely preferred to stay there than to launch out upon the uncertain trials that were involved in a long journey.[33] Reluctantly he left Ajmere on 20 November with his belongings strapped to eight miser-

---

[31] Ibid., p. 298.
[32] Foster, *Embassy*, Roe to the East India Company, 24 November 1616, p. 346.
[33] Roe, *Journal*, pp. 247–48.

able camels. In January he was still following "this wandering King" (as he called the Mogul) "over Mountaynes and thorough woodes" and was rapidly growing tired of the enforced journey.[34] Sir Thomas tried to continue his negotiations even while the court was on the move, but this proved difficult. He maintained contact with the English factories by means of messengers, but the average length of the entries in his journal decreased steadily and it is clear that the time spent in traveling was quite wasted insofar as the transaction of any business was concerned.

At last in March 1617 the court—and the English ambassador—arrived at Mandu, and it was with considerable relief that Roe learned that the Mogul intended to stay there for some time. He had gone there in order to observe at firsthand the operations that his forces were conducting against the kings of the Deccan. His son Parwiz, whom Roe had visited soon after his arrival in India, had been conducting the campaign but had met with little success because he appeared to be more interested in wine and pleasure than in soldiering. Now he was to be replaced as the commander in chief by Prince Khurram, and the Mogul himself had come to signify his interest in the efforts of his new commander.

Whenever the Mogul court went awandering it was accompanied by an incredible number of people. They traveled ten or twelve miles a day, depending on the availability of water, and at night they housed themselves in richly decorated tents that must have made a brave display.[35] It may be supposed that moving such a horde would have posed difficult problems of logistics, but the emperor solved these quite simply by refusing to concern himself about how his followers provided for their needs. Roe received no preferential treatment, and he was constantly having to worry about the most basic necessities of life such as housing and an adequate water supply. Under these

[34] Ibid., pp. 340, 375.
[35] Edward Terry, "A Relation of a Voyage to the Easterne Indies," in Purchas, *Purchas His Pilgrimes*, 9:50; Anonymous, "A True Relation . . . ," in *Harleian Miscellany*, 1:259.

circumstances he found it difficult to maintain the dignity that he was always so insistent about and he wrote in his journal that there was not a "misery nor punishment which either the want of Gouernment or the naturall disposition of the Clime gaue us not."[36] As a matter of fact, he was much better off than most of his fellow travelers, for in Mandu he was able to commandeer for himself and his immediate party reasonably good quarters in a deserted mosque. These were perhaps rather macabre surroundings, but at least they provided a solid roof and a minimum of comfort. Water was scarce, but in this respect too Roe was lucky, for he managed to make provision for his own party by arriving at an arrangement with a khan who agreed to let him draw "foure load a day."[37]

The summer and autumn of 1617 passed without any important occurrences, although there were two incidents that were of considerable interest and were reported by Roe in detail. In February he had a long audience with the Mogul. It must have been an exasperating experience for Roe, but for the readers of his account it is an amusing illustration of the icy equanimity with which Jahangir was likely to meet Roe's heated protests, and affords some insight into the provocations the ambassador had to bear.

In October, an English fleet had arrived in Surat bearing gifts that Roe confidently anticipated would strengthen his hand for the negotiations that lay ahead. When he had to leave Ajmere, Sir Thomas made arrangements for them to be sent from Surat under the care of the Reverend Edward Terry, the chaplain who had been sent to replace John Hall as his personal minister. Terry was to join the ambassador at Mandu, but on the way there his party was intercepted by Prince Khurram, who demanded to be shown the gifts that were being sent to his father.[38] Terry immediately notified Sir Thomas of what had happened and Roe complained to the Mogul. Jahangir,

[36] Roe, *Journal*, p. 393.
[37] Ibid., pp. 393, 402.
[38] Ibid., p. 380.

who was always quick to protect what was his, ordered his son
not to touch the gifts but to send them, under escort, directly
to him. This was done, and before Roe even learned that the
goods had arrived at Mandu, Jahangir had opened them and
appropriated all the items he fancied. Roe, in high dudgeon,
sought an interview with the emperor and proceeded to unburden himself:

> There were few things that I entended not to present him, but
> that I tooke it a great discourtesie to my Soueraigne, which I
> could not answere, to haue that [which] was freely giuen
> seazed, and not deliuered by my hands, to whom they were
> directed: and some of them were entended for the Prince and
> Normahall, some to lye by me, on occasions to prepare his
> Maiesties fauour to protect vs from iniuries that strangers were
> daily offered, and some for my friends or priuate vse, and some
> that were the Merchants, which I had not to doe withall.

With all the cleverness of a child who argues for a new toy the
emperor answered him point for point:

> He answered that I should not be sad nor griued that hee had his
> choyce, for that hee had not patience to forbeare seeing them:
> hee did mee no wrong in it, for hee thought I wished him first
> serued: and to my Lord the King of England hee would make
> satisfaction, and my excuse: the Prince, Normahall and he were
> all one: and for any to bring with me to procure his fauour, it
> was a ceremony and vnnecessary, for he would at all times
> heare me: that I should be welcome emptie handed, for that was
> not my fault, and I should receiue right from him: and to go
> to his sonne, he would returne me shomewhat for him, and for
> the Merchants goods pay to their content; concluding I should
> not be angry for this freedome: he entended well. I made no
> reply. Then hee pressed me whether I was pleased or no. I
> answered: His Maiesties content pleased me.[39]

Not satisfied with having appropriated Roe's entire supply of
gifts, Jahangir went on to request that the ambassador try to
get for him "a horse of the greatest size . . . and a Male and a
Female of Mastiffes, and the tall Irish Grey-hounds, and such
other Dogges as hunt in your lands";—and then, after all that

[39] Ibid., pp. 384–8

toward the end of the interview, to wonder aloud why the gifts Roe brought were "meane and inferiour" to those provided by his less exalted predecessor, William Edwards.[40] Before dismissing the ambassador, however, Jahangir did make such ardent protestations of his high regard for Roe and of his determination to grant his wishes that the ambassador reflected philosophically that perhaps he had been "happely robbd."[41]

The other incident that obviously made a deep impression upon Sir Thomas was the celebration of the emperor's birthday in September 1617 when, in accordance with an old custom, there was enacted the ceremony of the weighing of the king. Amid a scene of lavish pomp and splendor the emperor sat on one side of a massive pair of scales while on the other side "was put in against him many bagges to fit his weight, which were changed six times, and they say was siluer. . . . After with Gold and Iewels, and precious stones . . . then against Cloth of Gold, Silke, Stuffes, Linnen, Spices, and sorts of goods." The value of the goods thus presented to the king was so great that the ambassador grew skeptical and, noting that most of the precious stones were contained in bags, remarked that, since he had not actually seen them, they "might bee Pibles."[42]

The Mogul and his court remained at Mandu throughout the summer and during all that time Sir Thomas was given no chance to resume his negotiations. He sometimes broached the subject to the Mogul himself and never failed to receive the most verbose assurances of good intent, but he soon learned that these words meant nothing. On occasion he would receive satisfaction in some minor point—the payment of a debt or some demonstration of esteem—but nothing was accomplished toward the achievement of a permanent treaty.[43]

In October Prince Khurram returned from his successful campaigning and was received by his father with such honors

[40] Ibid., p. 390.
[41] Ibid., pp. 388–89.
[42] Ibid., p. 412.
[43] Ibid., pp. 415–17.

that his already proud nature became almost insufferable. When Roe went to offer his congratulations he was rudely rebuffed; but, while he huffed indignantly about his treatment, he recognized that the situation was not without promise, for the prince's puffed up attitude had served to alienate his friends and to weaken the confederation between him and Nur Mahal and Asaph Khan. Sir Thomas resolved to take advantage of this situation. By a number of carefully calculated favors (including the sale of a great pearl at low price and promises of other profitable bargains), he won Asaph Khan over to his side and received the minister's promise to do what he could to "make Englishmen content and happy."[44] Roe never deceived himself about Asaph Khan's reliability, but felt that the minister could be useful as long as his own selfishness and greed were being served. Roe detested the kind of diplomacy in which he was engaged and wrote in his journal of the "base and vnworthy men" with whom he was dealing, but the fact remains that Asaph Khan did prove useful and secured a number of limited concessions from the prince which Roe, unaided, might never have won.[45]

But even with the paid help of Asaph Khan, there was still no real hope that the treaty Roe wanted could be achieved, and the ambassador grew increasingly weary of his unprofitable employment. Late in October the Mogul left Mandu for Ahmadabad. Roe went on ahead of the main party and arrived at the city some three weeks before the emperor and his court. Upon arrival, Sir Thomas found a new shipment of gifts that

[44] Ibid., pp. 426–35.

[45] Foster, *Embassy*, p. 437, *n.* 1. On one occasion Asaph Khan's service to the English went quite beyond the call of duty. When Prince Khurram complained to the Mogul that he made no profits from the English and would be content to be rid of them, Asaph Khan defended the English hotly and told the emperor "that we brought both profit to the Port, to the Kingdome, and securitie: that we were vsed very rudely by the Princes seruants, and that it was not possible for vs to reside without amends: it were more honourable for his Maiestie to license vs [to depart?] then to intreate vs so discourteously" (Roe, *Journal*, p. 452). Such were the bewildering shifts in direction effected by the personnel of the Mogul court.

had been sent for his use from England. But he also found that the packages had been sealed at Surat by command of Prince Khurram, whom Roe described as having a "gredy desier of Presentes."[46] The seals clearly indicated that the packages were not to be opened unless the prince were present. Sir Thomas wrote for permission to open the goods, but when he realized that this was not forthcoming he boldly broke the seals and took possession of the merchandise. When the prince heard of this action he considered it an affront to his dignity, became extremely angry, and complained in strong terms to the emperor. The Mogul summoned Roe and with "an angrie countenance . . . told mee I had broken my word: that he would trust me no more (the Prince had desired him to doe so.)"[47] This was the first time the emperor had ever spoken roughly to his visitor, but Sir Thomas was apparently undisturbed by the severe reprimand and determined not to be intimidated. He replied that the gifts were intended for him to distribute freely as he saw fit; he had meant no offense, but if he had offended, it had been entirely due to his ignorance of their customs and not to any intentional design. His reply was apparently acceptable, for in a matter of days the unpleasant attitudes of the emperor and the prince were dispelled, and, after the distribution of gifts, friendship was restored.

But friendship did not connote any softening in the official attitude toward Roe's objective, and by February 1618, when he made his annual report to the company, Sir Thomas had abandoned hope of getting the Mogul to sign a formal treaty. This did not mean that he was ready to accept defeat, because he was still confident that he could gain all the necessary concessions through a series of firmans. There was good hope of this because of his recent reconciliation with the prince, but Sir Thomas was by now sufficiently realistic to know that there was a great difference at the Mogul court between promise and performance; and he told his "honourable

[46] Ibid., p. 301.
[47] Ibid., p. 458.

Frendes" of the company that he was as weary of flattery as he was of ill usage. He had tried every trick and blandishment he knew, but he recognized that the English were tolerated in India only because their naval strength was respected; and that the best that could be hoped for was a commercial relationship based not upon treaties and trust but upon craft and subtle coercion.

The last known entry in Sir Thomas Roe's journal was made on 22 January 1618. It is probable that he continued to keep some record of his activities, but a great deal of earnest searching on the part of both Samuel Purchas and Sir William Foster has failed to bring that record to light.[48] However, many of the ambassador's letters have been preserved and it is possible to reconstruct from them the story of the closing days of Sir Thomas's embassy to India.

While Roe was in Ahmadabad the city was stricken by a most severe plague, which caused a great deal of suffering and death. All the members of the English party—with the single exception of the ambassador himself—were taken ill and seven of the men died within the space of a week.[49] In August preparations were made for the removal of the Mogul and his followers from Ahmadabad to Agra. Sir Thomas saw that it would serve no useful purpose for him to accompany the court any further, for it was now quite clear that no amount of negotiation would succeed in binding the Mogul to a permanent trade treaty. Accordingly, the ambassador took formal leave of the emperor, receiving from him a letter for King James, full of compliments and assurances of lasting friendship for the English. The Mogul reported in the letter that he had given instructions to all his "subiects and vassalls" that English merchants were to be given freedom and residence and that they were not to be injured or molested in any way. They were to be allowed to trade freely throughout his dominions and their ships were to be free to enter his ports whenever

[48] Purchas, *Purchas His Pilgrimes*, 4:429–30.
[49] Foster, *Embassy*, p. 505, *n.* 4.

they wished to do so.[50] It was a substantial achievement to have received these assurances from the Mogul in writing, but Sir Thomas recognized that they were general and therefore left a great deal to be desired. He also recognized that the personal power of Jahangir was now in decline and that, as the emperor grew older, the importance of Prince Khurram increased.[51]

This being the case, Sir Thomas determined to devote his last days of the stay in India to the project of winning from the prince as comprehensive a firman as he could devise for the merchants at the principal English factory at Surat. The usual haggling negotiations ensued and, as had happened so many times before, an attempt was made to deceive the Englishman with an incomplete and ambiguous firman. But Roe's practiced watchfulness was proof against that sort of deception and in the end an agreement was drawn up that was reasonably satisfactory for English interests. The powerful prince (who was, of course, still the lord of Surat) publicly declared his friendship for the English and undertook to provide them with necessary supplies in the event of a falling out with the Portuguese. English factors were to be allowed to trade freely, English ambassadors were to be treated with honor and courtesy, and English goods were to pass without hindrance. Englishmen in Surat were to be allowed to live under their own religion and their own laws and to rent one or more "good, strong and sufficient" houses in the town. There was considerable argument over the prince's attempt to limit the number of Englishmen who would be allowed to carry arms in Surat, but Roe utterly refused to yield and said that he would reject the whole firman before he would accept such a dishonorable clause. The dispute was finally resolved in Roe's favor, although he was required to give his word that "our people should not land in Hostile manner to annoy the peace." The firman was drawn up and, to Roe's great satisfaction, he was

---

[50] Letter from the Great Mogul to King James, 8 August 1618, ibid., pp. 559–60.

[51] *C.S.P.C., 1617–1621*, Roe to the East India Company, February 1618, p. 119.

allowed to examine it before it was passed. He found it to be "according to promise, effectuall in most poynts . . . no materiall thing left out, and written clearly and rightly."[52]

With these very useful arrangements completed, Sir Thomas prepared for his journey to Surat. The emperor had left Ahmadabad early in September; Sir Thomas took his leave of the city toward the end of the month and made his way to the coast. At Surat he was provided with a suitable dwelling, and the courtesy with which he was treated was in marked contrast to the indignities he had suffered after his initial arrival there almost exactly three years before. Indeed, the heightened respect with which he was regarded was an indication of the success of at least one phase of his mission, and Roe must have been gratified to note the change.

It is impossible to construct any narrative account of Roe's activities during the months that he awaited the departure of the fleet that was to carry him home. It was believed in England that he used the time to visit Persia in an effort to "settle the trade in silks,"[53] and some modern authorities have accepted this as being the case.[54] Sir Thomas himself had, at one time, thought it likely that he would be required to go there,[55] and it is reasonable to believe that the shah might have been impressed with the earnestness of England's desire for trade if he had been approached by a fully accredited ambassador instead of by mere merchants. There is, however, other evidence to suggest that Sir Thomas did not go to Persia. He had made it clear that he did not want to make such a trip but

---

[52] The articles proposed by Roe, the prince's response, and Roe's comments about the ensuing negotiations are printed in Foster, *Embassy*, pp. 506–14.

[53] *C.S.P.C., 1617–1621*, Sir William Smithe to Sir Dudley Carleton, 7 January 1619, p. 232; ibid., G. Gerrard to Carleton, 9 January 1619, p. 234.

[54] Stanley Lane-Poole, "Sir Thomas Roe," in *D.N.B.*, 17:90; Sainsbury, "Preface," *C.S.P.C., 1617–1621*, p. lxix; Patrick S. McGarry, "Ambassador Abroad: The Career and Correspondence of Sir Thomas Roe at the Courts of the Mogul and Ottoman Empires, 1614–1628: A Chapter in Jacobean Diplomacy" (Ph.D. diss., Columbia University, 1963), p. 140.

[55] Roe to William Robbins at Ispahan, 17 January 1617, in Foster, *Embassy*, p. 374; same to same, 21 August 1617, ibid., p. 406.

that he would go if ordered to do so.[56] As far as can be determined no such instructions were ever sent to him and he seems to have contented himself with authorizing the factors already in Persia to act on his behalf.[57] With the great importance that Roe attached to protocol and proper procedure it is difficult to believe that he would have undertaken an official mission without a good deal of advance preparation. It is equally difficult to believe that some record of this preparation would not have survived. But there is no such record; neither is there any firm reference by Roe or anyone close to him to show that the ambassador ever visited Persia. Sir Thomas, upon his return to England, gave a meticulous accounting of his embassy to India. But at no time during his extensive report did he refer to any personal effort in Persia.

All these factors make it appear probable that Sir Thomas did not, in fact, visit Persia. At the very least they prohibit any firm assertion that such a trip was made. Sir William Foster, who has made by far the most careful study of Roe's Indian mission, assumes that Sir Thomas did not go to Persia. He gives no detailed reasoning to support his position, but merely states that the four months from October 1618 to February 1619 were spent in Surat awaiting the completion of the lading of the ships.[58] When all things are considered this appears to be the most tenable position.

In February all was in readiness for the homeward voyage and the ambassador and his party—changed and reduced by death from the group that had attended him upon his arrival—boarded the East India Company's ship *Anne.* On 17 February the little fleet put to sea and, after a voyage that was marred by something close to a mutiny, arrived at Plymouth toward the end of August. The lack of a suitable wind caused some delay there, and Roe was obliged to wait impatiently for more than two weeks until the ship could make its way into the Downs.

---

[56] Ibid.
[57] "Instructions given to our Louing Freinds [the factors in Persia]," ibid., pp. 430–34.
[58] Foster, *Embassy*, p. xlii.

On 14 September the *Anne* came to anchor and Sir Thomas stepped ashore to be greeted by the wife he had left so soon after their marriage. Transportation was provided by the East India Company and the couple was taken to Gravesend where they were officially greeted by some of the company's leading officials.[59] From there the party made its way to London and to the house that had been put at the ambassador's disposal until such time as he should report to the king and bring his embassy officially to a close.

No time was lost in arranging an audience. Toward the end of September, Sir Thomas presented himself at Hampton Court to report on his mission and to deliver the gifts sent to King James by the Mogul emperor. These included "two antelopes [and] a straunge and beautifull kind of red-deare"—gifts well calculated to appeal to a monarch whose interest in exotic animals was well known.[60] After his audience with the king, Sir Thomas asked for permission to go before the members of the East India Company so that he might "giue satisfaction to this Court of his procedings and seruice perfourmed" and "delyver vpp some Iornalls and accounts which he hath in his custodye."[61] The permission he sought was cordially granted and he went before the company to render some account of his proceedings. He began by describing the precarious state of the company's position in India when he had arrived there and, predictably, contrasted that with the much happier conditions that prevailed at the time of his departure. He urged upon the members the great potential of the other trades he had helped establish, told them how he had successfully collected all debts owed to the company and its agents, and concluded by having read a list that reported the holdings, in cash and in kind, of all English factories in India. It

[59] Court Minutes of the East India Company for 15 September 1619 in Foster, *Embassy*, pp. 520–21.
[60] *Calendar of State Papers, Domestic Series, 1619–1623*, John Chamberlain to Sir Dudley Carleton, 2 October 1619, p. 82 (hereafter cited as C.S.P., *Dom.* with appropriate dates).
[61] Court Minutes of the East India Company for 25 September 1619, in Foster, *Embassy*, p. 522.

was a detailed and polished performance that demonstrated effectively the care and the dedication with which Roe had discharged the task entrusted to him.[62]

In the days that followed this initial presentation a number of meetings were held between Roe and members of the company. They were naturally eager to glean from the ambassador as much information as possible about the state of their affairs in India. For this purpose a number of committees were appointed to confer with him, to hear his opinions, and to study and sort the many "wrightings" he had brought home. From these meetings it appeared how meticulous the ambassador had been in recording the details of his embassy—the money he had spent, the instructions he had given to factors, and the gifts he had bought for Indian officials. He had clearly taken to heart the company's initial request for frugality. When all his accounts had been examined, the company declared their conviction that he was "a very worthie gentleman that hath husbanded things exceedinglye well and very moderate in his expenses And one that by his modestie, honestie and integritie hath giuen good satisfaction."[63] In consideration of all these virtues they voted to give him a "gratification" of £1,500 and to reimburse him for some of the additional expenses he had incurred.[64] This seems a large sum but was, in fact, a modest reward, because Roe had actually used considerable amounts of his own money during his embassy, and much of the "gratification" was repayment for legitimate expenses that the ambassador had taken from his own pocket. The company sought to excuse its parsimony by referring to their small returns, but this was hardly convincing, since their records at the time of Roe's return to England indicate a net gain on the Surat trade of £200,000, or 120 percent on the capital employed.[65]

[62] Court Minutes of the East India Company for 6 October 1619, ibid., p. 524.
[63] Court Minutes of the East India Company for 12 November 1619, ibid., p. 528.
[64] Ibid.
[65] Foster, *Embassy*, p. 528, *n.* 1.

The size of the company's gift to Roe did not accurately reflect the members' estimate of his worth. They recognized the great value of his knowledge and experience and proposed an arrangement whereby Sir Thomas, in return for a payment of £200 a year, would make himself available for periodical consultation about their eastern trade. The offer was readily accepted, probably because Roe was glad to secure even this modest income. There are many indications that his finances were in anything but flourishing condition. By his own account he had wasted his patrimony, he had lost the royal friends who could have given him preferment, and he was unemployed. While in India he had sedulously resisted the temptation to line his own pockets and although, when he first returned to England, it was whispered that he had "come home rich . . . from the East Indies," the estimate was soon corrected and it became common knowledge that he had "not prouided so well for himself as was thought at first but must relie on the Companies liberalitie."[66] In view of his straitened circumstances it is a remarkable comment on Roe's charity and generosity to report that soon after his return home he offered to contribute £400 toward the building of a hospital or almshouse for men who had been maimed in the East India Company's service or for the relief of their families. The idea of the hospital had been raised earlier in the year and Roe hoped his offer would help it along. But nothing was done by the company until 1627 and Roe's donation was lost to the fund.[67]

After Sir Thomas had submitted his reports and met with many different committees to discuss the company's business, his contacts with the members became less frequent, although they occasionally called upon him until 1621, when new duties called him away from England. In the later years of his life he occasionally visited the company's modest headquarters and sat in on the deliberations, making available his advice and assis-

---

[66] Norman E. McClure, ed., *The Letters of John Chamberlain* (Philadelphia, 1939), pp. 264, 265.
[67] William Foster, "The East India Company's Hospital at Poplar," *The Home Counties Magazine* 12 (1910): 134.

tance to the company that had given him his first public employment.[68] The records of the East India Company make it clear that the members were well pleased with the performance of their ambassador. The modern historian, as he weighs the available evidence, is similarly inclined to conclude that Roe's embassy was a successful one and that it contributed significantly to the development of English interests in India.

It is true that Sir Thomas failed in his primary endeavor, that of bringing the Mogul to a hard and fast treaty. But Indian attitudes that were deeply engrained had rendered this goal unattainable from the start, for the conclusion of any form of treaty for commercial purposes was foreign to Indian ideas. Roe had had to fall back upon the less satisfactory firmans as a means of achieving his end, and, despite interminable delays and evasions, his persistence had brought success. From Prince Khurram (who had once been antagonistic toward the English) Roe gained concessions that established the factory at Surat in a strong position for future trade. From the Mogul himself he won dozens of minor firmans that had the effect of removing petty annoyances and grievances that the English had suffered for years. He took a firm stand against English pirates whose activities could have worked great damage to the attempts aimed at the establishment of a legitimate trade.[69] He

---

[68] *Calendar of State Papers, Colonial Series, East Indies and Persia, 1630–1634,* pp. 66, 67, 142, 167, 410, 495.

[69] In 1617 two ships belonging to the fleet of Robert Rich, earl of Warwick, were engaged in a piratical expedition in the Red Sea. They chased a large carack belonging to the mother of the Great Mogul. The capture of the ship and its cargo (which was valued at £100,000) was prevented solely by the chance appearance of an East India Company fleet. Warwick's ships were seized and converted to the company's use and a good deal of ill-feeling was generated. Roe was firm in the stand he took and Warwick held him responsible for his misfortune. But, as Sir Thomas pointed out, the earl was playing a game that could have caused incalculable harm to England's trade in the East. The Indians made no distinction between one Englishman and another and it would have been impossible for the ambassador to disavow the piratical act. In view of this friction between Roe and Warwick it is ironic that the earl later married Roe's cousin (Wesley F. Craven, *Dissolution of the Virginia Company: The Failure of a Colonial Experiment* [New York, 1932], pp. 83, 127–28; *C.S.P. Dom., 1619–1623,* Sir Thomas Wynne to Sir

played a prominent role in the extension of the company's activities to Persia and the Red Sea, and he brought some semblance of cohesion to the policies and practices of the English factories in India.

In terms of specific achievements, then, Roe's performance had been impressive; but it also has to be judged in more general terms: how did his embassy affect the overall position of the English in India? What differences did his mission make?

When Roe had first stepped ashore at Surat the English position had been precarious and uncomfortable. The Portuguese, implacably hostile to the English, enjoyed a clear primacy. Local officials regarded the English with scant respect and treated them accordingly. Prince Khurram, the governor of India's wealthiest province and the second most powerful man in the kingdom, took few pains to conceal his contempt. Indian merchants who had once been friendly looked unkindly on the English and came increasingly to regard them as dangerous competitors.[70] The residents of the factories misbehaved constantly and in doing so generated ill will among the population at large. The sum total of all these circumstances had been demonstrated by at least one incident that showed the English to be in real danger of being expelled from India.

By the time of Roe's departure some of these conditions had been materially altered. The Portuguese leadership had disappeared and, although they still could be troublesome, it was clear that England's principal rivals were now the energetic and aggressive "Hollanders." Sir Thomas recognized this fact and, despite a longstanding admiration for these brave (and

---

Dudley Carleton, 28 January 1619, p. 8; Roe to the East India Company, 14 February 1618 in Foster, *Embassy*, p. 480).

[70] This was not helped by the implementation of Roe's proposal for trading into the Red Sea area, for the Surat merchants feared that the English would take away some of the profitable trade they enjoyed in that area. Roe actually used a kind of blackmail to win the acquiescence of the Indians; he offered to protect their shipping en route to the Red Sea, but he implied in no uncertain terms that, if the offer of protection were spurned, the English would molest the Indian ships.

Protestant) people, he sought to convince the company that they had more to fear from their supposed friends, the Dutch, than from their old enemies, the Portuguese.[71]

To change the attitudes of a people was clearly beyond the power of one man, but Roe recognized that, in the Mogul Empire, the ideas of the people did not much matter if the attitude of high officials could be made favorable. He correctly perceived that the struggle for position in India would be won or lost at the Mogul court, "where local feelings had little influence, and where, if 'the King and Prince and great men . . . are pleased, the Crie of a Million of subiects would not bee heard.' "[72] Throughout his embassy Roe attached the greatest importance to the maintenance of a dignified bearing. He always insisted on being treated with the respect he felt to be due the king he represented. When the honor of his king or his country was at stake, Roe was unmovable and utterly fearless of consequences. It must have taken a great deal of courage to stand up against the anger of an oriental despot who could send men to their deaths with a nod of the head. At the Mogul's court he could depend upon none of the protections and guarantees recognized in European diplomatic practice, but Roe never weakened, and it may be that the most valuable (though least tangible) fruit of his mission was the heightened respect with which Indian officialdom came to regard the English. Other factors, obviously, were contributing to this transformed attitude, but, for the highest ranking officials of the empire, England was personified by a brave and determined man, intensely proud of his country and wholly committed to the performance of his duty. The emperor and his son, with all their faults, could and did appreciate such qualities, and "English prestige . . . was raised to a high pitch by Roe's gallant bearing and indomitable will."[73]

Another valuable contribution that Roe made to the ad-

[71] Roe to the East India Company, 14 February 1618 in Foster, *Embassy*, p. 481.
[72] Ibid., p. 480.
[73] Foster, *Embassy*, p. xliv.

vancement of the East India Company's fortunes came in the form of the steady stream of good advice he supplied. The advantage of hindsight permits us to recognize, perhaps more fully than Roe's contemporaries, the essential soundness of his opinions. This is not to say that they were disregarded at the time they were offered. G. M. Trevelyan has written that Roe was the first great Anglo-Indian statesman and that he "laid down the policy which guided the action of his countrymen in the East for more than a century to come."[74]

Roe was convinced that, except for resisting the encroachments of the Portuguese and the Dutch, the company should strive to follow a peaceful policy. "Warre and [trade] are incompatible," he told them, and "by my consent you shall no way ingage your selves but at Sea, where you are like to gaine as often as to lose." At one time he had thought that the possession of forts was vital, but he changed his mind and came to believe that the costs would be greater than the profits would warrant. His new conviction was based on the experience of the Dutch and Portuguese who had "never profited by the Indies, since [they] defended them." Sir Thomas was convinced that the English could trade peacefully and profitably without maintaining shore garrisons, but he was under no illusions as to the reason for their acceptance in India. From his own experience he told the company that they could never win the rulers of India by favors, for "they will sooner feare you then love you." This respectful fear he believed would be most effectively instilled by English seapower which would make possible the exertion of great economic pressures upon the most influential segments of the Indian community. (Roe must have been one of the earliest exponents of the doctrine that holds that seapower can exert a decisive influence on the destinies of even essentially nonseafaring states.)

Roe was unalterably opposed to the idea that the company should seek to control land in India. "You must remove from

---

[74] G. M. Trevelyan, *Illustrated English Social History*, vol. 2, *The Age of Shakespeare and the Stuart Period* (New York, 1942), p. 175.

you all thought of any other then a Trade at their Port," he advised. It was true that the Dutch were seeking to establish settlements in India, but even though they carried on a fine trade, their profits were small because of the expense of keeping soldiers there. His major dictum was that the English should follow a peaceful course and avoid unnecessary expense: "Let this be received as a Rule, that if you will profit, seeke it at Sea, and in quiet Trade: for without Controversie it is an errour to affect Garrisons and Land Warres in India . . . ; one disaster would either discredit you, or [involve] you in a Warre of extreme charge and doubtfull event. Besides, an action so subject to chance as Warre, is most unfitly undertaken . . . when the remoteness of place for supply, succours and counsels, subject it to irrecoverable losse."[75]

The East India Company followed the advice of its first ambassador for as long as it was possible to do so. Throughout the seventeenth century, while the authority of the Mogul Empire endured, the company followed the peaceful policy Roe advocated. It was only when India relapsed into anarchy and English merchants were faced with the clear alternative of fighting or leaving that the path of peace was abandoned. Roe's advice had been fundamentally sound and its application had some bearing on the fact that, when the ultimate struggle for supremacy in India developed, it was the English who won—obviously because of the genius of men like Warren Hastings and Robert Clive; less obviously, but just as surely, because of the firm foundation on which English interests had been built by Sir Thomas Roe and other unsung heroes.

The evaluation of Roe's mission can be concluded with the apt words of Sir William Foster, the most distinguished student of the early history of the British East India Company: "Roe was . . . the first of the long line of remarkable Englishmen who by their ability, their force of character, their unselfish adherence to lofty aims, have built up the British dominion

[75] Purchas, *Purchas His Pilgrimes*, 4:462–67.

in India; and looking down the ranks of his successors, it is not too much to say that few have equalled, none has surpassed him."[76] The words have the Victorian ring of the age in which they were written, but their estimate of Roe's contribution is surely just.

[76] Foster, *Embassy*, p. xlv.

CHAPTER 5
To the Ottoman Porte

Upon his return from India Sir Thomas Roe was faced with the problem of making a living. He had some resources—accrued investments in East India Company stock and the modest salary that the company had agreed to pay for the benefit of his advice. But these were wholly inadequate for the support of one who had been a courtier and recently held the title of royal ambassador. Dignity was a most expensive commodity in the seventeenth century, and although Roe was never in danger of starving, he had a constant struggle to support himself in a style appropriate to his rank. It was natural that the son of a distinguished City family, fresh from a term as the representative of England's greatest trading company, should turn in his search for funds to the world of commerce. Trade was no longer held to be incompatible with respectability and Roe already had some strong connections that gave promise of bearing profitable fruit.

As long ago as 1608 Sir Thomas had become involved with the group of merchants who, under the name of the Virginia Company of London, had been given a charter to organize a colony in North America. The extent of his interest was indicated by his appointment by the king as a member of the company's ruling council. His voyage to Guiana and his sojourn in India had temporarily broken his association with the company although, while he was in India, he was kept informed about its affairs through frequent letters from his friend Lord Carew, who was also a member of the council.[1]

Back in England, Sir Thomas prepared once again to become

active in the company. His investment in its stock had become quite substantial; he attended meetings fairly regularly, participated in the discussions of policy, and was appointed to a committee that was to select from the laws of England a body of law that would be suitable for the young colony struggling on the banks of the James River.[2]

By 1620, when this appointment was made, the Virginia Company was running a rocky course. After long years of desperate struggle against Indian attacks, crop failure, internal disorders, disease, and death, the colony's fortunes seemed at last to be improving; but it was still not growing and prospering as had been hoped, and—what was more to the point—the investors were not making any profit from their stock. Under the pressure of prolonged discouragement many of them had begun to lose interest while others criticized past policies and insisted that the company was in need of a thoroughgoing reorganization. Serious factions developed which reflected the opposing views in contemporary English politics. A "court party" led by Sir Thomas Smythe and Sir Robert Rich advocated the established church and the continuation of martial law in Virginia. They were opposed by a "country party" whose leading lights were Sir Edwin Sandys and the earl of Southampton who were in favor of allowing freedom of worship and the exercise of political rights by the colonists. The views of Sandys—and not merely his ideas about colonial government—made him anathema to King James. Some years before, in the Parliament of 1614 he had made an extraordinary speech in which he maintained that the origin of every monarchy lay in election, that a king's authority was dependent upon public consent, and that a king who pretended to rule by

---

[1] John MacLean, ed., *Letters from George Lord Carew to Sir Thomas Roe, Ambassador to the Court of the Great Mogul, 1615–1617* (London, 1860), passim.

[2] Susan M. Kingsbury, ed., *The Records of the Virginia Company of London* (Washington, D.C., 1906), 3:332; ibid., 1:395. In 1618 Roe's investment was somewhere in the region of £750. He held sixty shares which had originally been valued at £12. 10s.

any other authority should be dethroned.[3] The king's views about Sandys were well known, but the members of the Virginia Company were so dissatisfied with the performance of their present officers that they resolved to risk the king's displeasure, by making him the head of the company. The country party gained control and Sandys was elected to the treasurership almost unanimously.

His administration brought some improvement. At home he instigated an examination of company accounts which convicted Smythe of incompetence, if not worse.[4] In Virginia a number of reforms were introduced. The Assembly of Burgesses met in Jamestown, more men and women sailed to the colony from England, and efforts were made to introduce new manufactures that would lessen the colony's dependence upon tobacco. Sandys had been opposed for some time to the growing emphasis upon tobacco. He regarded it as a "deceavable weede . . . which served neither for necessity nor for ornament to the life of man, but was founded only on humor, which might soon vanish into smoke and come to nothing."[5] Sandys and the king agreed in their views on tobacco, if on nothing else.

Not all these new measures were successful and the company was by no means over its difficulties (indeed, desperately hard times lay ahead), but for the present most of the members were won over to Sandys's side, and when his term as treasurer expired in May 1620, they prepared to reelect him. But the king was determined that his wishes would not be ignored a second time and on 27 May he sent a message to the quarterly meeting of the company, naming four candidates whose election would be acceptable to the Crown: Sir Maurice Abbot, Alderman Johnson, Sir Thomas Smythe, and Sir Thomas Roe. Smythe was unacceptable to the members on the basis of his

---

[3] A. F. Pollard, "Sir Edwin Sandys" in *D.N.B.*; A. L. Rowse, *Shakespeare's Southampton, Patron of Virginia* (London, 1965), pp. 219-20.

[4] A. F. Pollard, "Sir Edwin Sandys," in *D.N.B.*

[5] Quoted in Oscar T. Barck and Hugh T. Lefler, *Colonial America* (New York, 1968), p. 50.

past performance and Johnson was tarred with the same brush because he was a supporter and associate of Smythe. Either Abbot or Roe would have been well suited to the task, but that was beside the point.[6] The members of the company deeply resented the king's interference in their affairs (which amounted to a breach of their charter), so they rejected the royal nominees and asked Sandys to retain his office temporarily while they sent a deputation to the king. James received them angrily. He said that the company was a "seminary for seditious parliaments" and that Sandys was his greatest enemy. His final blast to the company's representatives was "Choose the Devil if you will, but not Sir Edwin Sandys."[7] In the face of this bitter antagonism on the part of the Crown, Sandys withdrew his candidacy, but the members proceeded to elect as their treasurer his friend and supporter—indeed his "foremost backer"[8]—the earl of Southampton.

The position of treasurer of the Virginia Company would have been an influential, profitable, and congenial one for Roe, and his qualifications for the job were impressive.[9] But that door to security was now firmly closed. It was ironic that one who spent so much time pleading for advancement at the hands of the Crown should have been rejected now precisely because he was a royal nominee—and rejected by the kind of men he knew the best, the leaders of the merchant community.

So one road to security was barred, but there were others and Sir Thomas now turned to that most popular device of hardpressed courtiers and sought to have the king grant him a monopoly of the importation of tobacco into England. Mo-

---

[6] Abbot was the brother of the archbishop of Canterbury. Of more relevance in the present connection, he was an eminent merchant who became the governor of the East India Company, the lord mayor of London, and an extremely wealthy man.

[7] Pollard, "Sir Edwin Sandys," in *D.N.B.*

[8] Rowse, *Shakespeare's Southampton*, p. 247.

[9] J. A. Doyle, *English Colonies in America: Virginia, Maryland and the Carolinas* (New York, 1882), 1:165. Doyle writes: "Roe would have been unquestionably the best of the four [men nominated by the king]. He was the greatest of those half-commercial, half-political agents, who fill so large a space in the travels of that age."

nopolies were expensive and were obtainable only by those
with court influence. Sir Thomas could not have mustered the
funds necessary for such a grant, but he did have some influence in high places. Accordingly he joined forces with a group
of London merchants headed by Abraham Jacob and Nicholas
Leate, a wealthy man and the deputy governor of the Levant
Company. The association with Leate was to be a fateful one
for Roe, but for the present, the two men were merely business associates engaged in winning what they thought would
be a valuable grant from the king.

The prospect of getting a monopoly over tobacco imports
was a most attractive one, for the big cargoes had just begun to
arrive from Virginia and consumer demand was growing
steadily.[10] But only about half the tobacco used in England
came from Virginia. The rest originated in the Spanish colonies and was generally thought to be of superior quality.
Virginia tobacco was exempt from the payment of import
duty—a concession extracted by the politically powerful men
of the company—but the Spanish tobacco was not: it carried a
duty and an imposition that amounted to two shillings on
every pound of tobacco, but it still cost less than the Virginia
leaf and, because of that fact and its high quality, it retained its
full share of the market, returning a nice profit to those who
controlled its sale.

For some years the tobacco farm had been run by Roe's new
partner, Abraham Jacob, who paid an annual rent of four
thousand pounds for it. In 1619, speaking for the combine of
which he was a member, Jacob offered to double the rent if
taxes were extended to all tobacco, Virginian as well as Spanish. If the grant were made on the terms they sought, Jacob,
Roe, Leate, and their associates would have an absolute monopoly over the purchase and sale of tobacco in England.[11]

---

[10] Menna Prestwich, *Cranfield Politics and Profits under the Early
Stuarts: The Career of Lionel Cranfield Earl of Middlesex* (Oxford,
1962), p. 243 (hereafter cited as *Politics and Profits*).
[11] *Acts of the Privy Council of England, Colonial Series, 1613–1618*
(London, 1908), 1:32–33; Kingsbury, ed., *Records of the Virginia Company*, 3:265.

Such a grant would work against the best interests of the
Virginia Company. Roe and his friends were, in effect, asking
the Crown to bring to an end the privileged position the
company had enjoyed since its founding: the privilege of
being exempt from the payment of customs duties, impositions,
and quotas on its produce. It was a strange position for a
stockholder in the company to be in, but Roe must have
known that the Crown had launched a full-scale effort to make
the customs yield fresh revenue and reasoned that if the monopoly were going to be imposed anyway, he might as well
benefit from it as someone else.[12]

The request of Roe and his associates could not have been
made at a better time. In 1619 relations between King James
and the Virginia Company were strained. The king was not
much disposed to forego the revenue that a tax on Virginia
tobacco would produce in order to favor a company led by his
enemy, Sandys. Indeed, in 1619 King James was finding it
difficult to pass up any chance to increase his income; so he
permitted his dislike of tobacco, his dislike of the company,
and his need for cash to persuade him to approve an import
duty of one shilling per pound on Virginia tobacco. This
amounted to about 20 percent of its normal selling price and
was technically contrary to a provision in the company's
charter which promised that such tax would be limited to 5
percent.

The imposition of the tax, by itself, brought no satisfaction
to Roe and his group; their request for the monopoly had still
not been granted. In fact, no action was taken on their request
during 1619, so in April 1620 Roe submitted the request again,
this time to the Privy Council.[13] Action on the matter was
delayed for a time so that other interested parties could be
heard, but in July the Privy Council instructed the Commissioners for the Treasury to draw up the necessary papers. Roe
and his group did not get all they had requested, for the

[12] Prestwich, *Politics and Profits*, p. 242.
[13] *Acts of the Privy Council of England, Colonial Series, 1613–1618*,
1:32–33; Kingsbury, ed., *Records of the Virginia Company*, 3:265.

monopoly was granted for only one year and the rental was to be £16,000—a price that reflected the commissioners' efforts to squeeze every possible penny out of the customs.[14] The ever-observant John Chamberlain thought that, despite the steep price, the arrangement would be profitable for Roe and his friends, but he expressed a widely held sentiment when he wondered if, perhaps, "the general clamor [and] indignation . . . may bring that filthie weede out of use."[15] Chamberlain's letter went on to complain about the large number of patents of monopoly the king had granted since his accession. It thus reflected two notable opinions of the time: against monopolies in general and against tobacco in particular. The king's dislike of tobacco is well documented; and in 1621, the year after the grant to Roe, parliament prepared to unburden itself on the subject of monopolies.

King James had not wanted to call a parliament that year, but he was persuaded to it by his councillors. He hardly needed to be reminded that no parliament had sat since 1614, and it had been even longer since any subsidies had been voted. Yet now the threat of extraordinary expenditures was looming on the horizon. In Germany the Thirty Years War had begun. James's daughter and son-in-law were at the center of the storm and it seemed too much to expect that the winds would pass England by.

The crisis had been precipitated when the Elector Frederick rashly accepted the Bohemian Crown which had been offered to him by rebels. Hapsburg response had been swift and sure. Frederick's own Palatinate was invaded by Spanish troops. His forces in Bohemia were defeated by the emperor at the battle of the White Mountain. Frederick, along with his English wife and their newborn son Rupert, had to flee for his life. The brief, inglorious reign was over; the long exile had begun.

[14] Ibid., p. 365; *C.S.P., Dom., 1619–1623*, p. 170; Wesley F. Craven, *Dissolution of the Virginia Company: The Failure of a Colonial Experiment* (New York, 1932), p. 228.
[15] Norman E. McClure, ed., *The Letters of John Chamberlain* (Philadelphia, 1939), 2:310–11, Chamberlain to Sir Dudley Carleton.

In England there was general sympathy for the young couple, and sentiment for giving aid to Frederick ran high. The powerful anti-Spanish faction in the Council pressed for war; Buckingham and Prince Charles both urged the king to intervene; and the population at large regarded the Palatine family as Protestant heroes, suffering for their faith at the hands of a grizzly Catholic coalition. The people demonstrated more interest in foreign affairs than at any time since the Armada. In London enthusiastic rumors circulated that levies were to be made for men to be sent to Bohemia. Pamphlets and preachers played their customary role, and the sentiment came to be generally held that parliament should be summoned for the purpose of granting war subsidies.

The king's desire was for peace, and he was still inclined to place his trust in diplomacy. Encouraged by Gondomar, he persisted in his dream of a marriage alliance with Spain that would give him the diplomatic leverage he needed and, with a generous dowry, relieve at least the most pressing of his monetary needs. But at length the need for military preparedness became unavoidable, and with great reluctance the king prepared to move in that direction, submerging for the moment his vision of a world that settles its problems by the acts of diplomacy and peace. The Council of War was called upon to prepare estimates of what it would cost for England to intervene effectively on the Continent, and writs were sent out for the election of members of parliament.

The government made careful preparations for the session. The Council of War began its deliberations; a list was drawn up of men the Court hoped would be elected to parliament; and the king sent out a proclamation warning the towns and counties of England not to elect "curious and wrangling lawyers, who may seek reputation by stirring needless waters." The events of the next several months, however, suggest that the king's warning went unheeded in most of the towns and counties of England. The parliament that met early in 1621 had more than its share of curious and wrangling lawyers.

In the county of Gloucestershire it would have been hard to find a family with more electoral influence than the Berkeleys.[16] Since Sir Thomas Roe was related to this family through his mother's second marriage, it was not surprising that, when King James opened the third parliament of his reign, Roe was present as one of the burgesses from the city of Cirencester.

The first order of business was the consideration of the government's request for subsidies. The Council of War had advised the king that intervention in Germany would cost the staggering sum of £900,000 a year. James balked at asking parliament for such a figure and told the Commons that the army he needed would cost £500,000—a serious underestimate. But even this figure was enough to alarm the members who were in fact in a bit of a quandary. Most of them favored intervention, but they did not trust the king. They were not convinced that subsidies would be spent for the designated purposes; they were indignant over the king's extravagance; and they suspected that James (far from being convinced of the necessity of armed intervention in Europe) still pinned his hopes upon a marriage treaty. Accordingly, they did the predictable thing: they gave the king some money, but they did not give him enough— £160,000.

Sir Thomas Roe's career in the Parliament of 1621 was short, lasting only from the opening in January to the adjournment in May. During that time, however, and in spite of a brief illness, he was very active. He played a leading role in the debates. More than eighty of his speeches on a wide range of subjects were recorded. In the debate over subsidies Roe stood squarely on the king's side which, in this instance, coincided with the activist, Protestant view that Roe had always held. The issue was whether to grant one subsidy, one subsidy and two fifteenths, or two subsidies. He pleaded with his fellow members to vote for two subsidies: "Let us give liberally and

---

[16] D. Brunton and D. H. Pennington, *Members of the Long Parliament* (Cambridge, Mass., 1954), p. 133; W. R. Williams, *The Parliamentary History of the County of Gloucester* (Hereford, 1898), p. v.

freely that the Papists may see that the King and his subjects are in union and that the King hath the hearts, the hands and the purses of his subjects to help him."[17] Other members expressed similar sentiments and in the end the Commons voted for two subsidies.

He was active on committees too, serving on twice as many as the average member.[18] Although he was tied to the Crown by bonds of duty and affection, Sir Thomas took an essentially independent stand on the matters that came up for discussion. His speeches in the House of Commons usually inclined to what might be called the popular side, and the records of the parliament confirm the belief that Sir Thomas was an independent thinker. On one occasion he was a member of a committee to "consider of the best means and manner to acquaint the Kings Majestie with [a] breach made of the priviledge of this howse." The committee produced a draft of a "Petition for Liberty of speech" which affirmed that only the House of Commons could censure a member for an inappropriate statement and asked the king to make a public declaration to that effect. Roe was chosen to submit the committee's report to the House. Another time the king had sent to the House of Commons notice of his intention to fulfill a promise made to Spain to sell her a hundred artillery pieces. The king had been assured that the guns were to be sent to Portugal for use against pirates; but under the circumstances it was not surprising that members feared that they would, in fact, be used in the Palatinate and against English ships in the East. In the debate occasioned by the king's announcement Roe spoke out with telling arguments against the royal position.[19]

Although the impetus for calling parliament had been provided, in the main, by foreign affairs, the members actually

[17] Wallace Notestein, Frances Relf, and Hartley Simpson, eds., *Commons Debates, 1621*, 7 vols. (New Haven, Conn., 1935), 2:88 (hereafter cited as *Commons Debates*).
[18] Williams M. Mitchell, *The Rise of the Revolutionary Party in the English House of Commons, 1603–1629* (New York, 1957), pp. 90–92.
[19] *Commons Debates*, 2:26, 52; 4:37; 5:454; 2:71.

spent most of their time considering domestic matters. Warned against discussing foreign policy by the king, they gave their attention to the drafting of the Great Protestation and, above all, to complaining about monopolies. They spent more time on that than on any other subject, and on occasion the Palace of Westminster became a very uncomfortable place for Sir Thomas Roe because the members addressed themselves not only to questions about monopolies in general but also to the particular matter of the importation of tobacco. As a matter of fact, they passed a bill designed to exclude foreign tobacco from England. The measure failed to pass in the House of Lords, but it nevertheless demonstrated the extent to which the House of Commons disapproved the grant that had been made to Roe and his friends. We cannot know what effect this disapproval had upon Sir Thomas, but we do know that, while he spoke out in defense of the grant, he surrendered the patent when it terminated in September, and there was apparently no effort to have it extended for the seven-year period mentioned in the initial request.[20]

While giving his best efforts to his parliamentary duties Roe continued to ponder his future. The tobacco monopoly had not been as profitable as he had hoped and there were no developing prospects of suitable employment. Sir Thomas undoubtedly hoped that some sort of office or preferment would be forthcoming from the Crown, but the months passed and the Court preserved its silence. Accordingly, he directed his attention to an avenue he knew to be open to him—overseas service. Soon after his return from India he had been approached by the merchants of the East India Company who wanted him to undertake another embassy to the Far East. Roe had refused, saying that after so long an exile he was unwilling once again to take his leave of home, family, and friends.[21] However, in the absence of attractive employment at home,

[20] Ibid., 4:113; *Journal of the House of Commons*, 1:586; *C.S.P., Dom., 1619–1623*, p. 170.
[21] Foster, *Embassy*, p. 530, *n.* 1.

the wanderlust was making itself felt again; and Sir Thomas listened with increasing interest to his friend Leate, who was trying to persuade him to become England's ambassador and the Levant Company's representative at the Ottoman Porte.

The Levant merchants regarded Roe as a desirable man for the post. He had extensive experience of the workings of the eastern mind, and some of the negotiations he had undertaken in India had given him firsthand knowledge of Middle Eastern trade. Moreover, the essential objectives of the embassy would be similar to those of his earlier mission: English prestige in Constantinople had suffered from a succession of mediocre ambassadors; it needed to be restored by a man of dignity and resolution. In theory, English merchants enjoyed extensive trading privileges in the eastern Mediterranean, so the negotiation of commercial treaties would not be of great importance. However, the exercise of those privileges was being severely jeopardized by the activities of the pirates of Algiers and Tunis, and stern representations needed to be made to persuade the sultan to restrain his unruly subjects. Roe seemed to be the right man for the task, and the merchants of the Levant Company were well pleased when, in the summer of 1621, he indicated his willingness once again to serve his country "in partibus infidelium."

Roe was about to become one of a long line of Englishmen who worked to develop their country's trade in the Middle East. The beginnings of English trade in the area date chiefly from the fifteenth century, but the Levant Company (which was born in the amalgamation of the Turkey and Venice companies) was not chartered until 1592. At that time its members had been granted the exclusive privilege of trading for twelve years in the territories of Turkey and Venice. In 1605 the company was granted a permanent charter under which it was governed for more than two centuries.

The principal article exported by the Levant Company was English cloth, for which there was a steadily increasing demand at Constantinople, Smyrna, and Aleppo. Tin, lead, furs, and some East Indian products were also sent out; and these exports made it possible for the company to procure all the money it needed to buy the chief articles for importing into England: currants and indigo. This favorable balance of trade made the company the darling of the economists of the age: unlike the East India Company it was not forever sending bullion out of the country. At mid-century Lewis Roberts wrote in convoluted praise: the Levant Company "is the most flourishing and beneficiall Company to the commonwealth of any in England of all other whatsoever." The total volume of trade increased rapidly during the first half of the century, and by 1626 the value of exports to Turkey alone was put at £250,000. Unfortunately, there was one serious flaw in this otherwise flourishing trade. The whole imposing structure was built on currants, and the main sources of supply at Zante and Cephalonia were Venetian dependencies. This meant that the whole trade was unusually susceptible to outside interference. The Venetians were one of the company's principal rivals in the Levant, and they were now proving difficult. At first they had allowed traffic to flow at very reasonable rates, but once they became convinced that the eating of currants was a firmly entrenched habit in England, they began repeatedly to raise the duties that had to be paid. Roe, it seems, had rather a contemptuous attitude toward the humble currant. He called them "those trash berries"; but for all his disdain he would find himself spending a good deal of time in the next few years doing his utmost to protect and enlarge the company's trade in that commodity.[22]

The Levant Company was represented overseas by an ambassador and a number of consuls who were subordinate to him. The ambassador invariably resided at Constantinople. He performed a dual function, for he was the representative both of the English Crown and of the company. In his capacity as ambassador he had extensive jurisdiction over English nationals

[22] Alfred C. Wood, *A History of the Levant Company* (London, 1935), pp. 42–43.

living in the lands of the sultan. This jurisdiction was founded upon the "capitulations," negotiated between England and the Porte in 1592. Under these agreements, Englishmen were not subject to Turkish law, and they could be arrested or deported only by the order of their own ambassador. Disputes involving Turks and Englishmen were settled in accordance with the law of England as administered in the consular courts. This practice, which was not then regarded as a derogation of sovereignty, gave to the English ambassador at Constantinople a rather demanding and influential role to play. In his capacity as the representative of the Levant Company, Sir Thomas would be expected to give direction and leadership to the consuls who conducted the company's business in such places as Alexandria, Aleppo, Smyrna, and Salonika; and he would have the authority to discharge those officials in the event of any dereliction of duty. In its ambiguity and its duties his new position would thus be rather similar to the one he had recently held. In both instances, he had been the servant of the Crown and of a company of merchants. In India, his subordinates had been the factors, resident in the principal commercial centers; in Turkey, he would be the head of a similar network of agents, but they would be empowered to perform both political and commercial functions. His purpose, as in India, would be to build up English prestige, increase the volume and security of trade, and end the harassment of English subjects. In Constantinople, as in Ajmere, he would have to deal with a Muslim prince who was inclined to regard himself as being vastly superior in dignity and power to any other monarch. In at least one respect, however, the new venture promised to be more enjoyable than the last, for his new employers approved Sir Thomas's request that his wife be permitted to accompany him on his journey.

His official appointment as King James's ambassador to the Sublime Porte was contained in Letters Patent dated 13 September 1621. His instructions admonished him to protect and defend the interests of the Levant Company and gave him authority to direct and govern all English subjects in the territories of the Grand Signor. The goals of his embassy were only vaguely indicated, and it was clear that he was to be guided in large part by his own discretion. One or two specific objectives were indicated, however. He was to try to dissuade the sultan from waging war on Poland or Hungary, to which countries King James piously professed to be joined by the common bond of the Christian faith. He was to seek the release of certain Polish noblemen who were imprisoned in Constantinople and, as part of his efforts on behalf of the Levant Company, he was to aim at the suppression of the pirates of Tunis and Algiers.[23]

With these instructions in mind, Roe embarked in September 1621. The voyage was made in leisurely fashion, and the ambassador and his party frequently went ashore to visit sites of particular interest. At each port Sir Thomas and his wife were received with hospitality and respect. Roe interpreted these attitudes as reflecting admiration for the king he served. A few days were spent at Malaga in Grenada, and already Roe was becoming aware of the seriousness of the situation he had been sent to remedy. In a letter to Secretary Calvert, he conveyed something of the plight of the English merchants in the area and emphasized the necessity of strong action: "if all the trade from the North of the Cape to the Streight [*sic*] and from thence into the Levant be of any Consequence to his Mat^y or the Commonwealth of England there must be some speedy course taken for the suppressing of these Robbers, before they growe too powerfull at Sea for the Armys of Kings." If this is

---

[23] *C.S.P., Dom., Addenda, 1625–1649*, pp. 64–65; *State Papers Foreign, Turkey* (Public Record Office ref. SP97), bundle 8, f. 101. In subsequent references the bundle and folio numbers will be cited thus: 8/101. His instructions are printed in Thomas Carte, ed., (?) *The Negotiations of Sir Thomas Roe, in his Embassy to the Ottoman Porte, from the Year 1621 to 1628 Inclusive* . . . (London, 1740), pp. 2–4. This work will hereafter be cited as *Negotiations*. It consists of copies of letters received and sent by Roe and taken from collections now in the Public Record Office. The editorial work has been done so well that a study of the original materials adds little of substance to the story that can be pieced together from Carte.

not done the whole Levant trade will be lost: the pirates of Algiers already have treasure "above the Mynes of India."[24] Ideally, the solution would be for all the Christian princes to take joint action against the pirates, but, given the current condition of European affairs, there was not much hope of that.

They went ashore again at Messina where they watched in fascination "the fire of Aetna upon Sicily."[25] They were given a cordial reception by the local folk. Although Roe had "made no noyse" of his arrival, he was greeted by an armada of galleys and welcomed by the local dignitaries—"all the nobility of this little court," as he rather condescendingly put it. The prominent ladies of the town visited his wife. Accommodations were offered to them, but Roe decided to take the house of "an honest Englishman." All in all it was very satisfactory and Sir Thomas felt moved to purr in a letter home, "I think no minister of his M[ties] abroad ever received more courtesies nor honors."[26] While he was at Messina, Roe took advantage of an opportunity to secure the release of fourteen English captives from the galleys and, at his own expense, to send them back to England.[27]

The journey continued without further incident. Brief stops were made at Zante, a small island off the southwestern coast of Greece where the Levant Company had a factory and at "Sio" (perhaps Khios) off the western coast of Turkey. Finally, on 28 December 1621, more than three months after their departure from England, the ambassador and his party arrived at Constantinople. They had good reason to be thankful for their safe arrival, for in the early years of the seventeenth century a journey across the Mediterranean was a risky business because of the frequent raids of the Barbary pirates. Sir Thomas recognized this fact and commented on his good fortune in a letter to a friend: "in my way [I] saw noe enimie,

[24] *State Papers Foreign, Turkey,* 8/74.
[25] *Negotiations,* p. 37.
[26] *State Papers Foreign, Turkey,* 8/88.
[27] Ibid., 8/88–89.

though they wher often but a day too soone, or too latte, which is one of the happiest passages that ever shippinge made, and . . . a great blessinge of God.''[28]

During the first days that he spent in Constantinople, Roe was disturbed by the coolness of his reception. The Turkish ministers took no notice of him and Roe interpreted this as a studied insult against his king. He blamed his predecessors and the ambassadors of other Christian countries who, by their submission to repeated discourtesy, had earned the contempt of the Turks. Sir Thomas determined to "beginne a reformation," and wrote an angry letter expressing displeasure at the disrespect shown to former English ministers and indicating that he had no intention of submitting to similar indignities. He received no satisfaction beyond a polite letter from the vizier who apologized for former attitudes and extended a cordial welcome to the new representative of the English king. But this was not what Roe wanted. He had been in Constantinople for almost three weeks and no arrangements had been made for an audience with the sultan. Roe regarded this as a serious breach of protocol. He was determined that the first gesture of friendship should be extended by the Turks and, because he was convinced that the sultan "would rather strangle tenne viziers than risk a breach with England," he sent a strongly worded message telling the sultan that he was prepared to leave Constantinople unless the official attitude mellowed very quickly.[29]

This brought results. In February Sir Thomas was received with great courtesy by the young sultan, Osman II. The audience was conducted with a good deal of ceremony, but Roe took advantage of the occasion to outline the objectives of his mission. He made a brief formal speech himself, then had his interpreter read the list of English demands; first, that the capitulations be renewed, the privileges of the English in Constantinople extended, and certain injuries done to English mer-

---

[28] *Negotiations,* p. 37.
[29] Ibid., p. 15.

chants remedied. Second, Roe offered himself as a mediator between the Turks and the Poles and stressed his master's desire "to procure the generall quiett and peace of the Princes of Christendom." The third demand was that the sultan release certain members of the Polish nobility and "one Scottish gentleman" who were then his captives. Next, the ambassador demanded that the sultan make every effort to impose order on the pirates of Algiers and Tunis, and that a large sum of money, illegally taken from an English merchant named Arthur Galloway, be restored. Finally, he asked that the reply to his demands be made in writing; and at the close of the audience he informed the vizier that the English did not intend any longer to be deluded with words and promises.[30]

This was a bold and forthright start and Roe was equally blunt in his estimation of the young prince to whom he had presented his credentials. He was not much impressed and compared the Turkish ruler unfavorably with the Great Mogul: "[Here] I spake to a dumb image, and ther I treated familiarly with an affable and courteous prince."[31] Actually, this was hardly a fair comparison to make, for the Turkish prince was but a boy of eighteen. He had come to his throne in February 1618 at the age of fourteen years. His accession had almost coincided with the outbreak of the Thirty Years War, an event that presented a wide range of problems and opportunities to the ruler of the Turkish state. From its beginning the struggle in Germany had claimed the attention of the major foreign foes of the Ottoman Empire—Austria and Spain—and the young ruler had thus been able to turn his attention to the suppression of his domestic enemies. Foremost among these were the powerful Janissaries who had long been the backbone of the Turkish army, but whose power now represented a serious threat to the government. The only effective and practical way in which their strength could be reduced was by loss

---

[30] *State Papers Foreign, Turkey,* 8/117: "The demands made to the Grand Sig^{or} at my first Audience and delivery of your Maties Roiall Letters."
[31] *Negotiations,* p. 37.

in battle, and with this end in view Osman in 1621 had declared
war upon Poland. The young prince had returned from a
Polish campaign just two days before Roe's arrival in Constantinople, and Sir Thomas noted that he came home with "losses
and dishonour, his army almost mutined."[32]

The failure of the Polish campaign proved fatal to the young
sultan, for not long after the audience with Roe he was brutally murdered and his insane uncle, Mustafa, was dragged
from a cell and enthroned in his place. Sir Thomas saw that
Turkish affairs were not likely to settle down with a madman
on the throne. His mission had been made impossibly difficult.
No negotiations could be conducted, and for a while Roe was
more a commentator on Turkish affairs than an ambassador.
On every hand he saw signs of future revolution and unrest.
The leaderless soldiers wielded the sole power in the state.
Affairs were anarchical and chaotic. Roe could see no end to
the rebellions that were breaking out all over the country.
"What," he asked, "can be expected but ruyne?" He himself
anticipated nothing but trouble. "Every action is a prediction
. . . and . . . the fatall day is at hand." He described the
occurrences at the Porte as being "fitt matter for Ben Johnson." In a descriptive phrase that anticipated the famous re-
mark of Czar Nicholas I by some 230 years, Roe described the
Turkish Empire as being "yrrecouerably sick" and compared
it to "an old body, crazed through many vices, which remayne
when the youth and strength is decayed."[33]

Sir Thomas was proved correct in his predictions of future
upheavals; by August 1623 he was writing the news of Mustafa's deposition and the proclamation of the young sultan
Murad IV as ruler of the Ottoman Empire. He commented:
"Emperors are here made with less noyse than a proctor in
Oxford. . . . In fifteen months I have seene three emperours,
seaven great viziers, two capten bassas, five agas of the Janiza-
ries, three treasorers, six bassas of Cairo, and in proportion as

---

[32] *State Papers Foreign, Turkey*, 8/107; *Negotiations*, p. 15.
[33] Ibid., pp. 22, 126.

many chaunges of governours in all the provinces; every new
vizier making use of his tyme, displaceing those in possession,
and selling their favour to others."[34]

During these years of upheaval and revolt Roe and the other
Christians at Constantinople lived under the shadow of great
danger. The rampaging soldiers, immune to discipline, showed
themselves ingenious at devising refined forms of torture for
their enemies. A Venetian was staked out in front of a church
in Galata, his death intended as a gesture of scorn for all
Christians. Christians were robbed in the streets of Constantinople. The members of the English embassy were ordered
to keep indoors. Government officials were found floating in
the Bosporus. The residences of Christian consuls were attacked in many different parts of the empire. Europeans and
Turks, Christians and Muslims were ravished with fine impar-
tiality.[35]

There was little hope of bringing anything positive out of
such conditions, but with change so constant there was always
the possibility that the very chaos would produce a man
capable of ending it. Roe thought he detected such a man in
the person of the new sultan. The first time he saw him he
described him as "a youth of 14 yeares of age, fatt, and of a
lively countenance, and good stature, a prince of too faire hopes
for such a people: his actions . . . showe hee will soone knowe
himself and prove of a stirring virtue."[36] Roe was not often
wrong in his judgment of people and he proved to be right in
this case too. The young sultan, Murad IV, used the terrible
ferocity of his race to stamp out mutiny, master the army, and
extend his empire. He was the last of the great warrior-sultans,
and his accession brought about the restoration of normality
and the possibility of the resumption of diplomatic business.

During these troubled times, when the impotence of the
government made negotiation impossible, Roe developed his

[34] Quoted in Stanley Lane-Poole, "An Ambassador to the Sultan,
1621–1622," *Cornhill Magazine*, n.s. 3, 7:475.
[35] Ibid., pp. 473–75.
[36] Ibid., p. 475.

relationship with the English merchant community in Constantinople. Soon after his arrival he met with the merchants at the home of Edward Stringer to acquaint them with his instructions and intentions. These meetings became regular affairs and soon a procedural pattern began to develop. The meetings were usually called by Roe and began with the reading and approval of the report of the last meeting. After this "reading of the minutes," they would discuss the details of their trade, payments, loans, the capitulations, prevailing conditions, and markets—in short, anything that affected their business. Quite often Roe would report on the work he had been doing, and sometimes he was called upon to settle disputes between the merchants. A routine matter was the approval of agreements entered into by individual merchants. These were spelled out in a notebook kept for the purpose, and Roe would indicate his approval by writing in the margin: "I, Sir Tho: Roe, Ambass: for his Matie of great Brittaine affirm this bargain made before mee." To this he added a sketch of his coat of arms.[37] Most of the agreements were made with Jewish traders (for the Turks themselves had no interest in commerce), and the terms were painstakingly written out in both English and Hebrew.

Another item of business that periodically came before the meeting was the matter of the ambassador's salary. Roe was to be paid by the Levant Company, an arrangement that was a source of some embarrassment because it put him in the position of having authority over the merchants and at the same time being dependent upon them for his pay. Thus, for example, in November 1624 at "a court called by his Lordship and present all the Nation," Roe told the merchants that his salary for the Michaelmas quarter had not been paid and that something must be done about it. The treasurer said that he was in

[37] *A Journal of all the Courts, Actes, Contracts, Sentences, Ends of Controversies and other Business concerning the English Nation in the tyme of the Right Honorable Sr Thomas Roe, Embassadour resident from his Matie of great Brittayne at the Port of Constantinople, begunne the First of January 1621* (Public Record Office ref. SP105/102), passim (hereafter cited as *A Journal of all the Courts*).

no position to pay it, so Roe suggested three ways, "by one whereof it must be raised." All those present, "desirous his lordship should be forthwith paid, agreed to a donation," and the matter was settled.[38] All the evidence suggests that Roe's relations with the merchants in Constantinople were thoroughly cordial and that they were well pleased with his performance on their behalf. Throughout his embassy he watched over the little community of English traders with unremitting care and was able to safeguard their privileges with great success.[39] During his stay in Constantinople the volume of English trade with the Levant was to double—although it must quickly be added that those years were part of a longer period characterized by rapid growth and England's emergence as the leading commercial nation in the area.[40]

While his relations with the merchants seem to have been cordial, Roe found himself in a rather delicate situation with respect to his predecessor whom he met on a number of occasions during these early days. Not much is known about this man, Sir John Eyre, but the company had elected him as their ambassador in August 1619 and he was given the royal commission in December. By April of the following year he was in Constantinople. Soon afterwards he decided that the salary and allowances the company had arranged to pay him were inadequate; and moreover, he charged that the company was not paying him in advance as it had undertaken to do. In marked contrast to Roe's later sensible behavior in similar circumstances, Eyre had proceeded to recoup himself to the tune of £3,000 by seizing consulage from the merchants. They complained to the company in London. The complaint was relayed to the king, and in July letters of recall were sent to Eyre.[41]

Roe did not want to be drawn into the controversy: "as I am

[38] Ibid., sub. 11 November 1624.
[39] Wood, *History of the Levant Company*, p. 86.
[40] Ibid., pp. 42, 44.
[41] *State Papers Foreign, Turkey*, 8/43.

not his judge I will not be his accuser: there are enough prepared to that office." Since some sort of report was expected of him, he chose "to be a bare relater of what hath beene done since ye receipt of his M[s] letters [of recall]." In a letter to the Lords of the Council he reported that when the king's orders came Eyre had promptly turned over his seals, resigned his authority, and stopped dealing as a public official. He had not interfered in English affairs and, since Roe's own arrival, Eyre had treated him well and behaved as an obedient servant of the king.[42] He had heard it charged that Eyre had spoken slightingly of King James. Roe knew of no evidence for such an accusation beyond a little foolish bragging: "vanities and slipperynesses as if he had had great privacy with his majestie."[43] So Roe refused to kick a man who was down, and his testimony may have helped to influence the Council in Eyre's behalf. When the case came up in June he was treated generously. He was permitted to keep the money he had taken (even though it exceeded the amount due him) on the grounds that the merchants had been at fault in not paying him as they had promised and because his name had been subjected unfairly to damaging accusations.[44]

Roe's instructions had stipulated that, as a major objective of his embassy, he was to do everything possible to secure peace between the Ottoman Empire and Poland and to win fair treatment for certain Polish noblemen who were prisoners of the Turks.[45] When he arrived in Turkey the sultan was at war

[42] Ibid., 8/109.
[43] Quoted in Wood, *History of the Levant Company*, p. 86.
[44] *C.S.P., Dom., 1619–1623*, p. 413.
[45] On the basis of purely practical considerations, Roe's instructions on this matter are a bit puzzling. The Poles were allied with the Holy Roman Emperor who was despoiling the lands of King James's son-in-law. It seems that James would have been well advised to encourage the war, rather than to end it, and thus indirectly weaken the enemy of his family. His assertion that he chose an opposite course because of his devotion to the Christian faith and the interests of a brother Christian king has the ring of diplomatic hyperbole and in any case would not have carried much weight with the sultan. It may be that this suspicion does him an injustice and that he was acting from high principles. Perhaps he

with Poland, so from the beginning of his embassy Roe devoted his keenest efforts to arranging a treaty.

A Polish embassy arrived at Constantinople for the purpose of negotiating a treaty in October 1622; and soon afterwards both sides agreed to accept Roe as their mediator.[46] The first few meetings were filled with bitter harangues from both sides; but this, perhaps, was to be expected. More serious was the fact that negotiations were made almost impossible by the successive upheavals in the Turkish state. Each convulsion brought new people into office and much time had to be spent in briefing the minister of the moment about what had been done before his arrival on the scene. In the nature of things a new negotiator was suspicious of the agreements made by his predecessor, and the talks were constantly being set back. But total stagnation was averted by the realization on the part of both sides that there was little to be gained from the war. Both countries were deeply engaged in other areas, the Poles in the Baltic and the Turks in Persia and Syria; and the Turks in particular were feeling the strain of these multiple commitments. Roe's task in the talks was really just to keep the negotiators at their work and to smooth away the inevitable personal abrasions that developed. He encountered few major difficulties—although an annoying period of illness sidelined him for a time—and by March 1623 he could report jubilantly that the peace had been made.[47] The Polish prisoners were released, and Roe himself supplied them with money for their homeward journey.[48] Unfortunately, the detail about Roe's part in these successful negotiations is not known, for he made few references to them in his correspondence; but his

---

was trying to mollify the emperor; perhaps he was simply working in pursuit of his pacific ideals, believing that peace, even when so far away, was worth striving for; or, perhaps, the whole episode is just another illustration of the bewildering inconsistencies of James's foreign policy.

[46] *Negotiations*, p. 133; Roe to the archbishop of Canterbury, March 1623.

[47] Ibid.; a copy of the treaty is in *State Papers Foreign, Turkey*, 9/33.

[48] *Negotiations*, p. 129; Roe to Secretary Calvert, February 1623.

services were evidently recognized by the participants, for Sir Thomas was personally thanked by King Sigismund III for the good services he had rendered to the Polish state.[49]

While the treaty between Poland and Turkey was being negotiated, Roe was also involved in some business that was of more immediate interest to the members of the Levant Company. Before he arrived in Constantinople, the Turks had claimed the right to impose an "avenue," or fine, on silk shipped in foreign vessels. This was contrary to the capitulations and, although earlier ambassadors from England and other states had made no objection, Roe was determined to have the fine removed. To him it was part and parcel of the campaign to reassert the dignity of England; it was wrong in principle and must be fought.

The opportunity came in the summer of 1622 when, apparently at the instigation of a Jewish merchant, an English ship that refused to pay the fine was seized by the Turks. Roe angrily went to see the vizier, taking a copy of the capitulations with him. He got short shrift from the Turkish official who refused to look at the document and "with badd words bidd him to be gone and pay and that he would hang his secretary and Dragoman."[50] Roe predictably blazed up at this. He said that if the vizier was determined to ignore the capitulations and bring on a breach with the king of England, justice would be sought in some other way. And with that thinly veiled threat, he flung the capitulations at the vizier's feet and stalked out of the room.[51]

His next step was to call the merchants together to tell them what had happened. "If a rogue should pretend to raise a new imposition on our goods and show no reason but that he had a command contrary to our capitulations, they might as well get

[49] *Historical Manuscripts Commission: Report on the Manuscripts of Alan George Finch, Esq., of Burley-on-the-Hill, Rutland* (London, 1913), p. 320 (hereafter cited as *Historical Manuscripts Commission, Finch Papers*).

[50] *A Journal of all the Courts,* sub. 27 June 1622.

[51] Ibid.

a command to take ships and goods and all." The line had to be drawn, and he was not going to tolerate this. He would suffer no indignity at the hands of the Turk, but he was confident that before the business was closed he would "trouble the Vizier and hang the Jew."[52] He had communicated his intentions to the other ambassadors and, although they had all meekly tolerated the situation before, they now agreed to "go join and stand out with him to the uttermost, having all the like occasion." The merchants enthusiastically approved of Roe's resolve. They swore to stand by him in all things, and they urged him to press on "either for a Reformation or a finall dissolution."[53]

The struggle proved easier than expected, thanks to the vagaries of Turkish affairs. The vizier was deposed by soldiers and fled from the capital. His successor proved more tractable, and before long Roe was able to report his modest victory. He gained his point about the fine on silk and "gott a judgment in open divan, and I hope also to hang the Jewe that durst attempt to give cause of the breach of amity betweene his majestie and this state. I have obtayned a victory, which I hope may bring us much quiett, and make the best here wary to fall at difference with mee."[54]

The real victory, however—at least from Roe's point of view—was in the reassertion of the dignity of England. By taking the lead in the successful argument and by rallying the western ambassadors to his side, he had raised the stock of England both with the Turkish officials and within the diplomatic community. Every step in that direction would make his task easier and his mission more effective, and Roe never overlooked an opportunity to implement his conviction that at Constantinople the representative of the king of England should be treated with respect and that he should rank above the other ambassadors of Christian lands.

[52] Ibid.
[53] Ibid., sub. 2 July 1622.
[54] Quoted in Lane-Poole, "An Ambassador to the Sultan," p. 472.

Rivalry over precedence was one of the staple features of seventeenth-century diplomacy. In every capital there was interminable quarreling among the ambassadors who took it as one of their principal duties to preserve the dignity of their masters' crowns. At The Hague, for example, where Roe's friend Carleton was the ambassador, squabbles over precedence were carried on with great intensity, disrupting ceremonies, interfering with business, and even on occasion leading to blows.[55] Roe would have been thoroughly in sympathy with this kind of thing; he was a child of his age in that he attached great importance to seemingly trivial matters of decorum.

Not long after his arrival in Constantinople he was provided an opportunity to wage the war of precedence himself. A dispute arose among the Christian ambassadors on the order of precedence to be observed in their dealings with officials of the Ottoman Porte. The controversy was especially bitter between Sir Thomas and the French ambassador, a man named De Cesy, to whom precedence had been conceded by an earlier English representative, Sir Paul Pindar. Roe was determined that he would not accept second place and he began to lay plans for bringing about a "reformation."

The first step in his offensive was to write Secretary Calvert and inquire about the official relationship between the representatives of England and France in Constantinople. He received word that Pindar had, in fact, yielded precedence to the French, but that there had been no official sanction for his action. Sir Thomas himself was ordered not to yield on any account; and these instructions cleared the way for another demonstration of the stubborn persistence of which Roe was capable when he felt that some important matter of principle was at stake.[56]

[55] Green, *Elizabeth of Bohemia*, pp. 241–42, 256–57; Garrett Mattingly, *Renaissance Diplomacy* (London, 1955), p. 253; Maurice Lee, Jr., "The Jacobean Diplomatic Service," *American Historical Review* 72 (July 1967): 1274.

[56] *Negotiations*, pp. 60–61; Secretary Calvert to Roe.

It was not long before opportunity knocked. An incident arose that called for the concerted action of four ambassadors, and Sir Thomas Roe was asked to draft a letter which would subsequently be signed by the representatives of Holland, Venice, England, and France. No sooner was this done than an issue developed over the order in which the various representatives should sign the letter. Roe indicated his willingness to place his signature in a position equal to that of the French ambassador, but he rejected utterly the suggestion that his name should come beneath that of the Frenchman. But this was not good enough for France, and Roe's adversary demanded precedence. Sir Thomas refused to yield and suggested instead that, as a means of resolving the deadlock, each ambassador should send a separate copy of the letter. Just when it seemed that this solution would be accepted, another and greater difficulty appeared. This revolved around the matter of titles and was really basic in all the diplomatic wranglings of this kind between Englishmen and Frenchmen. The king of England in the seventeenth century still claimed the title "King of France," while the French king styled himself "Emperor of France." The claims implied by these titles were unreal and flippant, but it was part of the game of diplomacy that the pretense had to be maintained. Roe indicated his recognition of the charade when he pointed out that, by writing separate letters, all difficulties as to precedence could be avoided; and the French ambassador, in his letter, could, if he chose, designate his master as lord of Florida and Brazil!

Even this apparently sensible suggestion failed to win the representative of France, who still insisted that one letter be sent and that his signature be given precedence. With matters thus deadlocked, Sir Thomas wrote home and asked that an official protest be lodged with the French secretary. Following the dispatch of his letter, Roe suffered from a dearth of correspondence from England (a circumstance that often plagued him during his embassy) and so was left without instructions.

Eight months later he had still received no word, so he wrote again to Calvert, pleading for instructions and explaining that the situation had become very difficult, with the Frenchman doing everything in his power to force the issue. Meanwhile (he continued) the quarreling and disunity among the ambassadors of the Christian princes was weakening their collective power in the eyes of the Turks. He gave vent to some of his more personal feelings by engaging in some vituperative comments about the obstinate Frenchman whom he called "a montayneere that never wore a band, nor cuffes, nor, I thincke, linnen!"[57]

Even this outburst failed to bring an answer from England until May 1624. Then a letter came from Calvert, assuring Sir Thomas that everything possible was being done to obtain some concession from the French, but that, so far, no satisfactory results had been achieved. In the meantime, Roe was cautioned not to yield "one tittle," but to try to avoid any situation that would bring up the problem.[58] This can have brought little in the way of encouragement, but Sir Thomas persevered and, at last, the French ambassador weakened. He agreed that a single letter should be sent to the Turks; and, more importantly, he consented that the Englishman should sign first. Roe did not insist on being accorded precedence, but, wary of any possible duplicity on the part of the Frenchman, he signed his name in such a way that his rival could sign on a level with it, but could not possibly squeeze his signature above that of Roe himself.[59] The secretary of state, when told of these developments, was well pleased and wrote that the ambassador's conduct had "restored the honor of our kinge and nation."[60] This would have been extravagant praise if it had derived from the mere placement of signatures on a piece of paper, but for broader reasons it was well deserved. Roe

[57] Ibid., p. 209; Roe to Calvert.
[58] Ibid., p. 244; Calvert to Roe.
[59] Ibid., pp. 269–70; Roe to Calvert.
[60] Ibid., p. 60; Calvert to Roe.

could look back over his first two years in Constantinople with satisfaction. In spite of the most difficult circumstances he had made a good start toward achieving the goals of his embassy and strengthened his own position so there was realistic hope of success. He looked to the future with confidence.

CHAPTER 6

Pirates, Princes, & Patriarchs

THE objective of his mission to Constantinople in which Sir Thomas took the greatest personal interest, and one of greater import than disputes over precedence, centered around the plight of his countrymen who were the captives of the Barbary pirates. Roe, on his way to Constantinople, had obtained the release of a small group of prisoners and sent them back to England at his own expense. Further evidence of his interest in this problem is provided by a letter he wrote to the bishop of Lincoln, then Lord Keeper of the Great Seal, in April 1622. Sir Thomas suggested to the bishop that regular monetary collections be taken in London and the surrounding areas and that the funds thus realized should be used to buy the release of English prisoners who could be sent home "to serue God and their cuntry."[1]

Before Roe could receive an answer to his proposal, he received some orders from the Privy Council. He was to proceed immediately with negotiations aimed at obtaining the release of the English captives and bringing to an end the piratical activities that constituted such a hazard to English shipping in the Mediterranean. The members of the Privy Council pointed out that the ravages inflicted by the pirates were so serious that some British merchants were considering discontinuing their activities in that part of the world. It is said that between 1609 and 1616 the almost incredible number of 466 English ships had been captured and their crews enslaved.[2] A fleet sent out in 1619 to compel redress by force had been totally ineffectual, and the villainous plunder went on. In the face of these outrages Roe was ordered to make "a liuely representation of the same to the Grand Seignor," to demand that all the captive Englishmen be set free and that an order be given to the inhabitants of Tunis and Algiers to cease further piracy. The letter concluded with a passage that gave the ambassador authority to warn the sultan that, unless these demands were met, Sir Thomas himself, and all other Englishmen in Turkey, would be called home and reprisals taken at sea.[3] These threats were sheer bravado. The use of force was out of the question, for King James simply did not have the wherewithal to mount an expedition capable of dealing with the pirates, and the recall of all Englishmen and the resulting loss of trade would have been a blow that neither the king nor the country could afford.

On the basis of his new instructions Sir Thomas went to work with a will. He soon obtained a promise that action would be taken, but this was no great cause for jubilation because there were serious doubts as to whether the Porte would be able to enforce compliance from the pirates themselves. The Turkish Empire was so vast and ill governed that the sultans exercised only a vague suzerainty over many of the subject peoples, and the loyalty of the local Mohammedan dynasties seemed to vary inversely with their distance from Constantinople.

For a while it appeared that the ambassador's fears were

[1] *Negotiations*, p. 36. This plan was subsequently implemented on a large scale. The government periodically authorized the bishops to arrange collections like the one Roe had suggested. Well into the eighteenth century wealthy persons sometimes left in their wills sums of money to be used in liberating English prisoners from the Barbary pirates; see Alfred C. Wood, *A History of the Levant Company*, pp. 203–204.

[2] Ibid., p. 60, citing Corbett, *England in the Mediterranean*, (London, 1935), i, chap. 2.

[3] *Negotiations*, p. 52; Edward R. Turner, *The Privy Council of England in the Seventeenth and Eighteenth Centuries, 1603–1784* (Baltimore, Md., 1927), 1:145.

unfounded. Orders were sent to Algiers and Tunis that the English capitulations were to be enforced and English ships, captives, and goods restored. There were some protests, but the pirates gave a mild show of good faith by releasing a small group of English prisoners and declaring their intention of sending ten of their leaders to Constantinople for further discussions. Learning of these plans, Roe prepared himself for the meeting, at which he hoped to be able to bind the representatives of Algiers and Tunis to even more stringent terms by threatening them to their faces with retaliatory action in the event that the pirate raids should continue.

The meeting took place early in 1623, and although the records give us no information about the exact nature of the discussions, we do know that they resulted in a formal agreement made in March. All English slaves were to be released with compensation paid to their owners; Englishmen in Algiers and Tunis were to be afforded protection and good treatment; and in all waters English, Algerian, and Tunisian ships were to treat one another in friendly fashion and give the usual salutes.[4] It was further agreed that an English consul would be sent to Algiers to handle the details of the repatriation of the prisoners and to exercise authority over Englishmen living there and in Tunis. The Algerians would present to the consul a list of the names of their countrymen who were prisoners of the English, and these men would be released when the English captives arrived safely home. In explaining this action, Roe pointed out that he had agreed to this clause because he "could not auoid to make showe of a resolution in vs of reciprocallity"; further, he noted that, while the number of English prisoners involved was about eight hundred, the number of Algerians would not exceed forty, so that "the exchange is of great aduauntage if only the nombers bee considered."[5] Finally, the agreement of 1623 stipulated that English ships would not, with the consent

[4] *Negotiations*, p. 140; Roe to the Privy Council.
[5] Ibid.

of their government, transport goods for the enemies of Turkey. If they did so at all, it would be at their own risk and their conduct would not constitute a breach of the peace between the two governments.[6]

It may appear that Roe and the English government should have been well satisfied with these arrangements; but, as a matter of fact, there were strong rumbles of discontent from England, and the treaty was ratified only after a long delay. The government was apprehensive that a treaty with Algiers and Tunis might somehow be incompatible with existing agreements with Spain—and England's relations with Spain were in a very delicate state just then, Prince Charles and Buckingham having embarked on their romantic errand to Madrid. Roe had known of these sentiments even before he began his negotiations, but he was so genuinely concerned about the wretched plight of the English captives that he was willing to run the risk of mild displeasure in order to effect their release. At any rate, he defended his actions in letters home, spent £1,000 of his own money in the cause, and privately delivered himself of the opinion that the government's attitude was due to the excessive influence of the Spanish faction at court.[7]

The merchants of the Levant Company were not much happier with Roe's treaty than the government had been. The clause that prohibited them from legally carrying goods for the enemies of Turkey threatened to cut into their profits— profits which, presumably, they were paying their ambassador to protect. For a time they showed their displeasure by allowing Roe's pay to fall into arrears,[8] but he was convinced that he was right, and with almost no support from home he persevered until the treaty was signed.

---

[6] Ibid.

[7] *State Papers Foreign, Levant Company* (Public Record Office ref. SP. 105), 109/32, "Account of Money Spent on Algeria and Tunis," 23 July 1623; *Negotiations*, p. 177.

[8] Ibid., p. 141; Roe to the Privy Council.

In later years he spoke proudly about the results of his work. He wrote to Secretary Conway: "The Levant Company may in these seas hold up their heads as in former ages," and told his friend Dudley Carleton, "I have done what I came for, revived the traffic, made a peace and opened the seas . . . with Barbary."[9] It was not like Roe to blow his own trumpet so loudly, and we may suppose that he did so in an effort to justify his much criticized treaty. And indeed, he could be proud that as a result of his efforts eight hundred Englishmen were returned home and the pirate fleets were weakened by their loss. He could also claim that the Levant Company's trade had prospered in the years since the treaty. But he also knew, better than anyone else, that a treaty was a highly imperfect solution, that it was violated repeatedly, that it had almost no impact on the conduct of the pirates, and that, in plain point of fact, a treaty was not what was needed at all. Roe confessed as much to Conway when he told him that only cannon would produce any real effect.[10] In the Levant as in India, trade and all foreign policy had to rest ultimately on a base of strength. A treaty with pirates was not worth the paper it was written on unless it was backed up by the power to compel its observance. This was the heart of the matter: the fist inside the glove. Roe had seen the necessity for it, clearly and from the beginning. But it was to be a fact of fundamental importance in his life that the two kings he served did not see it—or, if they did, were unwilling, for one reason or another, to act as though they did. How costly the Stuart aversion to parliaments proved to be!

In the correspondence of Roe during his embassy to the Ottoman Porte there appears the first solid evidence of the deep and lifelong friendship that existed between the ambassador and Princess Elizabeth, the daughter of James I, who was

[9] Ibid., pp. 772, 243.

[10] Quoted in Patrick S. McGarry, "Ambassador Abroad: The Career and Correspondence of Sir Thomas Roe at the Courts of the Mogul and Ottoman Empires, 1614–1628: A Chapter in Jacobean Diplomacy" (Ph.D. diss., Columbia University, 1963), p. 218.

briefly (but to Roe, always) queen of Bohemia. Their affection for each other had been born at her father's court; it had survived her marriage and removal from England and had broadened to encompass her impetuous but likable husband. Sir Thomas regarded the princess with the utmost devotion and was deeply grieved by her misfortunes. Much of his life was spent in futile efforts to serve her. The Palatine family had no more steadfast or devoted champion than he. He found many reasons for disliking his isolation in the East, but he professed that "there is none more near my soule then that I can doe your Majestie, to whom I have bene devoted from your infancy and from whom I have received so undeserved favours, no such effectual service as that you should not only thereby know my heart, butt receive some fruict. O how happy should I bee if I could add one tittle or bring one contented thought to you!"[11] This, of course, was courtier's language, but it would be wrong for us to be cynical about the sentiments that it conveyed. There was little to be gained from devotion to the Palatine family. Their fortunes were so low that they had little to give, and King James himself gave small indication of sympathy for his daughter's plight. Besides, Roe's loyalty was much too persistent to be convincingly undermined by any charge of self-seeking, and Elizabeth knew that her "Honest Thom" was not guilty of courtier's hyperbole when he said, "I have not one dropp of blood in my hart which I will not shed for you."

She returned his affection and there was no other person with whom Elizabeth maintained a correspondence so free, so lengthy, or so intimate.[12] She never failed to address him in the friendliest possible tone. Her letters usually opened with such salutations as "Honest Thom,"[13] or "Honest fatte Thom,"[14]

---

[11] Quoted in Stanley Lane-Poole, "An Ambassador to the Sultan, 1621–1622," *Cornhill Magazine*, n.s. 3, pp. 477–78.

[12] Green, *Elizabeth of Bohemia*, p. 151.

[13] L. M. Baker, comp., *The Letters of Elizabeth, Queen of Bohemia* (London, 1953), pp. 53, 77, 79, 163, 164.

[14] Ibid., p. 80.

and they often included some teasing about his "Perte bulk,"[15] or "honest fatte boddie."[16] She confided in him all the forlorn hopes and schemes by which she hoped to bring about her family's restoration; she sent him pictures of both herself and her husband; and repeatedly she thanked him for the pains he was taking to advance her cause.

These efforts involved the strange and shadowy figure of Bethlen Gabor, the prince of Transylvania, who appears frequently in Roe's dispatches. Gabor had been elected to his position in 1613, just a short time before the Thirty Years War presented him with the opportunity to extend his influence into the other provinces of Hungary. While the Holy Roman Emperor was occupied with the Bohemian revolt that started the war, Gabor had led his armies into Hungary in pursuit of the dream of establishing a state that would be free of both German and Turkish domination. His action made him, in effect, the ally of the Bohemians, but when they were defeated at the battle of the White Mountain, he had quickly concluded a peace (the treaty of Nikolsburg) with the emperor and had returned home.

This was the situation at the time of Sir Thomas Roe's arrival in Constantinople. Translyvania and the empire were at peace, but it was clear that Bethlen Gabor was a man who stood to gain considerably from a successful war with the emperor, if he could find the support that would be necessary to give him any real chance of victory. From all these circumstances, Roe saw the possibility of rendering real service to the family of Princess Elizabeth. If he could persuade the English government to offer substantial assistance to Gabor, the Hungarian might become actively involved on the Protestant side and conceivably help bring about the eventual restoration of the Palatinate.

This was to ignore the point that his instructions imposed an opposite course: he was to be the instrument of his master's

[15] Ibid., p. 79.
[16] Ibid., p. 80.

Sir Thomas Roe

Elizabeth of Bohemia

Frederick V, King of Bohemia

William Laud

Prince Rupert

Sir Dudley Dorchester

quest for peace, not an agent for spreading war. There can have been few times in Roe's career when the calls of personal inclination and the demands of public service were so clearly opposed to one another. The only course open to him was to work in the spirit of his instructions and at the same time to try to urge a change of policy on the government at home. In the meantime, he assured Elizabeth that she could count on him to do everything he could "within the rule of obedience" to his king.[17]

His dilemma was borne in upon him in August 1622 when an ambassador of Gabor arrived at the Porte in search of support for a projected resumption of the war against the emperor. Unlikely as it may seem, the grand vizier (a man named Hussein) asked Roe to advise him as to how he should respond to the request. Should the Porte allow itself to be drawn into a war with the emperor? And could Roe confirm that, as other reports alleged, the emperor was raising a force of 150,000 men? Here was the tantalizing opportunity, but Roe did his duty and replied that war would be ill-advised and that the report about the men was almost certainly untrue. The Ottoman officials "gave me exceeding thanks, made me a good dinner and did me as much honor as I thinke ever was done to any . . . and I am persuaded that I have done the Emperor a service and diverted a war."[18] King James, for his part, wrote to his ambassador a personal letter of commendation:

> Trustie and welbeloved, we greet you well: Wee have been made acquainted with what you have latelie written to our secretary Sir George Calvert, and with the relation you have given him of your proceedinge upon the arrivall there of the ambassador from Bethelen Gabor . . . , and doe so well approve of your discreete carriage in that busynes and of the care you have had to divert the Turks entringe into the quarrell by the invadinge of Germany, and of your precise observinge our instruction on that behalfe as wee have thought fit to give you this testimony of our good acceptance, under our owne hand.[19]

[17] *State Papers Foreign, Turkey*, 8/205.
[18] *Negotiations*, p. 89.
[19] Ibid., p. 101.

Roe would certainly have had serious misgivings about helping to instigate a Turkish invasion of Christian countries, but it is difficult not to think that he must have been seriously tempted to use what influence he had to encourage the Turks against the emperor and in so doing add to the troubles of the enemies of Elizabeth.

Meanwhile Gabor's emissaries continued their attempts to win support from the Turks. But their efforts were counteracted by the inner turmoils of the Turkish state, by a new Turkish emphasis upon a war then being waged against Persia, and by the efforts of imperial representatives who were pressing for a league of peace between Turkey and the empire. In all these diplomatic crosscurrents Roe used his influence for the preservation of the general peace and tried to win assurances that the rights of the Elector Palatine would be respected.

In 1623 Gabor briefly resumed hostilities with the emperor. His campaign, however, was halfhearted and not coordinated with the efforts of other Protestant powers. In the spring of 1624 he once again made peace with Ferdinand. For a moment his policy followed an opposite tack, and he sought to gain his ends by asking for the emperor's daughter in marriage. This proposal bordered on the impudent; it was refused, and Gabor identified himself more decisively than before with the Protestant side.[20] From Roe's private point of view this was a step in the right direction, but it was still clear that Gabor would not play any significant role unless and until he received the firm backing of some other power.

By the spring of 1624 there was some realistic possibility of a change in the direction of English diplomacy. King James's plan for the Spanish marriage of his son—together with all the lofty hopes it carried—had fallen to the ground. Prince Charles and Buckingham had returned from Madrid without the infanta, and were hot for all-out war with Spain. Their influence

---

[20] Denis Sinor, *History of Hungary* (London, 1959), p. 194.

over the failing king was now so strong that they virtually ruled the country. When parliament met, anti-Spanish sentiment was running very high. But what the members wanted was war at sea with all its opportunities for plunder and riches. They were not sympathetic to the suggestion of launching an attack to recover the Palatinate and were inclined to agree with the member who dismissed it as "not fit for the consideration of the house in regard to the infinite charge."[21]

In spite of this opposition the prince and Buckingham pressed on with plans for war on a wider scale. A treaty was made with the Dutch, negotiations for a French marriage alliance were successfully concluded, and Count Mansfeld, a Protestant soldier of fortune, was given permission to visit England and recruit twelve thousand men at English expense.[22]

This new spirit soon showed up in the dispatches sent to Roe. In August he received these instructions from Secretary Calvert: "his Majesty thinks it now fit you . . . endeavor as much as you may to keep Bethlen Gabor in heart, by those courtesies you find in your power to do him in that court, and to stir up his friends to assist him; for that it concerns his Majesty's service to weaken the Emperor's party in whatsoever he may with whom in all likelihood is to have a war."[23] So now it was clear: Roe was to do everything he could to bring about a renewal of the war between Gabor and the emperor. The painful difference between what he had wanted to do and what he was required to do no longer existed, and it was all brought about by the pathetic collapse of the hopes of King James who saw that what he had always hoped for—cooperation between Spain and England that would let them dictate a settlement to Europe—would not come about. It was at last obvious, even to the king, that all his efforts at appeasement and all the talk of an alliance would

---

[21] Quoted in Godfrey Davies, *The Early Stuarts* (Oxford, 1949), p. 57.
[22] C. V. Wedgwood, *The Thirty Years War* (New York, 1961), p. 183.
[23] *Negotiations*, p. 244.

neither make him the peacemaker of Europe nor bring about the return of the Palatinate. There was nothing for him but to give in to the claims of those around him.

It was obvious that Gabor could not be expected to wage war against the emperor unless he had some firm assurances of support. Consequently, in the months and years that followed, and through many a tortuous time, Roe's diplomatic efforts fell into three broad categories. First, he tried to persuade Turkish officials that their interests now demanded supporting Gabor in pursuit of an active policy against the Hapsburgs. Second, he carried on a direct correspondence with Gabor, urging the prince to associate himself with a Protestant alliance and enter the field against the emperor. And finally, he wrote numerous letters home, arguing that the surest way to get Gabor into the war was to subsidize him directly.

He met with endless frustrations. Gabor himself was exasperating beyond belief, constantly changing his course and doing the unexpected. Roe confessed: "I haue diligently traced [him] in all his wayes at this court: and I must confesse, I cannott make a judgment: only I say, hee is a man whose witt and curage is known; and he will proue a notable instrument either of much good or euill."[24] Roe frequently lost patience with Gabor, but he never ceased to give him a grudging respect and to regard him as a potentially useful instrument.

He found the equivocal behavior of his own government even more trying. Though it seems incredible, he once went more than eighteen months without receiving instructions from home, and as a consequence found himself having to improvise, play for time, and postpone decisions. This was not

[24] *Negotiations,* p. 123; Roe to Sir Dudley Carleton. More recent estimates of Gabor reflect the same puzzlement. Denis Sinor, *History of Hungary,* p. 190, says: "Judgments on [Gabor] vary . . . and it must be admitted that during his lifetime his shifting, cunning, secretive political conduct put to a hard test the patience of friend and foe alike." David Ogg, *Europe in the Seventeenth Century* (London, 1956), pp. 124–25, characterizes Gabor as "one of those sudden apparitions from the fringes of civilization that sometimes startle Europe by a meteoric flight," and a man whose chief political quality was perfidy.

an unusual experience for the ambassadors of King James, but it must have been particularly infuriating for Roe at this stage of his career when he felt that so much was at stake and wanted so earnestly to see positive action taken to help the queen of Bohemia. The root of the trouble was money—always money. In their determination to avoid dependence upon parliament the Stuart sovereigns simply could not produce the hard cash which alone offered hope of tying Gabor to any consistent line of policy. This was where Roe had placed his hopes—in subsidies; but despite occasional promising signs they were not forthcoming. The Achilles' heel of Stuart government bedeviled its proceedings at Constantinople just as surely as it caused its troubles at home.

Late in 1626 the unpredictable Gabor at last joined hands with the Protestant union and, along with Mansfeld, put an army in the field against the emperor. It is quite impossible to estimate the extent of Roe's influence in this: all we can say is that his efforts were unremitting and that, in fact, his dispatches on the subject take up more space in his correspondence than letters on any other two subjects. But, hard as he worked, he was doomed to disappointment. Gabor won a minor victory, and Roe's hopes soared. But then Mansfeld was defeated by Wallenstein at Dessau and Gabor promptly negotiated a truce. He assured his supporters that this was only temporary and spoke bravely about taking the field again, driving deep into Austria and ending the miseries of Christendom. But all this proved to be an empty boast, and Bethlen Gabor never played any important part in the war. He died in 1629.

So Roe's efforts to aid Elizabeth by helping the enemies of the Hapsburgs had failed to produce anything of importance. It is true that he had helped to keep Gabor more or less attached to the Protestant side, and that for brief moments the unpredictable Hungarian had actually taken the field against the imperial army. But in the final analysis, Gabor's devotion to his own interests involved him in endless doubledealing and made him, at best, an unsuitable and unreliable ally. It was little wonder that Roe found it impossible to persuade him to commit himself to a consistent line of policy.[25]

Sir Thomas Roe was never happy at Constantinople. There, as in India, he found himself frequently yearning for the companionship of his English friends. It was ironic (but by no means unusual) that one who loved England so well spent so much of his life overseas. He found little pleasure in the company of the other western ambassadors at the Porte, although it seems that he was quite friendly with the Dutch representative. He longed for letters from his friends, and he assured them that their correspondence would be welcomed "like a shower in a dry spring."[26] Occasionally his loneliness and exile produced a real outburst, as when he told Lord Carew: "God knows I am as weary of the company of infidells as they would be of hell; and have now no ambition but of christian buriall."[27] He was impressed by the grandeur of the city of Constantinople and praised its outward beauty: "That seate is allmost incomparable. In breefe there is nothing in the world of that magnificence and delight." But for the people he had only contempt, and added to his comment about the city: But "if wee then consider the people that possesse yt, and the uncleanly order and government in yt, it is a sinke of men and sluttishness."[28] His sense of isolation was heightened by the frequent neglect he had to endure from the government at home. He knew that the surest road to advancement was through the favor of the king; and, although from time to time he was assured that his sovereign knew of his work and approved of his actions, he was driven almost to despair by the long official silences which his most earnest entreaties seemed unable to break.

Living conditions did not help matters much. The western

[25] There is a more detailed treatment of Roe's efforts with respect to Gabor in McGarry, *Ambassador Abroad*, pp. 225–69.
[26] *Negotiations*, p. 31; Roe to Sir Henry Wotton.
[27] Ibid., p. 39.
[28] Quoted in Lane-Poole, "An Ambassador to the Sultan," p. 479.

Christians in Constantinople made up a tight little community in which internal stresses and irritations were bound to occur. The principal bond that held them all together, in spite of their commercial rivalry, was the hatred and contempt with which the Turks regarded them and the risks they ran if they ever ventured onto the streets alone. It was not only at times of political crisis when all vestiges of law and order disappeared that a westerner ran the risk of being beaten, pelted, and spat upon. Things were even worse on religious holidays, for the Turks' arrogance was religious at its core. The meanest Mohammedan considered himself superior to any Christian, and even among men of rank "hog" was the word most often applied to westerners. Even at high official levels this arrogant contempt was clearly expressed. A man like Roe could not count upon the diplomatic immunity he would have been accorded in the West. A grand vizier once berated the French ambassador to his face, calling him a "hogge, a dogge, a turde eater"; and the usual method of signifying the outbreak of hostilities between the Turks and another power was to throw the ambassador of that power into the Prison of the Seven Towers.[29] There was always danger, and this was especially true in the tempestuous conditions that prevailed during the greater part of Roe's embassy. Financial extortion was universal and any appeal to the protection supposedly provided by the capitulations was foredoomed to failure unless it was accompanied by a payment called "peshkesh." So there was no possibility of developing any kinds of social contacts with the Turks, and the westerners inevitably turned in upon themselves. To a man like Roe, who had once moved freely in the highest circles of his own land the situation must have seemed intolerably restrictive, and we can understand and sympathize with the impatient outbursts that found expression in his letters.

The English ambassador at Constantinople lived in "a faire house within a large field and pleasant gardens compassed with

[29] Wood, *History of the Levant Company*, pp. 230–31.

a wall," agreeably situated on a hillside at Pera.[30] But the complimentary visits occasionally paid by other ambassadors were no substitute for the friendly conversations with his countrymen that Roe longed for. The English merchants in Constantinople lived in a large rectangular building called a "khan" situated in Galata, the commercial quarter of the city. There was good fellowship there, but Roe was separated from that both by rank and distance, so that he tasted in full measure the painful loneliness of the exile.

Loneliness was aggravated by the financial difficulty of which he complained in many a letter. He occasionally found it necessary to use his own funds for official purposes, and his difficulties were compounded by the fact that the Levant Company was very slow in paying his salary. On more than one occasion he wrote to the Privy Council and asked for financial relief.[31] A pension from the Crown, which hitherto had provided an important part of his income, was stopped without explanation in 1622, and Roe bemoaned that action which, he asserted, "takes away my bread."[32] He felt that he had served the king long and faithfully, but His Majesty, instead of thinking him worthy of some reward, had taken away that which the ambassador thought of as being his own.[33] There were undoubtedly people in England who suspected that he was getting rich during his embassy, but Sir Thomas emphatically denied that this was the case. He failed to see how he could possibly make more than a hundred crowns, and he knew many people in England who made more than that while they were asleep![34]

It is difficult to know how seriously we should take Roe's pleas of financial hardship. It is quite clear that complaints of

[30] Ibid., p. 238.
[31] *Negotiations*, pp. 119, 141.
[32] Ibid., p. 53; Roe to Secretary Calvert. Could the pension have been stopped in retaliation for the independent role he played in the Parliament of 1621? Or was it, perhaps, simply one of the minor economies of a hard-pressed king?
[33] Ibid.
[34] Ibid., p. 119; Roe to the Privy Council.

pecuniary embarrassment were frequent themes in the letters and reports that ambassadors wrote to their governments in those days.[35] It is certainly true that Roe complained on this score throughout his life, and since there is no evidence that he ever had to live in other than very comfortable circumstances, we are, perhaps, inclined to be skeptical about his protestations. However, dignity was an expensive commodity in the seventeenth century, and it required a handsome income to maintain a man in a style befitting the rank of ambassador. Viewed in the light of his needs, Roe's complaints become more convincing, and the cumulative evidence of a number of incidents suggests that Sir Thomas may indeed have experienced some "pecuniary embarrassment" during the time he spent in Constantinople. His pension was stopped, he used some of his own funds on official business, one of his tenants fell badly in arrears in the payment of his rent,[36] and for at least the first year and a half of his embassy, he received no payment from the Levant Company. Perhaps more convincing than any of these is the fact that for many months Sir Thomas tried to persuade the East India Company to buy a ruby that he held in joint ownership with Nicholas Leate.[37] It was rumored that the gem might be worth as much as two thousand pounds, and it might appear that in this respect, if in no other, Roe was moderately wealthy. But when the negotiations for the sale of the gem fell through, Roe proceeded to negotiate a loan from the East India Company, using the ruby as security.[38] This clearly suggests a pressing need for money. If we add to all this the simple fact that Roe had gone to Constantinople in the first place because he expected the appointment to provide a decent income, we are forced to acknowledge at least the possibility that his financial situation was as difficult as he described it.

[35] Garrett Mattingly, *Renaissance Diplomacy* (London, 1955), p. 111; Maurice Lee, Jr., "The Jacobean Diplomatic Service," *American Historical Review* 72 (July 1967): 1276–80.
[36] *A Catalogue of the Harleian Manuscripts in the British Museum* ([London], 1808–1812), MS 97, f. 125 (hereafter cited as *Harl. MSS*).
[37] *C.S.P.C. 1622–1624*, pp. 432, 452, 290–91.
[38] Ibid., pp. 450, 467–68.

Many of the letters Roe wrote to England during the years of his Turkish embassy had nothing whatever to do with his official business. During the seventeenth century wealthy Englishmen had become much attracted to the art of the East, and the collection of antiquities and manuscripts became one of the diversions of polite society. Frequently English noblemen would make their desires known to the overseas representatives of their country who were in a position to know where, and by what means, various works of art might be obtained.[39] Sometimes the initiative would be taken by the foreign representatives themselves, for they were understandably eager to be of service to men who could easily advance their interests. Sir Thomas Roe yielded to no one in his hopes for advancement, and it was not long before he was in correspondence with a number of prominent people, telling them of fine pieces of statuary, or coins, or manuscripts he could acquire for them. The earl of Arundel was his first patron, but he soon added the countess of Bedford (who was primarily interested in ancient coins), the archbishop of Canterbury (old books and manuscripts), and, most important, the duke of Buckingham, eager to buttress his high estate with rare statuary. The letters that passed back and forth were filled with such strange subject matter as "a marble negro," "six pieces of stories in a wall," and "a lyon to the wast, of pure white, holding a bull's head in its claws."[40]

Most of Roe's attention was given to the acquisition of such ornamental pieces as classical heads and antique pillars. He did not qualify as an expert in such things, and he conducted his search with more zeal than knowledge. Occasionally he must have been easy prey for canny Turkish traders, as for example when he exulted that he had "a stone taken outt of the old Pallace of Priam in Troy" and that he might, by stealth, be able to acquire more pieces from the same site.[41] But lack of

---

[39] David Mathew, *The Jacobean Age* (London and New York, 1938), p. 144; Lee, "The Jacobean Diplomatic Service," p. 1273.
[40] *Negotiations*, p. 154; Roe to Lord Arundel.
[41] Ibid., pp. 16, 154.

experience was apparently not an insuperable barrier to success, and Roe's efforts flourished to the extent that the acquisition of artistic pieces became too large a task for him to handle alone. It became necessary for him to engage assistants, and at one time he had three men busily searching in Greece, while the consuls at Smyrna, Aleppo, and Morea had been advised to be on the lookout for any valuable items.[42] Not surprisingly, Roe seems to have made his most determined efforts on behalf of that most favored of all royal favorites, the duke of Buckingham. The duke, with typical largesse, had given Sir Thomas a standing order for "marbles" and instructed him carefully as to the type of art he found most pleasing. "Laye not out much money vpon alabaster pieces," the duke wrote, "vnlesse they be figvres of exquisite cvriosity. . . . Neither am I so fond of antiquitye . . . to court it in a deformed or mishapen stone; but where you shall meete beauteye with antiquitye together in a statue, I shall not stand vpon any cost your judgment shall uallew it att."[43] The combination the duke sought was evidently not too difficult to find, for Roe sent him many shipments and promised to make for the duke "a noble collection."[44] His dedication to the interests of Buckingham necessarily undermined the confidence of some of his other patrons. The earl of Arundel, convinced that his needs no longer had prior claim to Roe's concern, sent out his own agent, and this man immediately became one of Roe's keenest rivals in the search for artistic treasure.[45]

Unfortunately the Turks were not always willing to see their treasure go west, and sometimes they refused to part with it. On such occasions, Sir Thomas was not above resorting to shady methods. Once he found it necessary to "corrupt some churchmen" with six hundred crowns; and on another occasion his efforts to obtain a particularly desirable piece involved him in an unsuccessful effort to bribe "the Bassa, the captayne

[42] Ibid., p. 497; Roe to the duke of Buckingham.
[43] Ibid., p. 534; the duke of Buckingham to Roe.
[44] Ibid., p. 818.
[45] Ibid., pp. 434–35; Roe to the duke of Buckingham.

of the castle, the overseer of the Grand Signor's works, [and] the soldiours that make the watch."[46]

Roe was sometimes aided in his search for *objets d'art* by the friendship that developed between him and Cyril Lucaris, patriarch of Constantinople. Cyril, whose name dominates the history of his church in the seventeenth century, had been patriarch of Alexandria before his election to the higher post, and he knew of some of the treasures that were available there. This information he made available to Roe, and on occasion he even assisted Sir Thomas in acquiring pieces that were of particular value.[47]

The two men, so different in background, were apparently attracted to each other, at least in part, by a certain similarity of religious conviction. This may seem an odd statement, since one was Anglican and the other was the highest official of the Eastern Orthodox Church. But it is clear that Roe and the patriarch shared pronounced Calvinist leanings and a strong antipathy to the Church of Rome. Calvinism was, for Cyril, perhaps the dominant fact of his life. His overriding purpose was to reform his church on Calvinistic lines. In 1629 he published his famous book *Confessio Fidei*, which was thoroughly Calvinist in doctrine.[48] The archbishop of Canterbury, Dr. Abbot (himself a good deal closer to Geneva than one would expect the occupant of Lambeth to be) described Cyril as "a pure Calvinist . . . full of piety and devotion."[49] It is not surprising, then, that the patriarch's ideas made him the target of repeated attacks by the orthodox members of his own faith and by the Jesuits, who were his bitterest enemies; nor that Sir Thomas Roe would enthusiastically give whatever help he could to one whose life was a crusade against the penetration of Roman influence into the Middle East. In doing this he

[46] Ibid., p. 445; Roe to Arundel.
[47] Ibid., p. 344; Roe to the duke of Buckingham.
[48] There is a fairly detailed analysis of the *Confession* in George A. Hadjiantoniou, *Protestant Patriarch: The Life of Cyril Lucaris (1572–1638) Patriarch of Constantinople* (Richmond, Va., 1961), pp. 95–100 (hereafter referred to as *Protestant Patriarch*).
[49] *Negotiations*, p. 110; the archbishop of Canterbury to Roe.

worked largely on his own initiative. It is true that he had valuable support from the Dutch ambassador and that he was urged on by the archbishop of Canterbury but he received no official authorization from his own government.

The first attack against the patriarch came early in 1622. A plot was discovered whereby the Jesuits, working with the French ambassador and certain elements within the Greek church, hoped to remove Cyril from his post and set up in his place a bishop who would introduce Catholic doctrine and slowly subject the Eastern church to the Pope. Cyril discussed the matter with Roe and other friends and, acting on their advice, excommunicated the bishop and made public his knowledge of the plot.[50] This drove his enemies to new courses. They approached the grand vizier with serious accusations against Cyril and, more effectively, the promise of twenty thousand dollars if Cyril should be expelled from his throne. This brought results: a sentence of banishment was procured and Cyril was sent to the island of Rhodes.

Roe was not unduly concerned by this unhappy turn of events. He was convinced that what had been done by bribery could be undone in the same way; and that moreover, if Ottoman politics ran their usual course, the grand vizier would not be in office for long. In this conviction he was soon proved to be correct. Some months later the vizier was strangled by order of the sultan, fittingly, in the very cell in which Cyril had briefly been held.[51] Sir Thomas and the Dutch ambassador combined efforts to persuade the new vizier to recall Cyril; the necessary sum of money was quickly subscribed by the Greek church and by September 1623 Cyril was back at his post.

Once back in Constantinople, Cyril resumed his efforts to spread Calvinist doctrines among his flock. One of the methods by which he hoped to accomplish this goal was the establishment in Constantinople of a Greek printing press. To this end there sailed from England in June 1627 a ship that carried a

---

[50] Ibid., p. 134; Roe to the archbishop of Canterbury.
[51] Hadjiantoniou, *Protestant Patriarch*, p. 61.

Greek monk named Metaxas, a fine collection of Greek books, and several large cases filled with all the equipment necessary for operating a printing house. The great difficulty that had to be overcome was to get this cargo safely through the Turkish customs. It surely tells us a good deal about the influence Sir Thomas Roe had developed with Turkish authorities when we note that Cyril, when he looked for help in this important matter, turned to Roe and that Sir Thomas was able to arrange an audience with the grand vizier and get permission for the valuable cargo to be brought ashore.[52]

Roe, in league with the Dutch ambassador (whose name was Cornelius van Haga), played the role of protector to Lucaris, who sought to spread a Calvinist gospel in the Middle East. Cyril was afraid of the reaction of the Jesuits against his printing house, and he asked Roe if the press could be set up inside the English embassy. Sir Thomas understandably thought this would be carrying things too far, but he did arrange to rent a house in which the press was set up under the direction of the monk Metaxas. In the months that followed, a remarkable number of books were turned out and the Jesuits became more and more alarmed at the damaging influence of the press. Metaxas began to receive threats to his life. He appealed to Roe for protection and was given a room at the embassy, where he would be safe.[53]

One night, when Roe was entertaining the patriarch and a number of others at dinner in the embassy, the printing house was ransacked by Janissaries. Roe was angry and chose to treat the action as a personal affront. In an audience with the grand vizier he reminded the official that he had arranged for the establishment of the press, and declared himself surprised and disappointed that the vizier had suddenly developed such suspicions of Roe's friends and permitted outrages to be performed against them. The vizier was apologetic. He assured Roe that he had intended no insult. He had been deceived by

[52] Ibid., p. 79.
[53] Ibid., p. 82.

false accusations against Metaxas. Roe perceived that he had won the upper hand and he pressed his advantage. He would not be satisfied until those who had been responsible had been punished and reparation made for the damage that had been done. He carried the day; for sometime later the Jesuits who had initiated the attack on the printing press were thrown into prison, and later an order was issued that all Jesuits were to be expelled from the territories of the empire.[54]

The deportation of the Jesuits by no means ended the troubles of Cyril Lucaris. The Roman Catholic Church renewed its attacks through new channels, but Cyril had to meet them without the help of his English friend who returned to England in 1628. The patriarch was fully aware of the valuable assistance that Roe had given and, as an indication of his gratitude Cyril gave him, for King James, a gift that probably outweighed in value all the statuary and coins and manuscripts that Roe had sent home. Sir Thomas described it as being "the entire bible written by the hand of Tecla . . . that liued with St. Paul; which [Cyril] doth auerre to bee authenticall, and the greatest relique of the Greeke church."[55] This document, which was probably written in the fifth century, is known today as the Codex Alexandrinus and is one of the prized possessions of the British Museum, where it was deposited with the old royal library.

The search for works of art provided Roe with pleasant diversions, but it could not change the basic discontent he had felt since his arrival in Constantinople. He had never become reconciled to the place, principally because he knew that the post was not highly regarded in England and that there was, therefore, little hope that it would lead to further advancement.[56] Roe considered this estimate of the position to be unjust, and, in a letter to Buckingham, sought to describe some of the difficulties encountered, and the qualities required, by

[54] Ibid., pp. 85–86.
[55] *Negotiations*, p. 344; Roe to the duke of Buckingham.
[56] Samuel R. Gardiner, ed., *The Fortescue Papers* (London, 1871), p. 205.

one who sought effectively to represent the interests of England at the Ottoman Porte. Apologizing for his lack of modesty he wrote: "It is not every man (though of great parts) that can fitt this place. It requires one well acquainted and tender of the affaires of merchants, one that hath experience and practicque with all nations: For though this imployment is slighted in England, yett . . . I can showe good reason that to discharge this duty well doth require as much sufficiency and honesty as any other whatsoever, and there is as much dishonor and danger in any miscarriage." He closed with the assertion that many of the other nations' ambassadors at Constantinople had had experience in the greatest courts of Europe before they were trusted with the Turkish embassy.[57]

These claims might have soothed Roe's ego, but they did nothing to improve his condition, and his dissatisfaction with his "sterile ymployment" deepened. In June 1625 a terrible plague spread over Constantinople. At the invitation of the patriarch Roe took refuge in a monastery, but even that was not considered to be wholly safe, and he later moved to an offshore island for almost three months.[58] This unpleasant experience deepened his resolve to return home, and most of his letters contained earnest pleas for recall.

His initial agreement with the Levant Company had been that he should serve for four years. His appointment was thus due to expire in December 1625, and as the date approached Sir Thomas anticipated it with great pleasure. In England the search was begun for a replacement. But the Levant merchants indicated that they wanted Roe to stay at his post, and they sent a letter to Buckingham asking him to plead with the king to retain him for two more years.[59] When Roe got wind of this request he himself wrote to Buckingham and asked that the duke use his influence to see that a successor was appointed. Before his letter arrived, the merchants took their case directly

[57] Ibid., p. 206.
[58] *Negotiations*, p. 414.
[59] *C.S.P., Dom., 1623–1625*, p. 493.

to the king and, in so doing, initiated an exchange of letters that had its comical aspects and, at the same time, demonstrated the stubborn character of England's new king, Charles I.

On 15 April 1625 the merchants of the Levant Company asked that Roe's appointment as ambassador at Constantinople be extended. Trade in the Levant, they said, had become dangerous, and, since they "had good experience of Sir Thomas Roe's sufficiency in his employment and of his great care to secure their persons and estates," they hoped the king would graciously extend his appointment. It was their opinion that, if Roe should be allowed to return before the work he had started had been finished, "it may fall greatly to the prejudice of your subjects and hazard the overthrow of that trade."[60] Ten days later the king replied to the merchants' letter and indicated that he had interpreted their request to mean that they wanted Roe recalled. It is impossible to see how the letter could have been given such an interpretation, but, at any rate, Charles went on to say that he would be pleased to give them satisfaction, recall Roe, and appoint as his successor Sir Thomas Phillips.[61] The merchants promptly wrote back to correct the "misunderstanding," and took the opportunity to reiterate their high regard for the services Roe was rendering.[62] The king's answer was that Roe wanted to return home, and in any case there were certain "affairs of state" that required him to send an ambassador with new instructions. For that position he had chosen Sir Thomas Phillips, and his mind was made up.[63] But the merchants were not easily dissuaded. They wrote to their ambassador and sent him a gift of five hundred pounds which, they hoped, would help persuade him to stay on.[64] They replied to the king's letter and showed signs of new determination by asking to have their "own free choice of an ambassador . . . as in the time of Queen Elizabeth and of your

[60] *C.S.P., Dom., Addenda, 1625–1649,* p. 4.
[61] Ibid., p. 5.
[62] Ibid., pp. 10–11.
[63] Ibid., pp. 12–13.
[64] *Historical Manuscripts Commission, Finch Papers,* 1:342.

royal father."[65] They even asked for an audience so that they would be able to press their case in person, but more than two months went by without any answer from the Crown.

On 19 July the merchants repeated their request for an audience and indicated that Roe had agreed to stay in Constantinople if the king would so order.[66] Later in the same month the merchants pressed still harder. They reminded the king of the value of the Levant trade which the company had initiated more than fifty years before. They pointed out that King Charles's progenitors had granted the company liberty to choose its ambassadors. Finally they played their trump card by presenting the financial part of their argument. In the past, they said, the company had borne the expense of gifts and ambassadors for the support of eastern trade. But since Roe had been in Constantinople for a little less than four years, they could not consider themselves able to bear the costs of sending a new ambassador so soon. They were, in effect, telling the king that, if he wanted to send a new ambassador, he would have to pay for him himself. Having shot this shaft home, the merchants closed their letter by rehearsing once again the virtues of their present ambassador and the gravity of the conditions in Constantinople that necessitated the presence of an experienced and able diplomat.[67] The king was unmoved and replied simply that he wished the merchants to approve Phillips without further ado.[68] Uncowed, the merchants wrote to the Privy Council to seek support for their position, but no action was forthcoming from that quarter.[69]

All this time the merchants were winning a *de facto* victory, since Roe continued to work in Constantinople. The king was apparently willing that this should be so, yet was unwilling to give official sanction to the situation. He was, in effect, display-

---

[65] *C.S.P., Dom., Addenda, 1625–1649*, p. 14.
[66] Ibid., pp. 34–35. Roe had, indeed, written to the duke of Buckingham in April and agreed to stay one extra year (*Negotiations*, p. 497).
[67] *C.S.P., Dom., Addenda, 1625–1649*, pp. 39–40.
[68] Ibid., p. 72.
[69] Ibid., p. 73.

ing the well-known Stuart tendency to surrender the reality of power for the shadow. Unwilling to back down from a stand once taken, he insisted on maintaining a hollow argument, even when it no longer bore any relation to the facts.

While this wrangling was going on at home Roe and his wife continued to live out their unwelcome exile. At the end of 1625 Sir Dudley Carleton was recalled from his post as ambassador at The Hague, and Princess Elizabeth tried to persuade her brother to appoint Roe in his place. But the appointment went to Carleton's nephew and Roe, undoubtedly disappointed, resigned himself to the bleak prospect of another year at Constantinople. He wrote Buckingham that he would stay, but expressed a fervent hope that a successor would be appointed before the end of the year.[70]

The months passed slowly for the ambassador and his wife, but when about half of the additional year had passed, word came from England that, although the merchants were still opposed, the king had promised the appointment to Phillips and had supplied him with a commission.[71] Roe's hopes rose abruptly, only to be rudely shattered by the sudden death of his intended successor and by the decision of the king, that, in order to ensure the smooth handling of state affairs and to protect the interests of the Levant merchants, Roe should stay in Constantinople for yet another year.[72] This was a hard blow, and even after his official reappointment Roe continued to write letter after letter that contained strong pleas. He spoke of his "dry and sterile ymployment" and begged Secretary Conway "to bring mee and my poore wife out of Egipt." He considered his continuing exile as a banishment designed to punish him for the vanity and prodigality of his youth.[73]

Thus, for some time, the situation remained. English official-dom remained cold, aloof, and, apparently, unfeeling; and it

[70] Green, *Elizabeth of Bohemia*, p. 254; *Negotiations*, p. 497.
[71] Ibid., p. 505; Sir Edward Conway to Roe.
[72] Ibid., p. 517; same to same.
[73] Ibid., pp. 536, 538, 544, 547, 570, 167; Roe to Sir Edward Conway and to his cousin Thomas Roe.

seemed to Roe that he would end his days at Constantinople. Eventually, however, word came from England that his requests were to be answered and that his official recall would soon be forthcoming. On receiving this notification, Roe jubilantly wrote to Conway expressing his pleasure at the prospect of returning home "to retyre . . . and to liue in the elysium and shades of his majesties grace."[74] This time his hopes were not disappointed. His successor, Sir Peter Wyche, arrived at the end of 1627. Sir Thomas spent a few months in instructing the new representative in the performance of his duties, and then was at last able to leave Constantinople on 4 June 1628.

The effectiveness of his mission there was convincingly proved in a general way by the merchants' reluctance to see him leave. He had served them well. On his arrival, the capitulations, which provided for the extraterritorial privileges of the English, were in a confused and imperfect state, but within a few months he had them redrawn in terms more favorable to the company. He won the approval of the Turks for the new arrangements and could claim to have won more concessions for the English than had previously been won in many years.[75] He had effectively resisted the additional levy on currants; brought about the release of hundreds of English captives and a few Polish noblemen; defended the company's rights against Venetian interlopers;[76] and secured the agreement with Algiers and Tunis which, if it did not bring an end to attacks on English shipping, did, apparently, result in some improvement. On the more purely diplomatic side, peace between Poland and the Turks had been made and he could claim some credit for its making. He had done all that could reasonably be expected to make use of Bethlen Gabor. His victorious tussle over protocol with the French ambassador and, even more, the powerful influence he displayed in helping Cyril Lucaris suggests that in Turkey as in India he had raised the reputation of

[74] Ibid., p. 630; Roe to Sir Edward Conway.
[75] *State Papers Foreign, Turkey,* 8/117; Lane-Poole, "An Ambassador to the Sultan," pp. 475–76.
[76] McGarry, *Ambassador Abroad,* pp. 219–22.

England to new levels, so that, by the middle of the seventeenth century, it was generally agreed that the ambassador of England was treated with more respect by Turkish officials than the representative of any other state.[77]

This may seem to be a sympathetic appraisal of Roe's work, but there is evidence that diplomatic circles in England also regarded his mission very favorably. Almost immediately upon his return, he was entrusted with more important negotiations; and many years later, his work in Constantinople was remembered with admiration. As late as 1664 (long after Roe's death) the earl of Winchilsea sought to justify some of his practices as ambassador to the sultan by referring to what Roe had done and describing some of the "great actions" he had performed.[78]

Having left Constantinople early in June, Roe and his party made their way to Smyrna. There they boarded a ship for Leghorn. The summer days passed without incident until 11 August, when the *Sampson* was becalmed near Malta. This was regarded as nothing more than an inconvenience until four strange galleys were seen rowing out from the harbor toward the motionless vessel. Ignorant as to the intentions of the crews of the strange ships, the crew of the *Sampson* prepared to fight. Their precautions proved to be wise, for without any warning, the Maltese galleys opened fire. The English ship was broadside to its attackers, presenting an easy target, but the captain, William Rainsborow, quick to take advantage of a light breeze that sprang up, swung the stern of his ship toward the approaching enemy. It was soon clear to the raiders that they would not be able to inflict a mortal wound on the English ship, so they decided to board her. As they approached, Captain Rainsborow ordered his men to hold their fire until the raiders were almost upon them. Thanks to this strategy, the *Sampson*'s broadside had a devastating effect and the galleys were forced to turn and make their way back to port.

---

[77] Wood, *History of the Levant Company*, pp. 231–32.
[78] *Historical Manuscripts Commission, Finch Papers*, 1:317.

The engagement had lasted for about seven hours, but only one man aboard the English ship—a Jewish passenger—had been killed. Sir Thomas Roe and his wife stayed up on deck throughout the engagement, and the ambassador had one very narrow escape. He was knocked down by a falling spar which had fortunately checked a shot that, had it not been deflected, might well have struck him. In writing of the engagement to Lady Roe's uncle, Sir Thomas boasted of his wife's bravery. "My poor wife," he wrote, "had little place of refuge, which much perplexed me. . . . This glory she hath, that she showed no fear or passion; but resolued, that seeing it was her portion, she would beare it. Some great shot fell about her, which moued her not."[79]

The rest of the journey across the Mediterranean was uneventful, but the ambassador and his party were thankful for their safe arrival at Leghorn. From that north Italian seaport the Roes traveled across the continent to visit the titular queen of Bohemia at Rhenen, a small town on the Rhine where Elizabeth and Frederick had built a villa that soon became their favorite summer residence. While there, Sir Thomas and his wife, at the request of Elizabeth, adopted the two daughters of Baron Rupa, an old supporter of the elector who had fallen on hard times.[80] From Rhenen, Roe and his newly enlarged family made their way to The Hague, arriving there in December 1628.

His visit with the queen of Bohemia (as he always insisted upon calling her) had stirred a new determination in Roe to do all in his power to aid her cause. Accordingly, he stayed at The Hague for quite some time and while there he presented to the prince of Orange a memorial suggesting the course that

[79] The account of the engagement with the Maltese galleys is taken from Richard Knolles, *The Generall Historie of the Turkes* . . . (London, 1638), pp. 1498–99, and from a letter written by Roe to Lord Grandison printed in *Negotiations*, pp. 826–27. Michael Strachan has written a detailed account of the engagement in *The Mariner's Mirror* 55, No. 3 (1969): 281–89.
[80] Green, *Elizabeth of Bohemia*, p. 264.

should be followed by the governments of England and the
United Provinces.

Roe started with the proposition that the successes of the
imperial forces in Germany were jeopardizing the freedom of
shipping in the Baltic Sea.[81] From the point of view of England
and Holland a more serious prospect could hardly be imagined,
for the Baltic was "the Indyes of the materialls of shipping"
and the basis of the "strength, riches, and subsistence" of the
two countries. The most effective way to combat this danger
would be to bring about an alliance between Gustavus Adolphus and Bethlen Gabor who would invade Germany from
north and south and relieve the imperial pressure against the
Hanseatic towns. Roe was convinced that, despite certain difficulties, such an alliance was practicable. A diplomatic mission
to the north would be necessary to extricate Gustavus from
the war he was then waging against the Poles; and both
Holland and England would have to undertake to support the
alliance financially. Roe, for his part, was convinced that the
importance of maintaining the freedom of the Baltic trade
dwarfed all other considerations. He hoped that, even while
the two governments were considering his proposal, they
would send a fleet into the Baltic to prevent its loss and to
hearten the king of Denmark.

This paper is of great interest because it sets out so clearly
the basic assumptions upon which Roe's ideas about foreign
policy were grounded. They were strikingly Elizabethan; they
proved to be remarkably constant and were absolutely central
in Roe's life because his stubborn fidelity to them condemned
him to a career spent in opposition, pressing for policies that
his government was determined not to pursue.

First of all there is the great concern about things commercial and maritime. England's trade and her strength at sea were

---

[81] "Memoir by Sir Thomas Roe," in Samuel R. Gardiner, ed., "Letters
relating to the mission of Sir Thomas Roe to Gustavus Adolphus,
1629–30," in *Camden Society Miscellany* (Westminster, 1875), 7:6–8
(hereafter referred to as Gardiner, ed., *Letters*).

always in the foreground of his thought, although in this instance they might have been advanced so forcefully because they provided the most likely base for the construction of an Anglo-Dutch alliance. Then there was his opposition to the House of Austria which is as clear and pronounced as his friendship for the Dutch. The Hapsburgs must be harassed constantly. If England herself would not engage in the struggle, then her diplomacy should have as its chief objective the stirring up of Hapsburg enemies in every quarter. Implicit in all of this is Roe's staunch Protestantism and his anti-Catholic bias. He had no faith in Catholic states. They were "papist-blinded," and any agreement with them would prove to be an "Egyptian reed." His great panacea was a Protestant alliance, an Anglo-Swedish-Dutch alliance. That objective he pursued relentlessly and it drove him almost to distraction that there was not more support for it in high places in England.

All these things were means, rather than ends. The Protestant alliance, the resistance to the Hapsburgs, an England strong in trade and at sea—these, to Roe, were simply measures by which the grandeur of England and her king should be made manifest. That was his goal. That was what stiffened him in his own diplomatic missions. The honor accorded an ambassador was the only test of the peacetime glory of a king, and Roe had been careful to exact in full measure the respect he believed to be due his sovereign. It was the reputation of his king and country he wanted to serve—and here lay the primary source of his deep and enduring frustration: that King Charles (like his father) chose to tread a path that did not accord with Roe's Elizabethan ideas of how glory was to be won.

These sentiments all came into focus on the question of the Palatinate. It was dreadful to reflect that since 1625 the heir to the English throne had been an exiled pensioner despoiled of lands and dignities by a Catholic coalition headed by Austria and Spain. It was an affront to the dignity of England; even without the powerful personal associations that were involved,

Roe would have been a leading advocate of intervention. But the unfortunate lady was Elizabeth, and this doubled his determination. The memorial he presented to the prince of Orange was, in truth, a part of his continuing effort on her behalf. For despite all its talk about the freedom of Baltic trade, it is quite clear that Roe's underlying idea was that an Anglo-Dutch alliance in support of Swedish intervention in Germany would advance the prospects of restoring the Palatinate to its rightful owners.

In all probability Roe made his proposals to the prince of Orange without the knowledge of his own government, for soon after his arrival in England at the end of February he prepared to submit a similar proposal to King Charles. His suggestions were endorsed by Sir James Spens, who was employed by Gustavus Adolphus and was the usual emissary between England and Sweden.[82] This had the effect of giving added weight to Roe's proposals, but the circumstance that made his ideas even more attractive was that there were definite indications that the king of Sweden himself would view with favor the course of action that Roe had outlined.

The result of all this was yet another overseas mission for the itinerant ambassador. Before he had been in England four months he was given instructions to mediate a peace between the kings of Sweden and Poland; and on this new mission, Sir Thomas Roe, at his king's command, set off for the North.

[82] Ibid., p. 5.

CHAPTER 7

A Northern Mission

WHILE Sir Thomas Roe had been away in Constantinople, England had been unusually active in the field of foreign affairs. The unpopular marriage negotiations with Spain had broken down in 1623 and the two countries had gone to war. But parliament's suspicion about royal intentions—and especially of the commanding role of Buckingham—caused the members to approve only a maritime war and to withhold the funds that would have made possible all-out intervention in Europe and perhaps resulted in the restoration of the Palatinate. As a consequence, Prince Charles and Buckingham, now the effective rulers of England, had turned to France in hopes of creating an alliance against Spain. Within three months of Charles's accession to the throne his marriage with Henrietta Maria took place, but it did not represent the firm alliance that the king and his favorite had been seeking. Indeed, the French had committed themselves to nothing beyond the payment of a dowry and some extremely vague promises about the Palatinate. On the other hand, Buckingham had made some extravagant commitments: British ships to help Louis XIII suppress Huguenots, concessions to Roman Catholics in Britain, and full freedom to practice her religion for Henrietta Maria.

Meanwhile, the war with Spain was proving to be a disaster. British hopes had been pinned on a naval expedition that would capture Spanish shipping, intercept the treasure fleet, seize an Atlantic port, and attack the Spanish Indies. But at every turn things went wrong. Inadequate resources, ill-trained and even cowardly troops, and maladministration led to frustrating failures. The fleet returned home, shattered and disgraced. The plight of the men who survived to reach England caused revulsion and anger in those who saw them, limping and dying, in the streets of southern ports. Parliament thought it knew where the blame belonged. Sir John Eliot, in a famous speech, declared: "Our honour is ruined, our ships are sunk, our men perished; not by the sword, not by the enemy, not by chance, but . . . by those we trust." An attack was launched against Buckingham and, to protect his favorite, the king dissolved parliament without getting from it the money that was so desperately needed for the war.

Buckingham now proceeded along the ill-advised course of provoking conflict with France, in hopes that a war in defense of the Huguenots would be popular and put a future parliament into the frame of mind to vote subsidies. One by one the promises that had been made to France in the marriage treaty were discarded. The concessions made to English Catholics were repudiated; the promise of ships for the king of France had to be broken when men refused to serve on them. Richelieu did what he could to avoid a breach with England, but Buckingham deliberately aggravated the disputes.[1] In April 1626 France made peace with Spain and put an end to whatever lingering hope there might have been of an Anglo-French alliance against the Hapsburgs. From that point relations grew progressively worse. Charles I expelled the French attendants of his wife, French ships were seized in the channel, and an embargo was placed on English ships in French ports. And so the two states, nominally allies months before, now drifted into war, and England found herself simultaneously engaged against France and Spain.

A forced loan raised nearly a quarter of a million pounds but caused widespread resentment. It nevertheless made it possible for Buckingham to plan another expedition, this time to give support to the Protestants of La Rochelle who were in revolt

---

[1] J. R. Jones, *Britain and Europe in the Seventeenth Century* (New York, 1966), p. 21.

against their king. The venture proved to be as disastrous as the earlier one against Spain and when a new parliament was summoned in 1628 it not only refused to grant subsidies but renewed the attack on Buckingham and was quickly prorogued. Hamstrung by lack of finances the war degenerated, on England's part, into a series of badly coordinated and largely ineffectual private sorties against enemy shipping.

This desultory warfare brought no comfort to men like Roe, who wanted to see their country work strenuously for the restoration of the Palatinate and for the Protestant cause. Ever since the accession of James I there had existed a group that held what could fairly be called an opposition foreign policy, and Sir Thomas Roe was one of its most forceful and persistent spokesmen.[2] This was the party of action. Its members were opposed to the Hapsburg power in both Austria and Spain, partly because it was Catholic and partly because it had despoiled the Palatinate. They drew considerable support from the queen's party at court, but any sympathies they felt for France were aroused more by convenience than by conviction. They detested France's Catholicism, but this was outweighed by their approval of her anti-Hapsburg orientation. Many members of this group had shown interest in projects of discovery and colonization and were, like Roe, supporters of what may be called the Elizabethan traditions. The conviction of England's greatness was bred in their bones and they were sorely at odds with the hesitant official policies of their day. Needless to say, only a handful of them held state offices under the Stuarts. We need not go so far as to accept H. R. Trevor-Roper's description of them as "ghosts after sunrise" to recognize that they were, nevertheless, rather uncomfortable and ill-fitting residents of an England that seemed to have lost its sense of daring and adventure.[3]

[2] David Mathew, *The Social Structure in Caroline England* (Oxford, 1948), pp. 30–35; H. R. Trevor-Roper, *Archbishop Laud, 1573–1645* (Hamden, Conn., 1962), pp. 129, 216–17.
[3] Trevor-Roper, *Archbishop Laud*, p. 12. Trevor-Roper also calls Roe and some others "irrelevant ornaments rather than protagonists in the

The ideas of the French group were opposed by the so-called Spanish party, whose central concern was the avoidance of a costly foreign war. They advocated negotiating with Spain for peace and for the restoration of the Palatinate. They were strongly royalist and their convictions were shaped by the recognition that war made the king dependent upon parliament. These men were isolationists in effect. They were undramatic, sober, and realistic—and they counted among their number most of the ministers of the Crown. Their influence had been temporarily eclipsed by Buckingham's star, but after his assassination in 1628 they regained the upper hand. The king shared their views and adopted what was to be the ruling principle of his policy for the next eleven years: to rule the country without the help of parliament and, as a necessary corollary, to disengage from present commitments in Europe and avoid any expensive new adventures. This kind of attitude obviously ruled out any chance that England would follow the course in foreign policy that Roe wanted her to take. But that was how things stood at the time of his return and his new assignment.

At first glance it appears strange that Charles I would choose to send on a diplomatic mission a man who supported an opposition foreign policy. But, as a matter of fact, there was no inconsistency. The king's purpose was to help to negotiate a peace between Sweden and Poland and so free the Swedish king from eastern involvement and make possible his intervention in German affairs. With this objective Roe was in complete sympathy. As a matter of personal conviction he would like to have gone beyond this and offered English assistance to Gustavus, but he was specifically ordered not to do this: no concrete commitments were to be made in the name of King Charles.[4] So, although Roe was not sympathetic with the general drift of

---

early seventeenth century" (ibid.). But in the case of Roe, at least, his later references are kinder and tend to refute his first judgment. He calls Sir Thomas "that brilliant and versatile diplomat" (p. 113), "the brilliant and cultured diplomat" (p. 128), and "this great diplomat" (p. 216).
[4] Roe's instructions are in S. R. Gardiner, ed., *Letters*, pp. 10–21.

his country's foreign policy, he was most anxious to see the Swedish king in the war and could be expected to press his negotiations with all the force and conviction at his command.

While Roe's ideas about foreign affairs might have given King Charles some pause, there were many considerations that pointed to him as a particularly appropriate choice for the mission being contemplated. Roe's appointment would do much to placate the king's sister, constantly pleading with Charles to act on her behalf and never more confident about her affairs than when they were in Roe's hands. Sir Thomas had already won the respect and gratitude of the Poles by the services he had rendered them in Constantinople, and this, presumably, would help smooth the way for the negotiations at hand. Moreover, Roe's appointment could be expected to please Gustavus Adolphus, for he was widely known as an ardent supporter of a vigorous foreign policy for England. The selection of such a man would at least suggest that England was preparing a more active program and that she would lend support to her Protestant allies.

These were compelling reasons, but there were more. Sir Thomas Roe was second to none in his knowledge of England's commercial affairs, and the embassy to the North was to have some secondary objectives that were commercial in nature. He was to arrange for the establishment of English embassies in both Sweden and Poland, do everything possible to advance English commercial interests in the Baltic region, and try to recover for King Charles the sum of ten thousand pounds which his father had lent the king of Poland.[5] As a matter of fact, the central aim of his mission had important commercial overtones. The war between Sweden and Poland had been harmful to England's trade in the Baltic and had brought about the closing of the port of Danzig. This was particularly damaging, for the foreign headquarters of the Eastland Company were there, and the closure of the port handicapped the company in its rather bitter rivalry with the

[5] Ibid.

Dutch. It was hoped that peace would bring the reopening of Danzig and of other ports that were vital to English interests.[6]

Roe left England in June 1629 and, in accordance with his instructions, made his way first to The Hague to acquaint the Estates General with the purposes of his mission. He received full approval of his objectives and then diplomatically asked for any advice the members might have to offer him. One of the men present had been on a similar, but unsuccessful, mission, and he warned Roe that the main stumbling block to the conclusion of peace was the haughty refusal of the king of Poland to acknowledge the king of Sweden. The Dutchman thought that the making of peace would be difficult and that the king of Sweden might be more amenable to the suggestion of a long truce with his ancient enemy. One of the mistakes that the Dutch envoy had made during his mission was to visit first the Swedish king and thus incur the anger and suspicion of the Poles. He advised Sir Thomas to send a representative to each king simultaneously, and then to invite the two parties to a neutral meeting-place.[7]

With these useful suggestions in mind, Roe left The Hague in the company of young Dudley Carleton, the nephew of his old friend, now Lord Dorchester. On 7 July he arrived at Rhenen and spent two days in deliberations with the Elector Frederick and in friendly consultation with Elizabeth. From Rhenen he made his way to Brabant, where the prince of Orange was encamped. More consultation followed before Roe moved on to Amsterdam and thence began the long eastward journey to Konigsburg and the seat of war. There was a short interruption for some brief and minor negotiations in Denmark, but on 18 August Sir Thomas arrived in Prussia and wrote to the two kings to offer his services as mediator.[8]

As a matter of fact, negotiations had already begun under the sponsorship of Baron Charnacé, an ambassador sent by

[6] Ibid., R. W. K. Hinton, *The Eastland Trade and the Common Weal in the Seventeenth Century* (Cambridge, Eng., 1959), pp. 66–68.

[7] Gardiner, ed., *Letters*, pp. 25–26.

[8] Green, *Elizabeth of Bohemia*, p. 269; Gardiner, ed., *Letters*, pp. 35–36.

Richelieu. France's interest in the northern war was very similar to England's. Richelieu regarded the Swedish king as a potential instrument to be used in his mortal conflict with the Hapsburgs and, like the English, wanted to free Gustavus Adolphus and make possible his participation in German events.[9] This being the case, it may be imagined that Roe and Charnacé would work harmoniously toward their common goal. But this was not to be, for in one vital particular French and English objectives were dissimilar. A cardinal aim of French policy was to avoid anything that might reunite the Catholic League and its chief, Maximilian of Bavaria, with the emperor. This could be done most effectively by extending to Maximilian certain guarantees, the most attractive of which would be the reassurance that he should keep the Palatinate and the electorate that went with it. France's war was with the House of Austria, not with the Catholic alliance. It was Richelieu's conviction that the continuation of the Catholic League and retention of the Palatinate by Maximilian were indispensable counterweights to the imperial power and necessary prerequisites to the eventual destruction of his enemy.[10]

This attitude had involved his ambassador in some difficulties with Gustavus, for the king from the beginning had included in his plans the restoration of the Palatinate to Frederick V.[11] Charnacé was an experienced, able, and much-traveled diplomat with the added advantage of having met Gustavus on an earlier occasion.[12] But the negotiations were not easy, for the Swedish king was naturally suspicious of Richelieu and his friendship toward Bavaria.[13] He saw that any concession to

[9] Lauritz Weibull, "Gustave-Adolphe et Richelieu," *Revue Historique* 174 (1934): 220.
[10] Gustave Fagniez, *Le Père Joseph et Richelieu (1577–1638)* (Paris, 1894), 1:563–64, 571.
[11] Lauritz Weibull, "Gustave-Adolphe et Richelieu," *Revue Historique* 174 (1934): 220.
[12] Fagniez, *Le Père Joseph et Richelieu*, 1:274–75. Charnacé's instructions are described in ibid., pp. 275–76. They were dictated by Father Joseph.
[13] Edmond Preclin et Victor-L. Tapié, *Le XVIIᵉ Siècle Monarchies Centralisées (1610–1715)* (Paris, 1949), p. 122.

French demands could easily bring about Sweden's alienation from the English and the Dutch and end all possibility of a genuine Protestant alliance. The English did everything they could to feed these doubts by making it appear that there was every likelihood of such an alliance being formed. Whether Gustavus believed this or not he was determined, at all costs, to preserve his freedom of action. He had no intention of becoming a tool in the hands of Richelieu.

Despite these difficulties (to which was added some personal animosity between Gustavus and Charnacé) the French embassy made some progress, and when Roe arrived on the scene he found things moving in the direction of a settlement. His appearance annoyed the French, and Richelieu afterwards complained that he disturbed things so much that the negotiations almost broke down.[14] Roe has nothing to say on this point, but it is reasonable to expect that he would seek purposely to sabotage negotiations that were being conducted under the aegis of his French rival. He referred to Charnacé as an "enterloping French ambassador," resented his presence, and initiated a dispute over precedence that consumed several days.[15] Gustavus himself refused to recognize Sir Thomas as an official mediator until certain disputes over titles had been settled. Roe was somewhat exasperated by this and expressed his belief that Gustavus had been given titles enough "for any Christian king." But he gave in and was accepted as a mediator by both sides.[16]

His primary purpose was to ensure that peace was negotiated between Sweden and Poland, but he was equally concerned to see that Gustavus Adolphus made no commitment that would stand in the way of the eventual restoration of the Palatinate. The first objective was achieved in a comparatively

[14] M. M. Michaud, ed., *Mémoires du Cardinal de Richelieu: Nouvelle Collection des Mémoires pour servir à l'histoire de France, depuis le XIIIᵉ siècle jusqu'à la fin du XVIIIᵉ* (Paris, 1838), 8:73 (hereafter cited as *Mémoires de Richelieu*).
[15] Gardiner, ed., *Letters*, p. 36; *Mémoires de Richelieu*, 8:74.
[16] Gardiner, ed., *Letters*, p. 36.

short time, the truce of Altmark being signed on 16 September 1629. The negotiations were evidently quite difficult. At one point Roe expressed his belief that "there never was in the world such a distracted treaty, so many wrangles, so many parts, so many difficulties, so much wresting to partiall ends."[17] Things were made especially difficult by the plague that was raging while the negotiations were being conducted. The ranks of all the delegations were thinned. Roe sent most of his servants to Danzig, thinking they would be safer there. He kept only four men to care for his needs.[18] These hardships cast a pall over the negotiations, but since Gustavus himself wanted peace, the outcome was never really in any serious doubt. The terms of the treaty provided for a five-year truce. This was not precisely what Roe had wanted, but the essential objective of his mission had been accomplished and the Swedish king was now free to embark on the career that altered once again the balance of power in Germany and affected the outcome of the war.

When the main treaty between Poland and Sweden was signed there were still some secondary matters to be settled. One of these concerned the arrangement of peace between Sweden and Danzig. Sir Thomas Roe took the leading part in these negotiations and a treaty was signed at Tiegenhof in February. It was a valuable document so far as Sweden was concerned because it provided that Gustavus should receive most of the money realized by a toll that was to be levied on goods passing through the port of Danzig.[19] From Roe's point of view the treaty represented a significant achievement. He well knew that Gustavus's primary need in preparing for the invasion of Germany was money.[20] His aim from the beginning had been to make that invasion possible, and he had

---

[17] Ibid., p. 37.
[18] Ibid., p. 38.
[19] Michael Roberts, *Gustavus Adolphus: A History of Sweden, 1611–1632* (London, 1958), 2:398–99.
[20] Preclin et Tapié, *Le XVIIᵉ Siècle Monarchies Centralisées*, p. 122; Gardiner, ed., *Letters*, p. 82.

always recognized that the end of the war with Poland, while a necessary preliminary, would not of itself accomplish that end. The treaty of Tiegenhof, although a minor settlement as such things are measured, did help to provide the Swedish king with the money that he needed. Of course, Gustavus might have undertaken his German adventure without the revenues that Roe helped to provide, but it seems unlikely; and it is almost certainly fair to say that Gustavus's principal gain from Altmark and the subsidiary treaties was financial.[21]

There is some question as to the relative importance of the contributions of the English and French ambassadors in bringing about the treaty of Altmark itself. In general, modern historians (when they have not ignored Roe altogether) have viewed his part as being secondary to that of Charnacé.[22] But there is contemporary evidence that suggests that they are mistaken in this attitude. Gustavus Adolphus himself acknowledged that he owed chiefly to Roe the suggestion he put into effect when he invaded Germany and placed himself at the head of the Protestant alliance. He referred to Sir Thomas as his "strenuum consultorem" and gave him a gift valued at £2,500.[23] This was in marked contrast to the king's known dislike of Charnacé, whom Gustavus once dismissed from his presence. The king's staunch friend and adviser, Chancellor

[21] Roberts, *Gustavus Adolphus*, 2:399.
[22] P. O. von Torne, "Poland and the Baltic in the First Half of the Seventeenth Century," in *The Cambridge History of Poland from the Origins to Sobieski*, ed. W. F. Reddaway et al. (Cambridge, Eng., 1950), pp. 485–86; Oscar Halecki, *Borderlands of Western Civilization: A History of East Central Europe* (New York, 1952), p. 200; W. F. Reddaway, "The Vasa in Sweden and Poland (1560–1630)," in *The Cambridge Modern History*, ed. Sir A. W. Ward et al. (Cambridge, Eng., 1934), 4:187; Fagniez, *Le Père Joseph et Richelieu*, 1:274–82, 560–71. Some historians have been more cognizant of Roe's part in the negotiations; see Gunnar Westin, "Negotiations about Church Unity, 1628–1634," in *Uppsala Universitets Arsskrift* (Uppsala, 1932), p. 83; Stanley Lane-Poole, "Sir Thomas Roe," in *D.N.B.*, 17:91. Roberts, *Gustavus Adolphus*, 2:397–98, speaks disparagingly of Roe's part in negotiating the truce of Altmark, but gives him full credit for his later work.
[23] Joseph Jacobs, ed., *Epistolae Ho-Elianae: The Familiar Letters of James Howell* (London, 1892), 1:285.

Oxenstiern, had a similarly high regard for Roe's contribution. He, like his master, acknowledged that Sir Thomas had been responsible for making possible Sweden's entrance into the German war.[24] In England there were no doubts as to the importance of Roe's part. He received a splendid welcome on his return and King Charles had a handsome medal struck in his honor.[25] But perhaps the most persuasive evidence of the quality of Roe's contribution comes from the ambassador's own evaluation of his work. He was not given to boasting about his achievements, but he did confide to the queen of Bohemia that he was extremely proud of his part in bringing Sweden into the war. He averred that he would rather have that achievement recorded on his tombstone than dearly bought titles; he went on to tell the queen that, although he had never publicly claimed credit for the treaty, he now felt compelled to speak up because someone else was trying to claim the honor.[26] It is not known to whom Roe was referring, but it does seem clear that he sensed, even then, that his contribution was being underestimated and that an honor that was rightfully his was in danger of being usurped.

Sir Thomas had always recognized that peace in itself would not guarantee Sweden's entrance into the German war. Long before he set out on his mission he had written that if nothing but a bare peace were arranged and no league, aid, or contribution made to Gustavus, the king might well be content merely to "enjoye his peace." He continued: "Simply to make a peace betweene Poland and Sweveland is a noble worke and becoming his Maties greatnes and goodnes of mynde, but hath a

[24] Ibid.; *C.S.P., Dom., 1631–1633*, Roe to John Dyneley, p. 276; ibid., Roe to Sir John Hepburn, p. 199.

[25] *C.S.P., Dom., 1629–1631*, p. 466. One side of the medal, with the date 1630, bears the shields of arms of the parties to the truce. On the other side the crown of England is upheld by two angels, and under the crown is a monogram combining the letters of the name of Sir Thomas Roe. Lady Roe presented the medal to the Bodleian Library after her husband's death (W. D. Macray, *Annals of the Bodleian Library, Oxford* [Oxford, 1890], p. 134).

[26] *C.S.P., Dom., Addenda, 1625–1649*, Roe to the queen of Bohemia, p. 422.

narrow extent of dessigne, and doth not assure nor conclude necessarilye any benifitt to the good cause. For though it pretends the setting free of the King of Sueveland it doth also enlarge the Pole, who is as much an Austrian as the other is opposite. . . . No man can convince me with reason why he should marry our quarrell for charitye and without a dower."[27] Here Roe was pointing his finger at the basic weakness of England's position in foreign affairs: King Charles's determination to rule without parliament eliminated any possibility that he could play an influential part. His ambassadors were condemned to deal from weakness; they had nothing to offer. The French were right: "Charles Ier ne comptait plus en Europe."[28]

The French themselves were more realistic. The ink was hardly dry on the treaty of Altmark before Charnacé was at work trying to arrange a Franco-Swedish alliance.[29] Gustavus Adolphus was hesitant. He needed the money, but he suspected the French. He would have preferred to get the necessary aid from almost any other quarter, but none appeared to be forthcoming. He was tempted, but he hesitated and, eventually, broke off the negotiations. And then, in July 1630, he invaded Germany. He had made his move as a free agent, and at least insofar as the Palatinate was concerned, his intentions were still much more nearly in line with English interests than with French. Charles I, however, could claim no credit for this fact, and there was no assurance of any kind that Gustavus would continue to regard the restoration of the Palatinate as one of his war aims.

To the French the situation appeared dangerous, if only because it was uncontrolled. Gustavus was no sooner ashore in Pomerania than Charnacé descended upon him and renewed his efforts to conclude an agreement.[30] But serious and persis-

---

[27] Gardiner, ed., *Letters*, p. 7.

[28] Jean H. Mariéjol, *Henri IV et Louis XIII (1598–1643)*, vol. 6, pt. 2 of Ernst Lavisse, ed., *Histoire de France depuis les Origines Jusqu'á la Revolution* (Paris, 1905), p. 297.

[29] Fagniez, *Le Père Joseph et Richelieu*, 1:560–70; Roberts, *Gustavus Adolphus*, 2:407–408.

[30] Ibid., pp. 464–65.

tent differences existed, and not the least of these concerned the attitude to be adopted toward Maximilian of Bavaria. Gustavus would make no promise about the Palatinate that would alienate him from the king of England.[31] He was still clinging to the hope of a genuine Protestant alliance. The interviews with Charnacé were tempestuous, and at one point Gustavus lost his temper and dismissed the ambassador. Charnacé had never been popular with Gustavus or Oxenstiern; they did not trust him.[32]

This latest breakdown in the negotiations between Sweden and France seemed to Roe to present England with one last, golden opportunity. Gustavus was safely ashore in Germany, but he had not yet conducted a successful or profitable campaign and his resources were perilously slender. He could not afford much longer to reject Richelieu's advances, but he presumably would have been most receptive to a promise of help from another, and preferably Protestant, source whose aims were compatible with his own. If Gustavus Adolphus were ever to be won over and persuaded, for a reasonable price, to give strong support to English interests, the time surely was ripe. Roe saw this and rather allowed his eagerness to get the better of him. The language in his dispatches became strong, not at all the kind of thing King Charles expected to hear from his ambassadors. Time and again he complained about the king's unwillingness to give effective support. "Ther is nothing wanting but a little reall encouragement."[33] Meanwhile the opportunity was slipping away and "it were a great dullness to know good councells when their oportunitys is escaped."[34] He hoped the king would pardon his plain speaking, but he never made any effort to conceal his frustration at having to speak with "leafe gold [rather] than solid mettall."[35] He summed it all up in a letter to Frederick: "what a miserye it is to lose such an oportunitye, the terror, armes, conduct,

[31] Fagniez, *Le Père Joseph et Richelieu*, 1:566; Mariéjol, *Henri IV et Louis XIII (1598–1643)*, p. 299.

[32] Roberts, *Gustavus Adolphus*, 2:465.

[33] Gardiner, ed., *Letters*, pp. 50, 52.

[34] Ibid., p. 48.

[35] Ibid., p. 34.

reputation and prosperitye of so brave a king and capteyne . . . the world must judge us blinded with perverse counsells or blasted with a ruynous fate."[36] He could not, or would not, admit to himself that the government he represented had no place in its plans for the kind of policy he wanted to pursue. It must have been difficult for him to resist the conclusion that King Charles was willing to make polite gestures (such as the sending of an ambassador) in his sister's behalf, but that there was not the slightest intention of making any meaningful sacrifice to bring about her restoration. Elizabeth herself, for all her optimism, felt the same way at times. Wryly she told Roe that she had received from her brother "the oulde kinde message . . . that he will never make peace with Spain without our full restitution."[37] Perhaps Roe was nearer to the truth than he knew when he confessed to Sir Robert Carr, "I know not how the game of State is playd."[38] The truth of the matter was that he had permitted his own enthusiasm for Elizabeth's cause to blind him to any appreciation of the king's policy which he could only attribute to "perverse counsells" and a "ruynous fate."

While Roe cursed the stars, Richelieu acted. He sent Charnacé strongly worded instructions to do everything necessary to bring the negotiations to a successful conclusion.[39] Accordingly, the ambassador presented himself at Gustavus's headquarters, and at Barwalde in January 1631 the treaty between France and Sweden was at last concluded.

Charnacé did not get all he had wanted. In fact, the treaty of Barwalde was, in many respects, a major reverse for Richelieu's foreign policy.[40] On the vital point of Sweden's relations with Bavaria, Gustavus did not yield. France had wanted to be

[36] Ibid., p. 82.
[37] Ibid., pp. 53–54.
[38] Ibid., p. 49.
[39] Fagniez, *Le Père Joseph et Richelieu*, 1:564; Roberts, *Gustavus Adolphus*, 2:466.
[40] This point is argued convincingly in Roberts, *Gustavus Adolphus*, 2:467–69, and the following paragraph is based upon his work. G. Pagès, *La Guerre de Trente Ans, 1618–48* (Paris, 1949), pp. 117–18, also stresses the extent to which Gustavus remained independent of French control.

certain that no war could develop between the two countries, for if this happened Bavaria would almost certainly be driven back into an alliance with the emperor. Richelieu had needed both Gustavus and Maximilian, and he had hoped to "allay Maximilian's nervousness by persuading France's protestant clients to recognize Bavaria's right to the Palatinate." But the treaty of Barwalde made this program impossible, for it left the future of the Palatinate an open question. Gustavus refused to accept the French position and cited once more his unwillingness to do anything that would alienate him from the king of England. The terms as finally written actually made a conflict between Gustavus and Maximilian more, rather than less, likely because they provided that Sweden's recognition of Bavarian neutrality would end when and if Maximilian attacked any of Sweden's friends or allies. The state of German affairs was such that this was quite likely to occur, and there was a distinct possibility that the eventuality Richelieu dreaded most would be brought about by the very treaty he had worked so hard to achieve. It seems likely that Richelieu believed the subsidy he was to pay Gustavus would act as a bridle on him. But as soon as the conquest of Germany got underway French money ceased to be of major importance, and Richelieu never gained the degree of control for which he had hoped.

All this meant that in a roundabout way, and through circumstances that were largely beyond his control, the main objective of Sir Thomas Roe's mission was accomplished. Gustavus Adolphus made his peace with Poland, he invaded Germany, and he did not abandon his original intention to work for the eventual restoration of the Palatinate. It is true that he made no firm undertaking with regard to this last point, but his demonstrated unwillingness to cast into the fire even the possibility of an alliance with England indicated a substantial degree of commitment. It would be presumptuous to suggest that Sir Thomas Roe was responsible for this attitude, but it would be unfair not to point out that in spite of his own misgivings, he never abandoned his efforts to make the king believe that an English alliance was possible.

This must have been a forlorn task. Plead though he might, he had absolutely no authority to make any commitments on his country's behalf, and even while he was engaged in his mission England's foreign policy changed so as to make his efforts almost irrelevant. Charles I engaged in an all-out diplomatic effort to placate Spain and to effect the recovery of the Palatinate by negotiation. Roe's work, which had seemed so important a few months before, was now neglected by English officialdom, and he found himself cut off, unpaid, and without so much as a dispatch to tell him of the turn of affairs in England.[41]

For a while he wandered among the Baltic states, attending to the less important concerns of his mission.[42] These kept him occupied until the summer of 1630 and at that time he returned to England. He was kindly received and was presented with the special medal that the king had coined in his honor. This must have seemed rather a barren reward for a man who always longed to be at the center of events, but the ways of English politics were such that his successful mission proved to be for him the prelude to a long period of inactivity and forced exclusion from public affairs. Sir Thomas made it very clear that he would have liked another diplomatic or political appointment but such a course was not available to him, and he had no alternative but to be patient and to await the pleasure of his sovereign.

The situation did not look promising. England's foreign policy, insofar as it was committed to anything, was following a course quite contrary to the one Roe advocated. The king's determination not to call parliament colored everything. Peace was made with France in April 1630 and a treaty with Spain followed in November. It was unlikely that a man of Roe's convictions would soon find employment under the English Crown.

[41] Gardiner, ed., *Letters*, p. 83.
[42] Hinton, *The Eastland Trade*, p. 68.

CHAPTER 8

English Interlude

AT first, Sir Thomas was quite content to accept his exclusion from the affairs of state, for after so many travels he was ready to "come to an anchor" and establish a proper home.¹ As a matter of fact, he divided his time among several residences. When in London he stayed at his house in St. Martin's Lane. This was a very fashionable address. Close to Whitehall, the street was lined with large, newly built houses, each with stables and a coach house.² Among his neighbors were some of the outstanding figures of the day, and while Roe was there the earl of Leicester built a home on the other side of the Lane and laid out the "very handsome, large square . . . graced with good built houses" that is now known as Leicester Square.³

To begin with Roe moved between this comfortable town-house and a country place at Stamford in Lincolnshire, but in the summer of 1631 he settled down at Bulwick, a secluded and lovely spot in Northamptonshire. The release from the cares of office that he found there was pleasing to him. He felt that, for the time being, he was far away from the world "and the distempers thereof," and he found contentment in what he called "the sweet air of a calm rest."⁴ During this period of retirement we catch a lone glimpse of Roe being anything other than serious and grave, of Roe relaxed and enjoying himself. He wrote to Sir John Finet: "I did not write last week because the noise of fiddles was not out of my head. [We] have had a houseful of lords and ladies and have danced away cares. . . . And you will not believe how the variety of life hath pleased me, for this is a new voyage and a new country to me."[5] As the nights lengthened and winter brought its fogs to London he could not resist wishing his friend in the city "all the joys of London which are full of smoke."[6] Lady Roe used these long winter evenings to work at the rich embroideries she presented to Stamford Church as a thank offering for their own preservation in the engagement with the Maltese galleys en route from Turkey.[7]

But even while he was professing enjoyment of his unaccustomed leisure, Roe was beginning to feel his inactivity to be irksome. In the autumn of 1631 there was talk of an English mission that was to be sent to Gustavus Adolphus with the objective of persuading the Swedish king, in return for a subsidy from England, to pledge himself to bring about the restitution of the Palatinate. This seemed to offer Roe both the public employment that he was beginning to want and an opportunity to serve the cause of the queen of Bohemia. He hurried to London, took part in a round of conferences about the forthcoming embassy, and contributed the useful information and advice that his earlier contact with the Swedish king made possible. Despite his earlier good work, it was by no

[1] *C.S.P., Dom., Addenda, 1625–1649;* Roe to Lord Treasurer Weston, 8 October 1631, p. 417.

[2] Sir George Gater and Walter H. Godfrey, eds., *Trafalgar Square and Neighbourhood (The Parish of St. Martin-in-the-Fields, pt. 3),* London County Council Survey of London 20 (London, 1940): 115–16.

[3] Norman G. Brett-James, *The Growth of Stuart London* (London, 1935), pp. 178–79.

[4] *C.S.P., Dom., Addenda, 1625–1649;* Roe to Sir John Finet, 17 July 1631, p. 414.

[5] Ibid., 15 January 1632, p. 432.

[6] Ibid., Roe to Sir John Finet, 24 October 1631, p. 419.

[7] Peter Whalley, *The History and Antiquities of Northamptonshire* . . . (Oxford, 1791), 1:583; Arthur Mee, ed., *Northamptonshire: County of Spires and Stately Homes* (London, 1945), pp. 304–305; Arthur Oswald, "Stanford Hall, Leicestershire, III," in *Country Life,* 18 December 1958, p. 1473. There is an intriguing tidbit in Whalley for which unfortunately I have been unable to find any shred of supporting evidence. He says that the Roes fled precipitately from Constantinople "on account of the Sultan's having discovered too great a regard for Lady Rowe who remarkably excelled both in the beauties of her person and her mind."

means sure that Roe would get the appointment. The court was divided as to whether the mission should be entrusted to him or to Sir Henry Vane. It seemed to be the consensus that King Charles leaned toward Vane, but most agreed that Roe would be the more acceptable to Gustavus, for it was widely known that the Swede had professed his esteem for Sir Thomas.[8] Roe had substantial supporters,[9] but the final decision rested with the king—and the king chose to send Sir Henry Vane. This rejection seems to have hurt Roe deeply. To the queen of Bohemia he wrote of having been "forsaken";[10] and he felt that Vane had been sent to finish the business he had begun and which he would have been better qualified to see to a successful conclusion.[11]

After this disappointment Roe returned to Bulwick, but now he regarded his country home as a "cell" in which he was being compelled to live out an enforced and unwelcome retirement. A career spent in the courts of emperors and kings had taken away the ability to find contentment in a quiet life. He wanted to be in action.

In February 1632 Roe's old acquaintance Lord Dorchester, formerly Sir Dudley Carleton, died. There was fevered speculation as to who would succeed him in his position as secretary of state.[12] There is not much doubt that in some ways Roe was well qualified for the post. His experience, his general knowl-

[8] *C.S.P., Dom., Addenda, 1625–1649,* p. 414; *C.S.P., Dom., 1631–1633,* Unsigned News Letter, 30 December 1631, pp. 211–12.
[9] Ibid., Sir John Suckling to Sir Henry Vane, 2 May 1632, p. 323. (In this letter Suckling speaks of Sir Thomas Roe's "cabinet.")
[10] *C.S.P., Dom., Addenda, 1625–1649,* 20 November 1631, p. 420.
[11] Ibid., Roe to Secretary Dorchester, 16 October 1631, pp. 418, 421; ibid., Roe to the queen of Bohemia, 20 November 1631, p. 421. Vane failed in his mission and even became involved in a personal quarrel with Gustavus Adolphus. John Dury put the blame squarely on Vane's shoulders (ibid., Dury to Roe, 4 February 1633, p. 446), but, as Mrs. Green points out (*Elizabeth of Bohemia,* p. 293, *n.* 3), Dury was a protégé of Roe and was probably jealous of Vane for winning a position that Roe had wanted. However, Mrs. Green herself adds: "Had the cautious and friendly policy of Sir Thomas Roe been in operation . . . the treaty had probably taken effect" (ibid., p. 292).
[12] Florence M. Evans, *The Principal Secretary of State* (Manchester, 1923), p. 92.

edge of foreign affairs, and his all-round ability and statesmanship made him a most suitable candidate.[13] But all these advantages were canceled by his stubborn advocacy of a course his king would not follow. Nevertheless, during the four-month period in which the selection of a new secretary was being pondered, Roe allowed himself to hope. He wrote innumerable letters to the king and to influential people at court. He did not mention the secretaryship specifically, but his letters were filled with the most earnest pleas for employment and it was pretty clear what he had in mind. Some of the letters were quite abject and almost pathetic, as for example when he pointed out that he had no children to make him desire riches and no affections or obligations to distract him from giving his all in the service of the king.[14] He insisted that the king would "never find more zeal, more sincerity nor more truth and honour" than Roe would bring to his service.[15]

All his pleadings and all his professions of devotion were in vain. On 15 June 1632 it became known that Francis Windebank had been sworn in as the new secretary. He was virtually unknown in political circles and his appointment took everyone by surprise.[16] It was, however, sufficiently explained by a short entry in Archbishop Laud's diary: "1632, June 15. Mr. Francis Windebank, my old friend, was sworn Secretary of State, which place I obtained for him of my gracious master, King Charles."[17]

If Roe had not realized it earlier he must surely have seen now that the only logical explanation for his having twice been

[13] John Bruce, "Preface," *C.S.P., Dom., 1631–1633,* pp. ix–x; Samuel Rawson Gardiner, *History of England from the Accession of James I to the Outbreak of the Civil War, 1603–1642* (New York, 1883–1884), 2:311; Evans, *Principal Secretary of State,* p. 92.
[14] *C.S.P., Dom., Addenda, 1625–1649;* Roe to Lord Holland, 15 February 1632, p. 433.
[15] Ibid., Roe to King Charles I, 15 February 1632, p. 434.
[16] Gardiner, *History of England,* 7:200.
[17] Bruce, "Preface," *C.S.P., Dom., 1631–1633,* p. viii, quoting *Laud's Works,* 3:215; G. E. Aylmer, *The King's Servants: The Civil Service of Charles I, 1625–1642* (New York, 1961), p. 359; Evans, *Principal Secretary of State,* p. 93.

overlooked was that he was out of favor at court and had been simply and unceremoniously put aside. He was somewhat bitter, but he tried to take it philosophically: "A new Secretary has been brought out of the dark," he wrote to Elizabeth. "These are the encouragements we receive that have laboured abroad; but for my own part I protest I envy not; I can make my own content as fit as a garment, and if the State be well I cannot be sick."[18]

Though he was now willing to admit to himself the reasons for his exclusion he still refused to alter his convictions for the sake of an appointment. In letter after letter he hammered out and elaborated his argument. England should immediately form an alliance absolutely independent of France and Spain.[19] A Catholic alliance would be suspect and liable to break because a Catholic ally would always harbor the ambition to "root out our religion."[20] It was useless and foolish to hope for anything from France and Spain. They cared only for their own interests and were "best employed like millstones to grind themselves thin."[21] The only fruitful alliance for England was in the North.[22] He could not agree with those who feared the ambition of the Swedish king: Sweden's power was not deep rooted, but depended upon the personal genius of her king; if that were taken away the power of Sweden would quickly return to its former modest level.[23] Time was of the essence. Writing to Elizabeth in the spring of 1631, he thought that the time had come for action. The king of Sweden needed their

---

[18] Gardiner, *History of England*, 7:200, quoting *State Papers, Germany*, Letter from Roe to the queen of Bohemia, 1 July 1632.

[19] *C.S.P., Dom., 1635*, Roe to Sir William Boswell, 6 April 1635, pp. 10–11; *C.S.P., Dom., Addenda, 1625–1649*, Roe to the queen of Bohemia, 24 May 1631, p. 410.

[20] *C.S.P., Dom., 1629–1631*, Roe to Sir Robert Anstruther, 29 October 1630, p. 369.

[21] Gardiner, *History of England*, 7:199, quoting *State Papers, Germany*, Letter from Roe to the earl of Holland.

[22] *C.S.P., Dom., 1629–1631*, Roe to the earl of Holland, 20 September 1630, p. 344.

[23] Gardiner, *History of England*, 7:199, quoting *State Papers, Germany*, Letter from Roe to the earl of Holland.

aid and support in order to be successful. Equally important, he felt, if the king were successful without their aid, how could he be expected to have any regard for England's interests when the time came for a settlement?[24]

Roe held these convictions with all the heat and impatience of a man who knows he is right, and he made no bones about expressing his views to the king himself. In March 1636 he drew up a long discourse on foreign policy and submitted it to the king. He persisted in advocating the need for a treaty with Sweden, Holland, and the Protestant states of Germany. He was bold enough to say that he thought the considerations of "blood and honour," as well as of policy, should persuade the king to that course.[25]

All his protestations and unsolicited advice fell upon deaf ears. Charles I was firmly committed to his policy of ruling without parliament, and this necessarily eliminated any consideration of the expensive and activist policy for which Roe was clamoring. Peace was essential. The advocates of expensive alliances and of war must not be heard—and they most certainly could not be placed in positions of influence.

Excluded from state employment, Roe found time heavy on his hands and he began to learn from hard experience that financial difficulties frequently stalked those who had lost the royal favor. He had received no payment from his most recent mission and was no longer getting the income from a pension he had purchased with his wife's dowry during the reign of James I.[26] The king also owed him money for some diamonds that Roe had bought in Constantinople.[27] To make matters worse Roe had incurred some considerable expenses since his

[24] *C.S.P., Dom., Addenda, 1625–1649*, Roe to the queen of Bohemia, 24 May 1631, p. 410.

[25] *C.S.P., Dom., 1635–1636*, "A second discourse by [Sir Thomas Roe] given in to his Majesty, how the Prince Elector may be made considerable in a war, or in a treaty in Germany," March 1636, pp. 342–43.

[26] *C.S.P., Dom., 1634–1635*, Roe to George Lord Goring, 16 May 1634, p. 27; *C.S.P., Dom., Addenda, 1625–1649*, Roe to Lord Treasurer Weston, 8 October 1631, p. 417; Gardiner, ed., *Letters*, p. 83.

[27] *C.S.P., Dom., 1635*, 3 July 1635, p. 245.

return to England and could not pay his debts until he received the money that was owed to him.[28] Repeatedly he begged for payment, writing, for the most part, to people of influence at court. He indulged himself in the polite and conventional deception that the king would right all his wrongs if his case were only brought to royal attention,[29] but even this delusion was shattered when one of his correspondents insisted that his case had been presented to the king with all diligence but that he would neither deny nor grant Roe's requests.[30] In the picturesque language that often characterizes his writing, Roe compared himself to an old ship that had brought in gold for others, but that now lies docked and drying in its own pitch.[31] To the king himself Roe pleaded that he had never tried to make his own fortune but had always sought conscientiously to discharge the services in which he had been employed by the king and his royal father. He asked that payment of his pension might be restored and pointed out that, despite his thirty-three years of service, he had never had any gift from the Crown but had spent a goodly fortune in its behalf.[32]

His financial straits caused him to plead still more persistently for state employment and from his home in Bulwick he bombarded London with letters. He cannot live "as the king has made him [i.e., as an ex-ambassador should] unless the king will breathe into him a new life by service or employment."[33] He would rather wear out or break in the king's service than rest at home and wear out by rust.[34] On one day he wrote letters to four different people at court, asking them to intercede for him. In 1634 the Swedish Chancellor, Oxenstiern, summoned an assembly of German princes to meet at Frank-

---

[28] *C.S.P., Dom., Addenda, 1625–1649*, Roe to Lord Treasurer Weston, 8 October 1631, p. 417.

[29] *C.S.P., Dom., 1634–1635*, Roe to Lord Treasurer Portland, 13 June 1634, p. 75.

[30] Ibid., Francis Lord Cottington to Roe, 17 July 1634, p. 156.

[31] *C.S.P., Dom., 1633–1634*, Roe to George Lord Goring, 8 April 1634, p. 543.

[32] Ibid., Roe to King Charles I, 8 April 1634, p. 543.

[33] Ibid., Roe to King Charles I, 7 January 1634, p. 399.

[34] Ibid., Roe to Lord Treasurer Portland, 1 June 1633, pp. 81–82

furt. The queen of Bohemia wrote to her brother, asking that Sir Thomas be sent to the meeting on her behalf, but Sir Robert Anstruther was sent instead.[35]

None of his efforts brought the slightest satisfaction and toward the middle of 1634 he realized that pleading from a distance was not likely to bring relief. In April he went to Newmarket and laid his suit before the king in person. The king answered most graciously and said that it was his will that Roe should be paid, but still nothing was done.[36] That autumn, despite his dislike of London's winter weather, he moved back to the capital because (as he said later) he wanted once again to be within the air of affairs and not to bury himself in the country and deprive the sexton of his fees.[37]

The new approach brought results. After a meeting of the Lords of the Treasury, Secretary Coke jotted in his notes of the proceedings: "Sir Thomas Roe to be remembered."[38] A month later an entry in the receipts and payments of the exchequer indicated that he was given some satisfaction: "to Sir Thomas Roe, in part of £2,500, remainder of £3,500 for two pendant diamonds by him sold to his Majesty, £500."[39] So he was paid only five hundred pounds but at least the rest of the debt had been acknowledged and, best of all, the maddening silence and indifference that had greeted his earlier pleas had, at last, been broken.

But still no position was offered him and the unwelcome retirement persisted. Some of the time was passed in reading

---

[35] *C.S.P., Dom., 1634*, the queen of Bohemia to Roe, 10 March 1634, p. 497; ibid., John Dury to Roe, 16 April 1634, p. 554.

[36] *C.S.P., Dom., 1633–1634*, Roe to Francis Lord Cottington, 8 April 1634, p. 543.

[37] *C.S.P., Dom., 1635*, Roe to the queen of Bohemia, 23 June 1635, p. 139.

[38] Ibid., 6 June 1635, p. 110.

[39] Ibid., 3 July 1635, p. 245. One thousand pounds had been paid to him in December 1633 at the time of the sale. So now almost half of the debt's principal had been paid, but in January 1636, Roe calculated that if the interest were figured he would still be owed £3,761 (*C.S.P., Dom., 1635–1636*, January 1636, p. 203). He asked that in lieu of his money he be granted a thirty-one year lease of 1,200 acres of fenland at a rent of 8 d. per acre (ibid.).

and in entertaining relatives and friends, but these things could not satisfy his longing to be active again. He involved himself in a number of projects and gave his biographer cause to be grateful by carrying on a heavy correspondence. Roe himself believed that good history cannot be written from letters,[40] yet his correspondence is wonderfully instructive both of its writer and of the age in which it was written. Indeed Roe has to be regarded as one of the leading letterwriters of his day. He certainly qualifies on the basis of the sheer bulk of his correspondence, but more important is the quality of his letters.[41] They are fluent, colorful, and studded with phrases that impress. As a good ambassador needed to be, he was a keen observer of places, events, and men. His letters offer penetrating insight into many of the personalities he encountered.[42] In everything he wrote there is somehow expressed a certain uprightness, an "elevation of character," that clung to him even in times of distress.[43] The people to whom he wrote were, almost without exception, influential in shaping the dramatic history of their age. Most of the subjects treated in the letters were important ones and they are illuminated by the seasoned and honest judgment that Roe brought to affairs both foreign and domestic.

[40] *C.S.P., Dom., 1631–1633*, Roe to John Dyneley, 23 February 1632, p. 276. "From letters a good history cannot be made, for we write often as we first take up reports, which experience after doth correct."

[41] The index to *C.S.P., Dom., 1633–1634*, indicates that the collection for those years contains more letters written by Roe than by any other single person except the king. The historical value of his letters is commented upon by Mrs. Green (*Elizabeth of Bohemia*, p. 262) and by John Bruce ("Preface" to *C.S.P., Dom., 1633–1634*, p. xxxv).

[42] His evaluation of Thomas Wentworth may be worth quoting, not because it is exceptional but because it illustrates Roe's ability to assess character and to describe it succinctly: "He is severe abroad and in business, and sweet in private conversation; retired in his friendships, but very firm; a terrible judge, and a strong enemy; a servant violently zealous in his master's ends and not negligent of his own; one that will have what he will . . . affecting glory by a seeming contempt; one that cannot stay long in the middle region of fortune . . . but will either be the greatest man in England or much less than he is" (*C.S.P., Dom., 1634–1645*, Roe to the queen of Bohemia, 10 December 1634, p. 350).

[43] The phrase "elevation of character" is David Mathew's (*The Age of Charles I* [London, 1951], p. 93). It has just the right flavor.

Like most letters these are interesting largely for what they say about their writer, who was by this time a corpulent man, in his mid-fifties, and troubled with gout. He was rather inclined to complain about how the world and his king had used him, and we must suspect that his mournful descriptions of financial difficulty painted the picture blacker than it was.[44] He emerges from his letters as grave and serious; yet, as though to warn us against generalization, an occasional shaft of wit shines through. After 1635 he had no immediate family except for his wife (about whom he almost never speaks) and his mind rarely wandered away from matters political.

The views that Roe was expressing in the 1630s were those of a loyal, yet critical, supporter of the Crown. He always manages to give the impression of being, in those times of sweeping political and social change, a representative of "the old school." He had spent only his youth under the great queen, yet somehow he remained essentially Elizabethan in his outlook.[45] He was a staunch Protestant but had no sympathy for the radical groups that had developed.[46] He was critical of some of the challenges that parliament, in recent years, had leveled at the Crown, believing, for example, that foreign affairs were exclusively the preserve of the king and his chosen advisers.[47] The gradually widening gulf between the king and parliament caused him agony of spirit, and he wanted, more than anything else, to see once again "good intelligence and love between the king and his people."[48] His views on foreign policy were perfectly consistent with this sentiment. He felt

[44] His finances were sufficient to support him comfortably. He did, after all, maintain four homes during this period, but he felt that he was unable to live in a style befitting one who had been an ambassador of the king of England.

[45] Mathew, *The Age of Charles I*, p. 77, says that Roe's language was Elizabethan.

[46] *A Catalogue of the Harleian Manuscripts in the British Museum* ([London], 1808–1812), MS 1901, f. 111b.

[47] *C.S.P., Dom., 1634–1635*, Roe to the queen of Bohemia, 10 December 1634, p. 349. "State affairs are like the ark; not to be touched without warrant."

[48] Ibid., p. 350.

sure that if Charles would commit himself to an active, Protestant policy, the people would rally behind the Crown and heal the distressing breach that had developed. Perhaps this was the explanation for the persistence with which Roe pressed his convictions about foreign affairs: if followed they would, at one and the same time, overcome difficulties both at home and abroad.

Reading, entertaining, corresponding; enough perhaps to keep boredom at bay, but still there was nothing to satisfy the yearning to be active and to be involved in great events. Occasionally he was visited by diplomats, English or foreign, who wanted to seek his advice or enlist his aid for their projects.[49] This was flattering no doubt, but at best it provided only a series of temporary diversions. Late in 1636 he was appointed by the king chancellor of the Order of the Garter, but this was a sinecure that paid virtually no money and carried even less political power.[50] It was clear that exclusion from official position was still to be his lot and that if he wanted to press the policies he felt so strongly to be right he would have to do so through nonofficial channels.

He turned first to a project that had commercial as well as political implications. His name was a respected one in the City, he had been intimately associated with England's greatest trading companies, and he was a keen analyst of economic issues. He could expect to command an audience and to be heard with respect.

Accordingly, in the mid-1630s, Roe became a leading figure in a movement to establish an English West Indies Company. It

[49] *C.S.P., Dom., 1633–1634*, Roe to Sir John Finet, 31 July 1633, p. 161; ibid., Roe to Henry, earl of Holland, 15 September 1633, p. 209; ibid., Roe to John Dury, 6 April 1634, p. 541.

[50] *C.S.P., Dom., 1636–1637*, Roe to William, earl of Exeter, 2 January 1637, p. 336; *C.S.P., Dom., 1638–1639*, pp. 518–19; *C.S.P., Dom., 1637–1638*, p. 214. Soon after Roe's appointment a yearly pension of £1,200 was attached to the office, but this was not for the chancellor's personal use. It was to be spent as ordered by the knights and an account was to be rendered each St. George's Day. When Roe left England in 1638 the pension was paid to someone else.

is not difficult to understand why such a project would attract him. He hoped it would appeal to the Crown because of its potential for producing sorely needed revenues. Even more important was the conviction that the formation of the Company would provide an advantageous way to make war on the king of Spain.[51] With stubborn optimism he continued to believe that Charles I would be willing to fight Spain if only a way could be found to do so without shouldering the expenses that would necessitate the calling of a parliament.

Roe seems to have felt that war with Spain would be a panacea for all England's woes. He had the merchants' belief that a naval war with Spain would fill England's coffers, the Protestants' belief that war with Spain was almost ordained by God, and the patriots' hope that war with Spain would make Englishmen stand together behind their king. He was absolutely convinced of the value and the wisdom of the enterprise and felt that if it were not translated into reality future ages would "wonder at our blindness and want of courage."[52] And yet he was never optimistic about the chances of his idea's being accepted. Two of his associates, the earls of Pembroke and Montgomery and of Arundel and Surrey, felt sure that the king would favor the project if he saw the nobility and the gentry investing in it;[53] but Roe himself, who was ordered to explain the project to the king, was aware of two major obstacles. The first of these was the well-known reluctance of the king and his advisers to risk the consequences of a breach with Spain; the other, significantly, was the mutual suspicion which Roe feared would prevent cooperation between the king and his subjects.[54]

He worked hard to prepare the project for presentation to the king. He used information about the structure of the Dutch West Indies Company as a guide in drawing up his

[51] *C.S.P., Colonial, 1574–1660*, p. 257.
[52] *C.S.P., Dom., 1637*, Roe to Colonel Ferentz, 20 November 1637, p. 554.
[53] Ibid., Roe to Charles Louis, Elector Palatine, 29 July 1637, p. 336.
[54] Ibid., Roe to Colonel Ferentz, 20 November 1637, p. 554.

plans. He was careful to make the proposal as attractive as possible to the king and suggested that one-fifth of the income from any mines or minerals taken by the company should be reserved to the Crown. He prepared an estimate of the profits and benefits that could be expected from the company and indicated how much capital he thought would be needed to float the enterprise.[55] He was happy to be working again,[56] but his pessimism about the fate of the project persisted—and it proved to be well founded. Sir Thomas submitted his proposals to the king at the end of 1637, but they must have been firmly rejected, for the records after that date contain no further mention of an English West Indies Company.

As Roe described it, the proposed company undoubtedly had much to recommend it, but it was ill-timed. The Covenant had recently been signed in Scotland and relations between the king and his northern subjects were deteriorating rapidly. Needing money for domestic purposes, Charles I could hardly be expected to give much support to a project whose cost had been estimated at £200,000 per year for the first five years.[57] Roe seems never to have understood the almost desperate financial straits of the government. All his plans called for the expenditure of large sums—although in this particular instance he would have argued that the initial outlay was an investment that would ultimately yield rich rewards. At any rate, the idea was a vision for the future, and it did not see daylight again until 1654 when Cromwell sent an expedition against the Spanish possessions in the West Indies.[58]

If Roe's plans for a West Indies Company had little real hope of success, the prospects of the other project he supported during these years were even more forlorn. During his

[55] *C.S.P., Colonial, 1574–1660*, 18 September 1637, p. 257.
[56] C. V. Wedgwood, *The Great Rebellion: The King's Peace, 1637–1641* (New York, 1956), p. 180, quoting Strafford MSS, 10, f. 251. The project afforded Roe "as much pleasure as if by his industry the Indies were already conquered."
[57] *C.S.P., Colonial, 1574–1660*, 18 September 1637, p. 257.
[58] Founding a West Indies Company was no part of Cromwell's plan, but the exploits of the expedition did bring on war with Spain.

mission to negotiate peace between the kings of Poland and Sweden, Roe had met, in 1629, a rather remarkable Scotsman named John Dury. This man had idealistically dedicated himself to a lifelong effort to effect the reunification of the various Protestant churches. Roe heartily approved of this goal which was so entirely compatible with his own dream of a political alliance among the Protestant states. He and Dury had many talks and the Scot's enthusiasm proved so infectious that Sir Thomas promised to do what he could to help forward his designs.

Religious disunity among Protestants was a source of concern to many people in the early decades of the seventeenth century. During those years there was a continual drift away from any theological or institutional unity. Discord was rife. In Germany—even in the face of the Counter Reformation and the Thirty Years War—relations between the Lutheran and Reformed churches became more unfriendly. The Calvinists of the Netherlands were divided over the teachings of Arminius; in England friction grew not only between Anglicans and Presbyterians but also within the Church of England itself. "Incessant controversy . . . and . . . the emergence of new religious denominations are the characteristic features of the church history of the seventeenth century."[59]

The circumstances of John Dury's early life were, in a sense, testimonies to the bitterness and intolerance that divided Protestants. His grandfather had been a strong supporter and close friend of John Knox, and his father had been a leader of the effort to resist the introduction of episcopacy into Scotland. He had been exiled for his pains and had settled at Leyden as the pastor of the English and Scottish refugees there. John Dury was ten years old when his family moved to Holland. He attended the University of Leyden and, through his studies, became more aware of the increasingly bitter differences among Protestants and the growing intensity of their theolog-

[59] Joseph M. Batten, *John Dury, Advocate of Christian Reunion* (Chicago, 1944), p. 3.

ical strife. In 1624, after further study at the Huguenot Academy at Sedan and at Oxford, Dury was called to serve as the minister of a small congregation of English and Scots Presbyterians connected with the factory of the English Company of Merchant Adventurers at Elbing in West Prussia. It was there that he first met Sir Thomas Roe and expounded to him his hopes for bringing about the reunification of the Protestant denominations on the basis of a general confession of faith.

As an earnest Christian layman, Roe saw the advantages the realization of Dury's plans would bring. As a farsighted diplomat, he saw that peace and union among Protestants would go far in helping to offset the gains of the Roman Catholic reaction, saving Protestantism in Germany and bringing about the realization of his fond hope for the restoration of the Palatinate.[60] He must have been keenly aware of the great obstacles in the way of success, but he found room to hope that the English church might offer itself as a mediator between Lutherans and Calvinists in the same way as he, even then, was serving as a mediator between Sweden and Poland. During his negotiations with Gustavus Adolphus, Roe had occasion to speak with Oxenstiern about Dury's work. The chancellor showed considerable interest and promised to use his influence to win Lutheran support for the project. Both he and Roe felt that the leadership should come from England, for since she had remained neutral in Germany's theological and political struggle, she could be expected to wield more influence over the various groups of German Protestants.[61]

It was clear to Roe that the first task should be that of winning the support of important Englishmen, and to that end he agreed to approach the leading figures in church and state and to place Dury's project before them. He persuaded Dury himself to give up his pastorate and to devote all his time to the reunion negotiations.[62]

[60] Ibid., pp. 21–22.
[61] Ibid., p. 22.
[62] Ibid.

Roe knew that his championing of this new project was unlikely to advance him in the eyes of the king, for conditions in England were not at all favorable to a scheme like Dury's. The High Church movement had grown during recent years and the differences between Puritans and Anglicans had spread from matters of liturgy to matters of dogma. There was a strong anti-Calvinist trait in Anglican theology; and the Church of England, which reflected increasingly the ideas of the fast-rising William Laud, was not disposed to unite with the Reformed churches on the continent.[63] Indeed, not a few English clergymen were more kindly disposed to Rome than to Geneva, and the king himself was well known for his High Church sympathies.

Thus in religious as in political matters Roe was associated with a cause that opposed royal policy, and his work for "ecclesiastical pacification" almost certainly contributed to his continued exclusion from court. But he remained true to the promise he had given Dury and worked diligently to further the cause. He had never been one to abandon a program merely because there was little hope of success. Now he believed that he was engaged in "God's worke" and protested that his course was determined by "error amoris, not amor erroris."[64]

When he returned to England from his mission to the North, Roe set about the task of bringing Dury's work to the attention of those officials who were in a position to help. The project was made known to the king, and a conference was arranged with Archbishop Abbot and Bishop Laud. There Roe defended the program very ably, but Laud, who despite his inferior rank was more important than Abbot, was not won over.[65] It was not that he was actively hostile to the plan; he was simply disinterested in ecclesiastical affairs outside the

---

[63] Gunnar Westin, "Negotiations about Church Unity, 1628–1634," in *Uppsala Universitets Arsskrift* (Uppsala, 1932), p. 95 (hereafter referred to as Westin, "Church Unity").

[64] Ibid., p. 183.

[65] Ibid., pp. 100–103.

dominions of the British Crown; and neither as a politician nor as an ecclesiastic would he support the effort to raise a Protestant combination against the Hapsburgs. Peace and no parliaments were much more important to him than any crusade, and he found it both embarrassing and irritating to have his support solicited by these advocates of a policy toward which he should have been sympathetic but was not.[66]

Denied any official support, Roe turned to the rank-and-file members of the Anglican clergy. He drew up a "testimonial" which certified that John Dury was employed in bringing about a reconciliation of the Lutheran and Calvinist churches, and invited all persons who supported this aim to send Dury a declaration of their willingness to join with like-minded people overseas to further the project.[67] Archbishop Abbot, at least, must have given a passive approval to this document because Roe was able to assure the clergy that they could indicate their support without giving "offence or scandall, eyther to the Church or to ye principall gouvernours therein."[68]

The testimonial brought a disappointing response. It would probably have been more effective if it had been written by some high official in the church, but the very fact that Roe wrote it indicated that such clergy were unwilling to come forward in support of the cause, and this undoubtedly inhibited many others. A few low church bishops approved the scheme and gave Dury their benediction, but the greatest response came from leading Puritans and other opponents of Laud. Once again, Roe was demonstrating his affiliation with a group that was unpopular with high authority. But he was not deterred, and for the rest of his life he did what he could to further Dury's work.[69]

[66] H. R. Trevor-Roper, *Archbishop Laud, 1573–1645* (Hamden, Conn., 1962), pp. 263–67; Gardiner, *History of England,* 7:314.

[67] *C.S.P., Dom., 1631–1633,* 12 June 1631, p. 75.

[68] Ibid.; Westin, "Church Unity," p. 107n.

[69] G. H. Turnbull, *Hartlib, Dury and Comenius: Gleanings from Hartlib's Papers* (Liverpool, 1947), Dury to Roe, 2 June 1643, p. 234 (hereafter referred to as Turnbull, *Gleanings*).

His commitment was occasioned in large part by the political advantages that religious unity would bring, and in this sense it was part of his effort to bring into existence an effective Protestant alliance. He thought that religious disagreement had contributed to the lack of success of the Protestant forces in Germany and that "there is no hope of keeping Germany in balance against the common enemy . . . but by taking away the schism, and acknowledging that they were one church in the foundation."[70] Unity of political action needed to be reinforced by unity of religious belief, and an agreement providing for church unity would have been "the greatest treaty of this age." The Protestant religion, he felt, could never be secure while it stood divided in the face of a united Catholicism.[71]

But Roe's support of religious unity went beyond merely political considerations. His travels had bred in him a tolerance that was strongly opposed to the theological hairsplitting and insistence on doctrinal orthodoxy then prevalent in England and on the Continent. He wanted to bury the names of Luther and Calvin, remove the schism, and allow "love and charity [to] take the chair from envy and dispute."[72] He felt that no man's doctrine should be regarded as absolute, but that there should be room to disagree on matters of detail.[73] There was little real substance to the present disputes. They were kept alive by ignorance, and they could be easily healed if common sense and good will were but given a chance.[74] A general profession of faith, acceptable to the major Protestant sects,

[70] *C.S.P., Dom., Addenda, 1625–1649*, Roe to the queen of Bohemia, 21 February 1633, pp. 449–50; *C.S.P., Dom., 1633–1634*, Roe to Baron John Oxenstiern, 30 April 1633, p. 36. (John Oxenstiern was the chancellor's son.)

[71] Ibid., Roe to Archbishop Abbott, 20 July 1633, p. 149; ibid., Roe to the queen of Bohemia, 24 April 1634, p. 565; ibid., Roe to Secretary Windebank, 8 January 1634, p. 403.

[72] Ibid., Roe to Bishop Laud, 31 July 1633, pp. 161–62.

[73] *C.S.P., Dom., 1634–1635*, Roe to Archbishop Laud, 4 August 1634, pp. 179–80; *C.S.P., Dom., 1636–1637*, Roe to Dury, 28 January 1637, p. 400.

[74] Turnbull, *Gleanings*, Roe to Dury, 27 September 1636, p. 185.

should not be beyond the wit of man to devise, and it could serve as an invaluable bond to preserve and protect the faith against the wicked attacks of the Hapsburg power.

These are refreshing sentiments, coming from an age that is not noted for its religious tolerance. Roe made no effort to conceal them, but he expressed them to Archbishop Laud and to almost anyone else who would listen.[75] We are obliged to respect the sincerity of his convictions, even while we recognize that they were unlikely to win the support of those powerful individuals who alone could have given the enterprise any realistic hope of success.

From the beginning of his association with Dury, Roe served as a kind of financial manager and overall adviser to the project. He felt unable to make large financial donations himself, but was constantly soliciting the support of people who were in a position to help. Contributors sent their donations to him, and he sent the money along to Dury. Supporters of the work held periodical meetings,[76] but as the years passed and success continued to elude them, attendance declined and donations were increasingly difficult to find. Roe complained of the fickleness of men who "love [only] what is new," and he reminded some of them, in rather strong terms, that they had promised their support and were now in default.[77] His own dedication did not waver, and from time to time he reassured Dury of his continuing support: "For money doubt not you shal not want I wil rather beg for you and give my owne but you shal have part. I wil live in the country to save."[78] "[It] were now a sinne and a shame to have the worke deserted in

[75] He even wrote to Secretary Windebank, a man whose Catholic leanings were fairly well known, and who that very year had negotiated with the Roman Catholics with a view to establishing a union between Rome and the Church of England. Windebank was important to Roe because of his influence with Laud (*C.S.P., Dom., 1633–1634*, 8 January 1634, p. 403).

[76] *C.S.P., Dom., 1636–1637*, Roe to Dury, 28 January 1637, p. 400.

[77] Ibid., *C.S.P., Dom., 1633–1634*, Roe to Bishop Morton of Durham, 24 January 1634, p. 430.

[78] Turnbull, *Gleanings*, Roe to Dury, 10 May 1634, p. 164.

the tyme of best hope. . . . [It] is G[od's] worke bee of good courage."[79]

It was almost inevitable that some friction should develop from time to time between Roe and Dury. Their commitment to their venture was never in doubt, but the frustrating absence of official interest sometimes frazzled nerves and shortened tempers. Dury occasionally expressed resentment of his dependence upon Roe and complained that he was too much concerned with the political aspects of the work.[80] He felt that his freedom was limited by the necessity of getting Roe's approval of every move.[81] But, even at times like these, Dury was ready to acknowledge that Roe was the only real patron he had and that he was absolutely indispensable.[82] He rarely made an important decision without consulting Roe and through a heavy correspondence kept him well informed of his activities.

Dury was inclined to be rather naïve and idealistic and to believe that the moral force of his cause would eventually lead to its success. To begin with, at least, he saw his work as an essentially personal crusade and was, on the whole, less aware than Roe of the political factors that necessarily complicated his task. Roe, on the other hand, was rather more alive to political reality and saw that the project for church unity was inseparable from existing political conditions. He was more convinced than Dury that they could not succeed without official support and that the weight of the Church of England was almost essential to success.

Accordingly, while Dury did most of his work on the Continent, Roe bent his energies to seeking support at home, and it is a sign of his persistence that his principal target

[79] Ibid., Roe to Hartlib, 1 June 1633, p. 154; ibid., Roe to Dury, 10 May 1634, p. 164.
[80] Ibid., Dury to Hartlib, 17 April 1640, pp. 205–206; ibid., Dury to Hartlib, 2 November 1638, pp. 189–90.
[81] Ibid., Dury to Hartlib, 3 May 1639, pp. 194–95.
[82] *C.S.P., Dom., 1633–1634*, Dury to Roe, 24 April 1634, p. 566; Turnbull, *Gleanings*, Dury to Hartlib, 17 April 1640, p. 207.

continued to be William Laud, who had lately been translated to the See of Canterbury. Roe's persistence did not grow out of any failure to perceive the real interests of the archbishop, but rather from his conviction that, without the support of the Church of England, the project was doomed. Laud had to be won over; and if he once refused his help, he must simply be asked again. Without his support, Dury would be a mere wandering scholar on a vain quest; with it he would be a plenipotentiary of the Anglican Church, able to speak with authority in negotiations with continental princes and church-men.[83]

But Laud remained cool to all advances. Sometimes he professed his approval of the work and promised to pray for its success.[84] Sometimes he claimed he was too busy to help.[85] Occasionally he grew irritated and said that he could not be expected to support every worthwhile cause that came along.[86] But, no matter what his particular excuse happened to be, he did nothing, and the project foundered.

In 1634, however, Dury and Roe renewed their efforts to win Laud's support. Their revived hopes centered on a meeting of the Heilbronn League, shortly to be held in Frankfurt. This league was composed of Sweden and the Protestant German states, and it was expected that the assembly would be strongly influenced by Axel Oxenstiern, who had recently succeeded Gustavus Adolphus as the leader of Swedish affairs. Oxenstiern, in turn, was known as a supporter of the idea of church unity;[87] and it therefore seemed likely that the climate of opinion at the forthcoming meeting would be receptive to Dury's proposals and that the general confession of faith he desired might receive some consideration. Nor was this all. An English ambassador was to attend the Frankfurt meeting. For a

---

[83] Trevor-Roper, *Archbishop Laud*, p. 265.
[84] *C.S.P., Dom., 1634–1635*, Archbishop Laud to Dury, no date, pp. 148–49.
[85] Ibid.
[86] *C.S.P., Dom., 1633–1634*, Dury to Roe, 15 March 1634, p. 509.
[87] J. M. Batten, *John Dury*, p. 22; Westin, "Church Unity," pp. 85–88.

time Roe hoped that he would be chosen and that he would be able to use his official status to advance the cause of church unity. But he was disappointed, for the choice fell upon Sir Robert Anstruther. All was not lost, however, for Sir Robert was known to be privately sympathetic toward Dury's aims, and there was still room to hope that much might be gained.[88]

In view of the possibilities presented by the Frankfurt meeting, Dury and Roe were resolved that the former, at least, should plead his cause before the delegates. But they saw that there was little hope of success so long as he was merely an unofficial observer. What was needed was for Anstruther to be officially instructed to support Dury's efforts. This did not seem much to ask, but Laud remained unmoved; and with England's lethargy so clearly demonstrated, continental enthusiasm cooled rapidly. Roe did his best to keep Oxenstiern interested, but the Swede had never really wanted religious unity for its own sake. He saw it as a bond that could strengthen and consecrate a fighting alliance; and when he saw that no such alliance was forthcoming from the England of Charles I, his interest in religious unity went by the board.[89] In an effort to win influential converts, Dury spent his days on "a continual pilgrimage among the antechambers of princes and statesmen";[90] and Roe continued to supply him with money and encouragement.

But it was futile. They were idealistic men in a hardheaded world, and they were trying to sell an idea in which their age had little interest. Their cause attracted some people who did it more harm than good,[91] and there was never any real hope of

[88] *C.S.P., Dom., 1634–1635*, Dury to Roe, 22 June 1634, p. 89.
[89] Great Britain, Historical Manuscripts Commission, *Fourth Report*, 162; Trevor-Roper, *Archbishop Laud*, pp. 267–68.
[90] Ibid., p. 264.
[91] *C.S.P., Dom., 1636–1637*, "Account of Sir Nathaniel Brent, Vicar General, of his metropolitical visitation of the diocese of London," p. 545. This report tells Laud that a certain Mr. Marshall, "a cunning & dangerous person who conforms outwardly but hath an incomformable heart" and who governs the consciences of all the rich Puritans in a wide area, is a supporter of Dury.

success. There is something both admirable and pathetic in their perseverance and dedication. Dury gave a lifetime to the pursuit of his dream, but he died in 1680 fully aware of the completeness of his failure. "The only fruit which I have reaped by all my toils," he wrote, "is that I see the miserable condition of christianity, and that I have no other comfort than the testimony of my conscience."[92]

Roe, too, retained until his death an active interest in the work for Christian union. In leisure hours his thoughts would turn in that direction, and he would, perhaps, write to Dury some words of encouragement and enclose some small amount of money.[93] But Roe was never thrown back entirely on the bitter reflections of failure. There were other things to occupy his mind, for in 1638 he was rescued from his long and unwelcome retirement by yet another summons to overseas duty.

[92] Quoted in John Westby-Gibson, "John Durie," in *D.N.B.*, 6:262.
[93] *C.S.P., Dom., 1636–1637*, Roe to Dury, 28 January 1637, p. 400; *C.S.P., Dom., 1633–1634*, Dury to Roe, 16 April 1634, p. 554; Turnbull, *Gleanings*, pp. 154, 164.

CHAPTER 9

Hamburg & Westminster

THE diplomacy in which Sir Thomas Roe was now to become involved was part and parcel of the tortuous intricacies that characterized European politics during the Thirty Years War. Sir Thomas had a personal interest in the course of the war because of his warm attachment to the queen of Bohemia. Ever since he had been sent to Constantinople in 1621 he had sorrowfully watched the decline in the fortunes of Elizabeth and her family.

That decline had really started in 1619, the year in which Elizabeth's husband, Frederick the Elector Palatine, had unwisely accepted the crown of Bohemia, offered to him by the Protestant party that was unwilling to accept as king the ardent Catholic Hapsburg, Ferdinand of Styria. Frederick's enjoyment of his new throne was brief, for in 1620 the imperial army had crushed his forces at the Battle of the White Mountain and quickly succeeded in overrunning Bohemia. The royal family had fled to safety, but the vengeance of the emperor followed them. The imperial troops of Spinola and Tilly fell upon the Lower Palatinate while Maximilian of Bavaria, eager to attain the dignity of an imperial elector, conquered the Upper Palatinate. By the spring of 1623 all Frederick's possessions had been wrenched from him, and he was grateful to accept the refuge offered at The Hague by the prince of Orange.

Further humiliation fell to Frederick when the ban of the empire was called down on him and his territories were given in trust to Maximilian of Bavaria. He was exiled and destitute, almost universally criticized for having accepted the crown in the first place, and widely ridiculed as the "winter king," or "le roi de neige." The only thing he had left was his electoral dignity, but even this was in jeopardy, for the emperor had pledged to give it to Maximilian. However, when he tried to do so at a Diet held in Ratisbon in 1623 he ran into a good deal of opposition, and that opposition illustrates effectively some of the complexities of European diplomacy at that time.

Most of the Protestant princes opposed the transfer of the electorate on the grounds that it would give the Catholics a clear majority in the electoral college. Spain, which for this very reason might have been expected to support the transfer, in fact opposed it, because she was anxious to stay on good terms with Frederick's father-in-law, James I of England. On the other hand, French diplomacy supported the emperor because the government in Paris believed that the transfer of the electorate would ultimately cause dissension between the Hapsburgs and the powerful Wittelsbach dukes of Bavaria. Some princes undoubtedly made their decisions on the basis of principle, being guided by their understanding of ancient and legal practices, but by and large the discussions at the Diet of 1623 were prophetic in that they indicated that expediency would rule most actions in the war that lay ahead, and that the Palatinate and its future would be used as a pawn by the competing powers. Frederick had no power to influence the struggle one way or another. All he could do was plead for assistance from the courts of Europe, and he was to find them more calculating than sympathetic.

After much wrangling a compromise was reached at the Diet, though not without causing deep resentment against the duke of Bavaria, who got his way for the good and simple reason that he held the land. It was decided that Maximilian should have the electorate for his lifetime and that the question of its permanent disposal should be decided at a later date. At any rate, in 1623 Maximilian became an elector, but perhaps without realizing the high price he had paid for his elevation.

He had gained his advantage at the expense of the very liberties by which he and all the other princes of Germany maintained their power; "he had sacrificed the constitution of Germany to the ambition of Bavaria."[1] As the leader and founder of the Catholic League he already had the Protestant princes against him; now the Catholics opposed him too. It was really a triumph for the emperor who had weakened a dangerous rival while seeming to favor him.

For almost ten years the Palatinate lay under the twin heels of Bavaria and Spain, but then in 1631 and 1632 it was taken by Gustavus Adolphus. With the country once again in Protestant hands it seemed that there was some possibility of effecting the restoration of the Palatine family. But their fortunes were of minor importance in the grand design of the Swedish king. For several months Frederick followed Gustavus and pressed his cause. He was treated with respect and was at last rewarded with Gustavus's declaration that he intended to restore the winter king. But there were terms. Gustavus demanded a guarantee of toleration and protection for Lutherans in the Palatinate. He also required that Frederick should make a public statement saying that he owed his restoration solely to Sweden. This seemed reasonable enough, but Frederick summoned up a dignity he could ill afford and refused. The differences between the two men were never reconciled, for they died within a few days of each other in November 1632.

Gustavus Adolphus was succeeded as the director of Sweden's affairs by his capable chancellor, Axel Oxenstiern. Despite the battle of Lutzen in which Gustavus had met his death, the Swedes were still in possession of the Palatinate. But, deprived of their great king, their cause was more desperate than before. They needed help. Roe, and others like him, felt that if England would commit herself decisively to Sweden's aid, there might be some real hope that the restoration of the Palatinate could yet be achieved. For a while events seemed to

[1] C. V. Wedgwood, *The Thirty Years War* (New York, 1961), pp. 162–63.

be moving in that direction. In 1633 the Heilbronn League, headed by Sweden and comprising most of the Protestant princes of Germany, agreed that the Palatinate should be restored to Frederick's young son, Charles Louis.[2] But then came disaster. At Nordlingen in 1634 the Swedish forces were routed. Practically all the conquests of Sweden were lost. The Palatinate was overrun by imperialist troops, and in 1635 the Treaty of Prague restored both Protestants and Catholics to the lands they had possessed in 1627. This meant that the Palatinate was once again given into the hands of the Catholic duke of Bavaria, and the restoration of its former rulers seemed as far away as ever.

Charles I, who had been little more than a spectator to these actions, prepared at once to protest to the emperor. The earl of Arundel was sent to the imperial court at Vienna with orders to demand the restoration of both the lands and the electorate of the Palatinate. The negotiations were long and predictably fruitless, so that when Arundel passed through The Hague on his way home he had to tell Elizabeth that there was little to be hoped for from Vienna and that all would be lost unless King Charles could be persuaded to intervene on her behalf.[3]

Even while the earl of Arundel was negotiating at Vienna another English embassy was at work in France. In May 1636 the earl of Leicester had been sent to Paris. His mission was complementary to that of Arundel, for he was to seek an active alliance with France so that, if Arundel's efforts should fail, the English and French together could take by force what the emperor refused to give up by persuasion.[4] When the Vienna

[2] Charles Louis was still a minor, so the territory actually was to be administered by his uncle, Philip Lewis, duke of Simmeren.

[3] *C.S.P., Dom., 1636–1637*, the queen of Bohemia to Roe, 21 December 1636, p. 239.

[4] *Calendar of State Papers and Manuscripts, Relating to English Affairs, Existing in the Archives and Collections of Venice, and in Other Libraries of Northern Italy* (London, 1921), 23:557 (hereafter referred to as *C.S.P., Venetian*); Allen B. Hinds, "Preface," *C.S.P., Venetian*, 24:xii. A second consideration was that the emperor might be more pliable if he knew that Anglo-French talks were being held and suspected that an unfriendly alliance was in the making.

talks did in fact break down, the negotiations with France naturally assumed great importance, for everything now depended upon them.

But the inability of Charles I to make firm commitments deviled the proceedings and the French got the impression that (as Richelieu said) the English "want to suit themselves; to avoid pledging themselves and do nothing while we do a great deal."[5] Charles was, indeed, trying to get the French to agree not to make peace unless the Palatinate were restored; at the same time he was refusing to pledge himself to make any specific contribution. His foreign policy was out of touch with reality. While professing to be concerned about his sister's plight, he consistently refused to do anything that offered any hope of improving it. Elizabeth almost overstepped the bounds of propriety in begging him to abandon fruitless negotiations, but Charles continued on his uncharted course, continued in what has been called his "weak and silly foreign policy."[6]

The French made a firm offer: if England would declare war on the emperor, France would be satisfied if she provided thirty ships, six thousand foot soldiers, and between fifteen hundred and two thousand horses.[7] These were modest enough requirements but Charles was still unwilling to plunge into war and sought agreement on a more limited alliance—one that would provide for indirect English support and would not necessitate an English declaration of war. He would undertake to provide Charles Louis with a fleet that could be used against Flanders and Spain and to defend the French coasts. He would also allow the French to levy six thousand volunteers in England. In return for these favors the French would have to agree not to make peace without including the interests (both lands and dignity) of the Palatine house.[8] The French were far from satisfied with these proposals and insisted that any such ar-

[5] Ibid., p. 191.
[6] Green, *Elizabeth of Bohemia*, p. 283; H. R. Trevor-Roper, "Historical Revision No. CVII, Archbishop Laud," *History* 30 (1945): 188.
[7] C.S.P., *Venetian*, 24:192.
[8] Ibid., p. 233.

rangements for "minor support" would have to be submitted for the approval of their allies, Sweden and Holland. A meeting with them had already been arranged to take place in Hamburg, and the French suggested that the English offer could be discussed there.[9]

This, then, was one of the purposes of the projected conference at Hamburg. But there were others. It had already been agreed by the three allies that they should discuss the claims of all the princes involved in the war and attempt to adjust them; it was also agreed that they should talk about the nature of the role to be played by the various powers opposed to the "common enemy." Thus the conference was intended to discuss broad, wide-ranging problems—problems that could be expected to give ample opportunity for disagreement and delay. Moreover, it was to be attended by four powers, each of which had its own private ends to pursue, each of which was to some extent suspicious of the aims and the good faith of the others, and each of which had some petty quarrel afoot with the others.[10]

Under these circumstances the outlook for the conference could hardly be described as promising, and it was widely recognized that the negotiations would be complex and difficult.[11] But little time was lost in getting the embassy underway. Roe's appointment had been announced on 14 May and just one week later he left for Hamburg. Before his departure he had a long private interview with the king at which his instructions were clarified. His first task was to be that of winning Swedish and Dutch approval of the agreement already

[9] Ibid. The French and Swedish ambassadors were already in Hamburg. In March they had signed the Treaty of Hamburg which had spelled out their mutual commitments in the war (G. Pagès, *La Guerre de Trente Ans, 1618–1648* [Paris, 1949], pp. 210–11).

[10] Ibid., pp. 233–34. The Dutch protested English molestation of their fishermen (ibid., p. 105); the Swedes were suspected of negotiating a separate peace with the emperor (ibid., p. 227); the French and English were wrangling over a number of maritime disputes (Allen Hinds, "Preface," ibid., xvii), and all the powers felt that England was not doing her fair share in the struggle (ibid., p. xvi).

[11] *C.S.P., Dom., 1637–1638*, the queen of Bohemia to Roe, 4 December 1637, p. 7.

achieved (but not ratified) between England and France. Some difficulty was anticipated on this point and Roe was authorized to ease the way for its acceptance by offering the Swedes material assistance and promising the Dutch satisfaction for their complaints about English interference with their fishermen. A secondary objective of the mission was that of treating with Denmark and the princes of Germany and trying to win their support for the Palatine family.[12]

Roe took up his task with apparent enthusiasm and expressed confidence in the success of his mission. But it is difficult to believe that his optimism was genuine, because prior to his leaving England Charles I imperiled the whole enterprise by trying to reduce his already modest commitment to France. The original agreement had called for England to supply both land and naval forces, but soon after it was concluded the Venetian ambassador in England was advising his government that King Charles had withdrawn the offer to supply soldiers and munitions.[13] Charles was still obsessed by the fear of becoming involved in a full-scale war with the Hapsburgs, and had determined that if war must come it would be a naval war only on his part. "In this way," wrote the perceptive Venetian, "they calculate that if war is made it cannot inconvenience them much, and if the treaty cannot be made on these conditions it is better for it to be dissolved, because the royal purse cannot bear such expenses alone and the king cannot put his hands into those of his subjects any further without parliament."[14]

These new developments gave Roe's mission, from its inception, an air of futility. The government itself was not determined to press the negotiations to a successful conclusion and was not prepared to make realistic sacrifices to achieve its desired ends. Reduced to its simplest terms Roe's task was to persuade France, Sweden, and Holland to spend blood and treasure for the restoration of the Palatinate while committing

[12] *C.S.P., Venetian*, 24:412–13.
[13] Ibid., p. 309.
[14] Ibid.

his royal master to provide nothing more than a fleet of ships that would not even fight in England's name.[15] This would have been difficult enough if England's influence and power had been high, but it was common knowledge that Charles's financial difficulties, coupled with growing discontents in Scotland, were sapping the country's strength and lowering her potential for effective action overseas. England was entering a period in which, on the international scene, her voice scarcely commanded respect. Roe's mission was nothing more than a gesture of concern on the part of King Charles for the fate of his sister.

Roe left England on 21 May 1638 and went first to the newly established trading center of Gluckstadt on the Elbe. There he had an audience with King Christian IV and sought, in accordance with his instructions, to persuade the Danish king to exert himself on behalf of the Palatinate and the Protestant cause in general.[16] This, however, was little more than a courtesy call, and Roe was soon on his way to Hamburg. Once there, he reiterated his confidence in the success of the pending talks and declared that his king was ready to make every effort to consummate the alliance.[17] He was graciously received and, to all outward appearances, the conference was off to a cordial start.

Friction started even before the talks began. Soon after his arrival, Roe and the French and Swedish ambassadors became involved in such an obstinate dispute for precedence that at least one observer thought it doubtful that they would ever meet to negotiate. This obstacle was overcome, but then, at the very first conference Roe was asked bluntly whether or not England intended to break openly with the House of Austria. This was an eventuality that Charles I wanted to avoid if at all

[15] The fleet was to be employed by the Elector Palatine and to fight under his flag. Charles I seems seriously to have believed that he could thus "make war under his nephew's cloak" and not give offense to Spain; S. R. Gardiner, *History of England from the Accession of James I to the Outbreak of the Civil War, 1603–1642* (New York, 1883–1884), 8:204.

[16] *C.S.P., Venetian*, 24:429.

[17] Ibid., p. 431.

possible, so Roe answered evasively that the question could be discussed after England's alliance with France had been settled.[18] That night he wrote home asking for fresh and precise instructions, for he wanted to know what his course should be if the other negotiators continued to press him on the matter of England's declaring war on Austria.

This was an aspect of the central issue of the conference: to what extent was England willing to commit herself to the anti-Hapsburg league, and would that commitment be sufficient to induce the other powers to accept obligations with respect to the Palatinate? This question, however, was constantly obscured by a host of minor issues and by a web of mutual suspicion and distrust. Clashes between English and Dutch shipping in the Channel kept relations between those ambassadors strained.[19] Roe suspected that the Swedes were involved in secret negotiations with the imperialists.[20] The French blamed Swedish obstruction for the delays that plagued the meetings, but the Swedes, with equal acrimony, put the responsibility on the French.[21]

All these things were annoyances, pretexts for delay, and, perhaps, the normal accompaniments of diplomatic jousting. But the principal substantive point that separated the representatives was the Swedish insistence that England's commitments, as laid down in the agreement with France, were insufficient, and that Sweden would undertake no promises about the Palatinate unless the English contribution were materially increased.[22] Charles had promised to provide ships—"thirty well-armed ships cruising in the Channel to cut off Spanish

[18] Ibid., p. 439; *Great Britain, Historical Manuscripts Commission Fourth Report,* "The Manuscripts of the Right Honourable the Earl de la Warr (Baron Buckhurst) at Knole Park, Co. Kent" (London, 1874), p. 293.

[19] C.S.P., *Venetian,* 24:442.

[20] Ibid., p. 439.

[21] Ibid., p. 502.

[22] Gardiner suggests that the French had accepted England's terms because they believed that even the modest English participation provided for in the treaty would inevitably lead to a full-scale involvement. The Swedes evidently did not share this belief (*History of England,* 8:204).

supplies to Flanders"—but ships, said the Swedes, were always at the mercy both of the winds and of their commanders' greed. What they wanted from England was money and men, or, better still, an English declaration of war against Austria.[23] They wanted to push Charles beyond the commitment he had made to France, but, as conditions in England deteriorated, the king became increasingly determined not to go beyond what he had already promised.[24] Around the English court the conviction grew that the Hamburg talks could not now be successful, and it was even said that the Spanish were sending an ambassador extraordinary to England to offer assistance in reducing the Scots.[25] So far did Charles I appear to be from getting into an anti-Hapsburg alliance!

With the English king adamant in the stand he had taken, there was no room for maneuver and no possibility of compromise. The negotiations were hopelessly deadlocked. Roe was bound by his instructions, but, knowing his eagerness to see his country committed to a dynamic alliance, we can imagine how he must have chafed at his inability to bring the negotiations to a happy conclusion.

Late in 1638 he was ordered to leave Hamburg temporarily and make his way to Gluckstadt for more talks with the king of Denmark. While he was there he lavishly entertained the prince elector who had recently sustained a serious military defeat at Gohfeld. The two men discussed at length the gloomy prospects for the prince's restoration.[26] From these conversations Roe went on to his talks with the Danish king. They were principally concerned with some financial matters that had arisen between the two crowns and with efforts to recover some valuable jewels that had been pawned to the Danish king.[27] Roe was successful in settling these affairs, but his efforts to negotiate a treaty of commerce between the two

---

[23] *C.S.P., Venetian*, 24:463, 481.
[24] Ibid.
[25] Ibid.
[26] Green, *Elizabeth of Bohemia*, p. 341.
[27] *C.S.P., Venetian*, 24:484, 567.

kingdoms were not brought to completion even though they were followed for several months by the efforts of other negotiators.[28]

Roe did not stay long at Gluckstadt, and when he returned to Hamburg he found the negotiations as badly snarled as ever. He recognized the impossibility of a successful completion of his mission; so he wrote home and asked to be recalled.[29] His request, however, was refused, presumably because Charles I did not want to be the first to admit the futility of further negotiations.

Throughout 1639 Roe occupied himself with minor tasks, the nature of which reflected the worsening situation in England. He was instructed to purchase supplies of arms and ammunition for his government, so, partly at his own expense, he rounded up supplies of pikes and muskets and shipped them to England. Once there they were found to be of inferior quality and Roe was not fully reimbursed for the expense he had incurred.[30] Other instructions asked Roe to do everything he could to prevent arms being sent from Hamburg to the Scottish Covenanters, and to "use the most powerful persuasions" to induce Scotsmen who had been fighting on the Continent (usually in the Swedish armies) to return to England and join the king's forces, which were being prepared to move against the Covenanters.[31] Sir Thomas performed a useful service in these areas, and in the process he seems to have built up an effective network of informants who were to prove useful in an important way in later months.

In March 1640 Roe was finally granted permission to return to England. He was not immediately employed by the govern-

---

[28] *C.S.P., Dom., 1640–1641*, Secretary Vane to Roe, 30 September 1640, p. 120; ibid., Secretary Vane to Secretary Windebank, 1 October 1640, p. 128; *C.S.P., Venetian*, 24:567, 568–69, 576.

[29] Ibid., p. 510; *C.S.P., Dom., 1639–1640*, Secretary Windebank to Roe, 24 January 1640, p. 371.

[30] Ibid., November 1639, p. 137; *C.S.P., Dom., 1640*, June 1640, pp. 374–75.

[31] *C.S.P., Dom., 1639–1640*, Secretary Windebank to Roe, 24 January 1640, p. 371.

ment although a number of interesting positions became available. Just prior to Roe's return Sir John Coke had resigned as secretary of state, but by the time Sir Thomas reached England the desirable post had been granted to Sir Henry Vane. This must have been a disappointment to Roe, his hopes for office renewed by his recent assignment, but he soon heard that he was being considered for the position of comptroller of the king's household. There was competition for the job; it was known that Sir Peter Wyche, the ambassador in Turkey, had offered £6,000 for it, but Roe was given to understand that he could have it for only half that amount.[32] Presumably some measure of royal favor or belief in his personal merit inclined the Crown in Roe's direction. As a matter of fact it was some time before the post was filled, and when it was it was given to Wyche; by that time, however, Roe himself was being used in another capacity.

From the time of his recall from Hamburg there had been little danger that he would have to endure another period of protracted inactivity. Archbishop Laud, in writing to tell Roe of the king's wish that he should return to England, had said that, although it was too late for him to take a seat in the parliament shortly to assemble, he felt sure that Roe would, nevertheless, be able to help the king's cause.[33] Clearly, he was being looked upon by the Royalists as a man who would be useful to them.

It is not hard to explain the improved relations between Roe and the court. The dissolution of the "Short Parliament" only three weeks after its first meeting had dramatized the deterioration in England's domestic affairs. In any split between king and people it would have been natural to regard Roe as occupying a middle position; for while it was true that most of his life had been spent in the service of the Crown, it was also true that his name had long been connected with the City and the mercantile interests, that for a full decade he had been in

---

[32] Ibid., Sir Richard Cave to Roe, 27 March 1640, p. 589.
[33] *C.S.P., Dom., 1639–1640*, Archbishop Laud to Roe, 6 March 1640, p. 525.

basic disagreement with the unpopular foreign policy of the government, that he had taken an independent line in parliament, and that he was closely identified in the public mind with two people who in England approached the stature of national heroes—Elizabeth of Bohemia and Gustavus Adolphus. Roe thus had about him the attractiveness of the intelligent moderate. It was reasonable to believe that his appointment as an adviser to the Crown would meet with the approval of both parties.

Changed domestic circumstances undoubtedly help to explain Roe's newfound favor in royal eyes, but foreign affairs also played their part. It was in this area that Roe was particularly well qualified and knowledgeable. This must have been an influential general factor, but further developments made Roe's appointment seem even more appropriate. In October 1639 the Dutch had shattered a Spanish fleet in the Downs. This decisive engagement had been followed in England by a marked trend in the direction of a Dutch alliance and a corresponding coolness in Anglo-Spanish relations. By mid-1640 a marriage alliance was being negotiated between Princess Mary of England and young William of Orange. English policy belatedly was beginning to approximate what Roe had long felt it should be, and as it did so an important cause of his estrangement from the court was dissolved.

All these considerations—and any number of others that might have entered the mind of King Charles—brought Roe to the summit of his career. In the summer of 1640 he was appointed a member of the king's Privy Council. At a time of critical importance in the life of the English state he entered the innermost circle of government, one of forty men whose task was to advise the sovereign. The Venetian ambassador understood that the appointment had come "as a testimony of satisfaction with the services rendered to the crown in many embassies," and, in his dispatch, went on to say that at that time Roe "enjoys great credit at Court."[34] Sir George Radcliff

---

[34] *C.S.P., Venetian,* 25:63.

commented upon the appointment in a less serious vein: "We have had two councillors lately sworn, the Earl of Cork . . . and Sir Thomas Roe. . . . Some say the King is now furnished for all things, even to the telling of strange stories, wherein these two shall vie wonders with any three in Christendom."[35] The queen of Bohemia sent her congratulations and expressed the hope that Roe would go on to still higher things.[36]

Roe was in ill health when the appointment was made. The gout, which had troubled him for a number of years, suddenly struck with renewed ferocity, and reluctantly he retired to a house he had recently purchased in Low Leyton, the town of his birth. It was not, however, an impressive homecoming, for so straitened was his financial condition that he could not afford to furnish his new home and was obliged to live in a cottage nearby.[37] The king owed Roe a large amount of money, but the return to royal favor indicated by his recent appointment had no beneficial effect on his economic condition.

His illness did not immobilize him. He made frequent trips up to London and took part in much of the business of the Privy Council. He also maintained contact with the agents he had established in Hamburg, and in the autumn of 1640 they were the source of some rather important information. Roe learned from them that a number of experienced Scottish army officers who had been employed in the forces of Sweden had obtained their release and were preparing to sail to Scotland with arms and ammunition, there to join the Scottish rebels.[38] He communicated this information to Secretary Windebank who passed it on to the lord admiral, the earl of Northumberland, whose responsibility it would be to prevent the conjunc-

[35] *C.S.P., Dom., 1640*, Sir George Radcliff to Edward Lord Conway and Killutagh, 4 July 1640, p. 447.
[36] Ibid., the queen of Bohemia to Roe, 9 July 1640, p. 461.
[37] A. P. Wire, "An Essex Worthy: Sir Thomas Roe," *Essex Review* 20 (1911):142; *C.S.P., Dom., 1640*, Roe to Secretary Vane, 7 August 1640, p. 565.
[38] Ibid., Roe to Secretary Windebank, 26 September 1640, p. 101.

tion of the two forces. Although the government seemed to appreciate the gravity of the situation, they took insufficient precautions, and the Scots from the Continent made their landing without being molested.[39]

These activities occupied Roe during the summer of 1640, a time when political events in England were moving fast. The Short Parliament, obstinate in its determination that the settlement of its grievances should have priority over the satisfaction of the king's needs, had been dissolved on 5 May. But dissolution was no solution to the problems of Charles I. The Scots, who were almost unanimous in their support of the covenant, had raised highly skilled professional armies and were encamped on the northern edge of England. Under the shadow of this danger Charles's need for money grew more desperate, but, urged on by Strafford, he continued to favor an offensive war and the reduction by force of the Scots. Any number of devices were tried to fill the royal coffers, but Charles simply could not raise an army that was fit to stand on the same field with the Scots. In August 1640 the Scots had crossed the Tweed at Coldstream, occupied Northumberland and Durham, and then refused to budge unless they were granted their own terms and a very substantial sum of money. Money, as they well knew, could be obtained only from parliament. A new parliament, having seen the king's plight so convincingly demonstrated, was certain to be even more angry and formidable than the last.

The king, however, was still strongly averse to calling a parliament and summoned instead a great council of peers. This group negotiated with the Scots the Treaty of Ripon

[39] One of the men that Roe had named specifically in his warning was David Leslie. Leslie became a major general in the Scottish army commanded by his namesake, Alexander Leslie, later earl of Leven. The failure to prevent Leslie's landing cost the government dearly, for he went on to become one of the most successful officers of the parliamentary armies. He has been credited with a major role in the Parliamentarians' victory at Marston Moor (T. F. Henderson, "Leslie, David, First Lord Newark," in *D.N.B.*, 33:86).

which provided that the Scots should remain in possession of the two northern counties and receive £850 per day until a permanent settlement could be reached. The treaty was a humiliation for the English Crown; moreover, it was obviously nothing more than a stopgap measure, which in no way alleviated the necessity of calling a parliament. Its terms served to aggravate the financial distress of the Crown; and in making the treaty, the Scots had clearly implied that they would not accept a final settlement that did not have the assent of the English parliament.

At last, in the autumn of 1640, Charles I reluctantly capitulated to his pressing financial needs, and writs for the election of a parliament were duly sent out. Both sides—the court and the leaders of the opposition—recognized the critical importance of the impending session. Each engaged itself in efforts intended to secure a House of Commons favorable to its cause. Pym rode around the country "to promote the elections of the Puritanical brethren." The king, his household, and the officers of state gave strong support to their candidates.[40]

As a privy councillor Sir Thomas Roe had a special interest in the impending session of parliament. The role of the councillors was particularly critical in the autumn of 1640, when there were major areas of disagreement between king and parliament. They provided a channel of communication and were vitally important factors in any royal effort to sway the deliberations and decisions of the lower house.

With their notions of divine right the first two Stuart sovereigns had not been as sensitive to the importance of the privy councillors as their Tudor predecessors had been. Relying on the power of their authority and scorning the need for persuasion, they had been inconsistent in their efforts to place councillors in the Commons. James and Charles seem vaguely to have understood that it would be wise to have councillors there as guardians of their interests, but they had not regarded

[40] R. N. Kershaw, "The Elections for the Long Parliament 1640," *The English Historical Review* 38 (1923):508, 502.

this as a matter of first-rate importance and, generally speaking, they had chosen carelessly and been poorly represented by their councillors in parliament.[41]

In 1640 the Privy Council was large, having about forty members. It was made up almost entirely of peers however, and the number of councillors eligible for election to the House of Commons was small. Indeed, as the elections for the Long Parliament took place only four privy councillors were involved: Secretary Windebank, Sir Henry Vane, Sir Thomas Jermyn, and Roe.[42] It could be assumed that the Crown, recognizing the crucial nature of the forthcoming session, would do everything possible to get privy councillors elected and that, because the number of eligible councillors was so small, its efforts on behalf of those few would be especially determined.

During the reigns of the first two Stuarts, privy councillors rarely contested open constituencies where public opinion could be freely expressed. As opposition to the Crown had increased the councillors had been driven more and more to seek election in constituencies where royal influence was particularly strong.[43] During the reign of Charles I two such constituencies were to be found in the universities of Oxford and Cambridge.

The universities had first been granted parliamentary representation by James I in 1604. Within a short time the tenure of a university seat had come to be regarded as a special honor, although both James I and his son had shown an increasing inclination to interfere with the elections. Charles I in particular seems to have regarded the university constituencies as royal pocket boroughs, and in the early years of his reign influence and pressure from outside the universities had been effective in ensuring the election of men acceptable to the

---

[41] D. H. Willson, *The Privy Councillors in the House of Commons, 1604–1629* (Minneapolis, Minn., 1940), p. 56; Wallace Notestein, "The Winning of the Initiative by the House of Commons," *The Raleigh Lecture on History* (London, 1924), pp. 23–53.

[42] Willson, *Privy Councillors in the House of Commons*, p. 63.

[43] Ibid., pp. 68–69.

government.[44] The universities' subjection was epitomized in
the fact that Laud was the chancellor of Oxford and Buckingham had been the chancellor of Cambridge. Of the members they had sent to parliament since 1621 about three-fourths
had been privy councillors or other royal officials.[45] And yet,
through this period of excessive royal influence, the universities had managed to retain a measure of electoral freedom and,
by 1640, two unwritten agreements seemed to have become
accepted. One of these was that the chancellor should have the
right to propose one of the university's burgesses—but only
one; the other, that the burgesses sent to parliament should
represent a compromise between the court candidate and the
university favorite.[46]

So the Crown could expect to have one of its nominees
returned from each university. But in the Oxford election for
the Long Parliament there were not one, but two candidates
with court connections. One of these was Roe, a privy councillor; the other, ironically, was Sir Francis Windebank, the
man who, in 1632, had been given the secretaryship that Roe
had coveted and who had also been appointed to the Privy
Council. There were two other candidates. One of these was
John Selden, a scholar and jurist who in earlier parliaments had
been a vigorous champion of the liberties of the subject, and
who had suffered imprisonment for his convictions on more
than one occasion. Selden had a great zeal for learning and his
candidacy may be supposed to have exercised a strong attraction to those in the university who were similarly inclined. The
fourth candidate was Sir Nathaniel Brent, the warden of Mer-
ton College and champion of the sizable and organized Puritan
faction of the university.[47]

The four candidates for the two Oxford seats were thus

[44] Millicent B. Rex, *University Representation in England, 1604–1690,*
Études présentées à la Commission internationale pour l'histoire des
Assemblées d'états, 15 (London, 1954), pp. 49, 57, 60 (hereafter referred
to as Rex, *University Representation*).
[45] Ibid., p. 97.
[46] Ibid., pp. 115, 121.
[47] Ibid., p. 146.

equally divided: two of them had connections that made it logical to regard them as the nominees of the Crown; two were more properly looked upon as representatives of the university's interests. Thus, in view of the tacit compromise between university and court, the essential task of the university voters in 1640 was to decide between Windebank and Roe on the one hand and, in what might be regarded as almost a separate contest, between Selden and Brent on the other.

Windebank and Roe had much to recommend them to the voters. Roe, it is true, had had very little contact with the university since his student days and his principal pursuits had been far removed from the academic life. He had, however, shown himself to be a friend of learning by making some gifts to the new Bodleian Library, and in a broad sense he fit fairly well the mold of the typical university member of parliament.[48] He had attended the university himself and had spent some time in the study of the law. His family was a prominent one which, although identified primarily with the city, had nevertheless put its roots down into a number of landed estates. Extensive diplomatic experience and far-ranging travel had developed in Roe the ability to see more than one side of a question, to judge calmly, and, on the whole, to act wisely. He was tolerant, but undoubtedly had the courage to stand up for his own convictions. In his religious convictions, he was free of the bigotry that characterized his age. Urbane, respected, experienced, something of a scholar, thoroughly upright, and dedicated to the interests of his king, Sir Thomas Roe must have held a strong attraction for the "masters and scholars" of Oxford University.

But his opponent was a strong one—not so capable as Roe, perhaps, but with a long record of powerful patrons, high office, and great influence. Windebank was the only heir of a prominent and fairly ancient family. Like Roe, he was an Oxford man who had studied law after his university days.[49]

---

[48] "The typical university member" is characterized in ibid., p. 40.
[49] Though, unlike Roe, Windebank had graduated B.A.

He had traveled on the Continent but acquired little political importance until 1632 when his friendship with Laud had brought him the secretaryship vacated by Lord Dorchester. In his new post he had become extremely influential. Subtly he had elbowed aside the other secretary, Sir John Coke, and soon practically all correspondence relating to England's foreign affairs passed through his hands.[50] Windebank was pro-Spanish and Catholic in his sympathies, so he epitomized the kind of thinking that had kept Roe in the political wilderness for a decade. In Weston and Cottington (the lord treasurer and the chancellor of the exchequer) Windebank had found men who shared his views. Throughout most of the 1630s this trium-virate had exercised great influence over the king. However, late in the decade, a breach had begun to develop between Windebank and Laud over some corrupt practices the arch-bishop strongly disapproved.[51] The disagreement between the two had not been sufficiently serious to prevent Windebank's representing Oxford University in the Short Parliament, but it was enough to throw into doubt the matter of Laud's support in the election now pending.

Roe was optimistic. The events of recent years indicated that his long estrangement from the court party was at an end and, although Laud had previously failed to recommend him for advancement, the two men had for many years carried on a cordial correspondence.[52] Moreover, Windebank was coming under increasingly heavy criticism. His performance as the university's representative in the Short Parliament was spoken of disparagingly, and his known political convictions were not now so popular as they had been but a short time ago.[53]

---

[50] Florence M. Greir Evans, *The Principal Secretary of State* (Man-chester, 1923), pp. 94–95.

[51] A. F. Pollard, "Windebank, Sir Francis," in *D.N.B.*, 62:162–64.

[52] In 1634 Roe had given his impression of the new archbishop to the queen of Bohemia: "[He is] an excellent man . . . very just, incorrupt, and above all mistaken by the erring world." Elizabeth's reply was that she was glad Roe commended Laud so much, for "there are but few that do it" (*C.S.P., Dom., 1634–1635*, 10 December 1634, pp. 349–50; ibid., 11 February 1635, p. 509).

[53] Rex, *University Representation*, p. 145.

The candidates did not know which way Laud would throw his support. They both took the precaution of having their names put on the ballot in other constituencies—no point in having the few privy councillors who were eligible to sit in the House of Commons eliminating each other in electoral battles.[54] But at the last moment in Oxford, Laud must have given his endorsement to Roe. If there was a letter, it has not survived. But Dr. Thomas Read, Windebank's nephew, gives us a pretty good idea of what happened: "most of our Doctors and the principal men of the University were well inclined towards [Windebank], but I am informed that some higher power was directly or indirectly interested in the election" of the other candidate.[55] It seems a reasonable assumption that the "higher power" was Laud, moving behind the scenes. At any rate, before the poll was held Windebank withdrew and Roe stood at the top of the list as a unanimous choice, leaving Selden and Brent to fight it out for the remaining seat.[56] Selden won and joined Roe to form the representation of the University of Oxford in the most famous of all English parliaments—the Long Parliament.

From Laud's point of view, and the king's, there is room to question whether Roe was the best choice. It was not that he lacked ability. He was easily the most able of the councillors in the House of Commons. But he continued to exercise the right of independent thought and experienced deep misgivings about the wisdom of the king's course. He never allowed himself to become merely a defender and apologist for royal policies. Moreover, he did not serve for long: yet again, illness and a diplomatic mission overseas called him away, and his departure left the king without a single trusted councillor in the House

[54] Miss Rex (ibid.) says that the Oxford archives contain no letter of recommendation from Chancellor Laud for any of the candidates. This excellent book contains a careful analysis of the forces that were at work in the Oxford election. Roe ran, and was elected, at Windsor; Windebank was returned for Corfe Castle in Cornwall. Roe's election at Windsor was subsequently voided by the House.
[55] Willson, *Privy Councillors in the House of Commons*, pp. 75–76.
[56] Rex, *University Representation*, p. 146.

of Commons—and that at a time when effective liaison was desperately needed. There were only four councillors in the House when the session began, and one by one they dropped away. Windebank was charged with being unduly lenient toward Catholics and fled the country. Sir Henry Vane went over to the opposition. Sir Thomas Jermyn ceased to attend when his son's involvement in the "first army plot" was disclosed.[57] All in all, it was a striking example of Charles I's ineptitude in the handling of parliament.

The Long Parliament began its deliberations on 3 November 1640 and from the very first meeting Sir Thomas Roe figured prominently in its activities. He was not to be there long, but while he was present his name ranked with those of more celebrated men for the frequency with which the clerks and diarists were obliged to jot it in their journals. At the opening ceremonies he appeared with the earl marshal of England and the other royal officials who, at the opening of each session, administered the oath to new members.[58]

The first order of business on 6 November was to make preparations for a public fast. This procedure had become a tradition, but nevertheless all the appropriate formalities were observed; there were resolutions in the Commons, messages to the Lords, and petitions to the king. All these arrangements were entrusted to a committee of which Roe was the head. Before long Sir Thomas had become recognized as the Commons' chief messenger to the House of Lords, and he was frequently given the task of reporting to the Commons the results of meetings between representatives of the two houses.[59]

It was not long before he was engaged in more weighty business. In the early months of the Long Parliament a good deal of attention was necessarily given to the matter of the Scottish armies that still occupied Northumberland and Dur-

---

[57] Willson, *Privy Councillors in the House of Commons*, pp. 67–68.
[58] *Journals of the House of Commons*, 2:20 (hereafter cited as *Commons' Journal*).
[59] Ibid., pp. 22, 23, 27, 30, 33.

ham. The Treaty of Ripon had been only a temporary agreement, and the negotiations that had begun there had still to be concluded. For this purpose Scottish commissioners and theologians made their way to London to negotiate with representatives of the two Houses of Parliament. A necessary adjunct to the proceedings between the two sets of commissioners was a series of frequent meetings between representatives of Commons and Lords, and in these meetings Roe was a prominent participant, acting as a member of the Commons' delegation and usually serving as the reporter of the proceedings.[60] His experience in diplomatic negotiations must have stood him in good stead during these sessions and we may reasonably surmise that he contributed substantially. Unfortunately, it is impossible to be more precise about the part he played, for while the reports that have survived record the consensus of the meetings Roe attended, they say nothing about individual contributions. This lack of information is especially annoying because a more detailed knowledge of the conferences would, in all probability, give valuable insight into the matter of Roe's political allegiance at this time.[61]

Throughout the period of his attendance in parliament Roe was in ill health, but he managed to follow a rigorous schedule. He served on at least eight committees,[62] spoke frequently,[63] and offered numerous motions.[64] At least two of his speeches were published separately and attracted a good deal of attention. One of them was directed against the debasement of the

[60] Ibid., pp. 27, 30, 32, 33; Wallace Notestein, ed., *The Journal of Sir Simonds D'Ewes from the Beginning of the Long Parliament to the Opening of the Trial of the Earl of Strafford* (New Haven, Conn., 1923), pp. 39–40.
[61] In the negotiations with the Scots the interests of parliament and Crown were divergent. The continued presence of Scottish armies in northern England was almost a guarantee to the parliament that it would continue to meet; Charles could hardly afford a dissolution while the Scots remained and received £850 per day. Thus in the negotiations the parliamentarians delayed the proceedings for as long as possible, while the royalists pressed for a speedy settlement.
[62] *Commons' Journal*, 2:39, 48, 49, 52, 54, 80, 86, 87.
[63] Notestein, *D'Ewes' Journal*, pp. 5*n*, 24, 33, 39–40, 81, 87, 117.
[64] Ibid., 3, 18, 49, 51, 55, 56, 76, 80.

coinage, a measure that was being considered by the king as a means of raising revenue independently of parliament. Roe was considered to be the principal opponent of the idea, and he defended his position with such vigor in the Privy Council that Strafford, an advocate of the scheme, quite lost his temper.[65] The second speech was a perceptive review of some of England's commercial problems. It is worthy of some detailed comment because it serves to illustrate Roe's competent understanding of those problems and sets forth the remedies he proposed.[66]

Like other Englishmen of his time Roe was concerned about the movement of English gold and silver overseas. This, he felt, could be blamed in part upon the deteriorating relationship between king and parliament. The restoration of tranquil conditions was a most important prerequisite for the restoration of healthy trade. (From this time until the time of his death the need for compromise, for an accommodation, between the king and his people would be Roe's main theme.) There were, of course, more specific, commercial reasons for the decline of England's trade, and Roe focused on the cloth industry in order to point them out. Excessive impositions were making English cloth too expensive abroad. The purchase of French goods "of little bulk . . . but of dear price" was taking money out of the kingdom. "Pressures upon tender consciences" were causing many English clothiers to leave the country, taking their skills with them "to the inexpressible detriment of the commonwealth." Bad practices—"falsemaking and stretching and such-like"—were discrediting English cloth and causing

[65] *Sir T. Roe's Speech at the Councel Table about the alteration of the Coyn, in July 1640; with some observations thereon* (London, 1695). The speech was actually delivered before the Privy Council. Lady Burghclere, *Strafford* (London, 1931), 2:206.
[66] "Sir Thomas Roe's Speech in Parliament. Wherein he sheweth the Cause of the Decay of Coin and Trade in this Land, especially of Merchants Trade: And also propoundeth a Way to the House, how they may be increased," in *Harleian Miscellany* (London, 1809), 4:433–37. This speech has survived in a number of forms; see *The British Museum Catalogue of Printed Books, 1881–1900* (Ann Arbor, Mich., 1946), pp. 46, 264.

people in other countries to manufacture their own. And the state, in making treaties and enforcing them, was giving insufficient attention to the needs and interests of English merchants established abroad in factories.

Having listed what he considered to be the causes of England's commercial problems, Roe proceeded to the matter of remedies. Again he impressed upon his audience the need for tranquillity in the state. Then he turned to some more strictly commercial proposals. England must concentrate upon developing her great staple commodities, of which wool was the most important. The price of wool should be kept high on the home market, and the quality of woolen goods made for export must be uniformly excellent. But, while doing everything possible to increase the trade in wool, England's merchants must realize that woolen goods are "heavy and hotwearing and [serve] but one cold corner of the world." They should try to produce, along with the traditional woolen goods, lighter fabrics that would enjoy broader markets. In this effort Dutch skills and experience would be invaluable, and Roe felt that Dutch craftsmen could be attracted to England. He proposed that they be offered land in the fens which were even then in the process of being drained. This area would be suitable for growing flax and hemp; and Roe believed that the manufacture of linen could be centered in England if the Dutch craftsmen were offered land at rents markedly lower than they paid at home, and if they were assured of being allowed to practice their own religious rites— "so [long] as they be not scandalous," he was careful to add.[67]

He recognized that many of his proposed remedies could be

[67] Although it runs counter to everything we know of him, it must be pointed out that Roe held a lease on some fenland and that it is possible to impute a measure of self-interest to his proposals. It is true that he suggested the land be made available to the Dutch at the modest rent of ten or twelve shillings an acre, but it is also true that Roe himself paid only pennies an acre for his holdings. See *C.S.P., Dom., 1635–1636*, Roe to the Lords of the Treasury, January 1636, pp. 202–203; *C.S.P., Dom., 1660–1661*, Petition of Lady Elinor . . . Rowe to the king, December 1660, p. 429.

enacted only by the state. This was not objectionable to the mercantilist age in which he lived, but Roe wanted to leave the solution of England's problems as much as possible in the hands of the merchants themselves. Let each company of merchants be invited to list its grievances and suggest the causes of decline in its particular trade. Let these statements be considered by a parliamentary committee and then invite the companies to suggest remedies, "which materials having altogether, and comparing one with another, we shall discover that truth which we seek: that is Whether trade and money decay or not? And how to remedy it." Roe ended his speech by moving that a committee be named to solicit the desired information from the merchants.

This speech, like Roe's letters, is of interest mostly for what it tells us about the man who gave it. He is a servant of the Crown, but he criticizes some of the policies that have emanated from it. In an age of bigotry he expresses his concern for "tender consciences" and is willing to see a number of foreigners bring their alien religious practices to the very corner of England in which he lived. In his speech, and in his parliamentary career generally, Roe as one of the members for Oxford University, demonstrated "that balanced judgment, that thoughtful approach, which—according to modern standards, at least—might be felt to be the chief contribution of the university mind to public affairs."[68] Certainly a number of people, contemporaries and later commentators, have expressed a high regard for Roe's talents as a parliamentarian.[69]

On 18 December 1640, when Roe had been sitting in the House of Commons for about six weeks, Archbishop Laud was accused of high treason. Here, perhaps, was the first sharp stab of personal pain that Roe was to suffer because of England's misery. There is nothing to suggest that the two men were close personal friends. They held conflicting views on a number of important issues and spent little or no time in each

---

[68] Rex, *University Representation*, pp. 143–44.
[69] Notestein, *D'Ewes' Journal*, pp. 51, 87; Willson, *Privy Councillors in the House of Commons*, p. 67; Rex, *University Representation*, p. 148.

other's company. But they were acquaintances of long standing, and their correspondence had frequently gone beyond
merely the official. There had been an exchange of affectionate
pleasantries and many expressions of good wishes from Laud to
Roe and his wife. Laud had, upon occasion, stayed in Roe's
home, and he had known Lady Roe ever since boyhood.[70] The
reader of their correspondence is justified in suspecting that a
measure of mutual respect existed between the two men. But in
all probability Roe was absent when the chain of events that
ended on Tower Hill was begun in the House of Commons.
D'Ewes ascribed Roe's absence to sickness;[71] but, although he
was certainly not in good health at this time, we are surely free
to conjecture that he may have stayed away simply because he
chose not to witness a distasteful act that he was powerless to
prevent.

His absence from the House lasted some eight weeks. He
returned early in February and served on some minor committees,[72] but it seems that another absence quickly followed until
17 April 1641, when he was again appointed to a committee.[73]
The House of Commons was, by this time, discussing the Bill
of Attainder drawn up against the earl of Strafford. But Sir
Thomas Roe took no part in the debate, for his parliamentary
career was once again cut short by a royal summons.

On 24 April 1641 he informed the House that the king had
ordered him to attend the Diet of the German Princes, which
was then being held at Ratisbon. He requested permission to
be absent from the House but asked that, even during his
absence, he should still be considered a member. These requests
were granted and Roe took his leave of the assembly. He was
never to return.

[70] *C.S.P., Dom., 1636–1637*, Archbishop Laud to Roe, 4 August 1636, p.
86; H. R. Trevor-Roper, *Archbishop Laud, 1573–1645* (Hamden, Conn.,
1962), p. 128, where it is said that Lady Roe's father, Sir Thomas Cave,
had been the patron of Laud's earliest living.
[71] Notestein, *D'Ewes' Journal*, p. 330.
[72] *Commons' Journal*, 2:80, 81, 85, 87.
[73] Roe is not mentioned in the *Commons' Journal* between 17 February
and 17 April.

CHAPTER 10
The Last Journey

In 1641, when Sir Thomas Roe took his leave of the House of Commons, the war in Germany had entered its last and most cynical phase. All pretense of fighting for principle had long since been abandoned, and Germany's anguish was being prolonged by the selfish ambitions of France, Sweden, and some of the German princes. Reasonable solutions to the religious and constitutional troubles of the empire had been achieved by the Peace of Prague, which had settled the issue of the ownership of church lands, decreed the dissolution of all armed leagues, and arranged territorial settlements that were soon approved by all the important estates and princes of Germany.

But the treaty made at Prague had not brought peace, for it had failed to resolve at least two important issues. It had not satisfied the territorial claims of France and Sweden, and it had not settled the difficult problems surrounding the claim of the Palatine family to the restoration of its land and titles. These were practically the only questions left as causes for the continuance of the war,[1] so any steps taken toward their solution would presumably move Europe closer to a general peace. Here lay the larger significance of the negotiations in which Sir Thomas Roe was soon to participate.

The fighting in Germany had become confused and, seemingly, aimless. Men wandered from one regiment to another driven, not by the cause that was represented or the religion that was followed, but by rumors of higher wages and a more plentiful food supply.[2] Captains sold their services to the highest bidder. Campaigns were not coordinated. Fighting erupted spasmodically here and there, like scattered and sputtering brush fires. The armies lived off the land like parasites, carrying famine and death to the peasant population. They drew their supplies from the territories through which they passed, then laid waste the land so it could afford no succor to an enemy.

By 1640 it had become clear that this kind of warfare held little promise of substantial gain, so Emperor Ferdinand III had begun to plan for peace. With the approval of the seven electors he arranged to summon a Diet to meet before the end of the year. It was his expressed intention to seek a general settlement on the basis of the Peace of Prague. In that treaty the emperor had agreed to do all in his power to maintain Maximilian of Bavaria as an elector and to ensure that the dignity would stay forever in the possession of his family. Maximilian's electoral title had been won at the expense of the Elector Palatine whose family had persistently refused to recognize its transfer as legal. Now, the forthcoming Diet threatened to sanction the alienation of the title and to strip it irrecoverably from its former holders.

News of the emperor's intentions quickly reached The Hague, where Elizabeth was as alert as ever to any development that might affect the welfare of her family. In May both she and her son wrote letters to Charles I imploring him to send a representative to the Diet to press their interests, and to choose Sir Thomas Roe for the task.[3] The king agreed to do this, and in April 1641 Sir Thomas was appointed to attend the meeting of the Imperial Diet that the emperor had opened some six months earlier in the ancient city of Regensburg.

When the news of the appointment became known some misgivings were expressed about the wisdom of the mission

[1] R. B. Mowat, "The Mission of Sir Thomas Roe to Vienna, 1641–42," *English Historical Review* 25 (1910):264 (hereafter cited as Mowat).
[2] C. V. Wedgwood, *The Thirty Years War* (New York, 1961), pp. 420–21.
[3] *C.S.P., Dom., 1640*, queen of Bohemia to Roe, 21 May 1640, p. 194; ibid., Sir Richard Cave to Secretary Vane, 22 May 1640, pp. 208–209.

and the choice of the ambassador. Charles I had insisted for so long on playing a nondescript role in foreign affairs that it seemed inconceivable that he really meant to assert himself on behalf of his nephew when his own affairs were in such critical condition. The Venetian ambassador was not alone in suspecting that Roe's appointment was little more than an empty and inexpensive gesture designed to convince Elizabeth and her son of Charles I's continuing concern.[4] John Dury, who probably knew Germany as well as any Englishman, also took a gloomy view. He believed that the emperor did not really want peace, that the Diet accordingly would make no real progress, and that there was little prospect of a satisfactory settlement of the affairs of the Palatine family.[5] Even people who were inclined to be more optimistic were obliged to recognize that England's internal dissensions would necessarily weaken her hand at any international conference table. The crowned heads of Europe were not likely to pay much attention to the representative of a king who was having a great deal of difficulty in controlling his own subjects.

Quite apart from these general reservations about the prospects for the Diet, there was more specific criticism of the king's choice of an ambassador. Sir Henry Vane was confident that the king had chosen wisely,[6] but there was no reason to believe that he was a particularly competent judge, and some people who were, perhaps, more objective than the secretary of state were not so sure. It was widely known that Roe was in ill health at the time of his appointment, and his frequent absences from parliament suggested that the gout now had a firm hold on him and made it impossible for him to engage in long periods of sustained work. No one in England could reasonably have questioned Roe's tenacious loyalty to Elizabeth and her cause, but there were people who feared that his

---

[4] *C.S.P., Venetian,* 25:135.

[5] *C.S.P., Dom., 1640,* Dury to Roe, 24 July 1640, pp. 510–12.

[6] *C.S.P., Dom., 1639–1640,* Secretary Vane to Roe, 28 February 1640, p. 494.

very eagerness to serve the queen might lead him to insist on a full restitution and blind him to the possibility of reasonable compromises. Perhaps some less zealous person would have greater chance of success. That these misgivings were widespread and genuine is indicated by the fact that the earl of Arundel and Surrey took the trouble to try to reassure Count Leslie, an adviser of the emperor, of Roe's fitness for the mission:

> For the ambassador, I will give you this true character of him . . . I do verily think that he goes with all possible desire to accommodate this business. I know well he has been formerly thought to be very averse, and do all ill offices to this business, but I assure you he now goes wholly the other way; for he agrees with me that the Prince Elector has never had wise nor well-disposed ministers, that he must accommodate himself to what may with honor be gotten now and hope for the rest by further treaty . . . . In sum I pray be confident of the ambassador as my friend.[7]

Elizabeth and her son (who was still persistently referred to as the "Elector Palatine" in all English correspondence) did not share these misgivings and were well pleased at Roe's appointment. They had leaned heavily upon him for advice in their adversity and felt that they could speak more freely to him than to almost anyone else.[8] There was not the shadow of a doubt of his absolute dedication to their cause, for he had been its champion now for no less than twenty years, and the family had good reason to believe that if anyone could plead its case effectively it was this experienced and loyal old diplomat. They were anxious and eager for him to be about his work.

Some delay was necessitated by Roe's ill health,[9] but by 7 May he had made his way to Gravesend and two days later he

---

[7] *C.S.P., Dom., 1640–1641*, Thomas, earl of Arundel and Surrey to Count Leslie, 9 May 1641, pp. 572–73.

[8] Ibid., Charles Louis to Sir Richard Cave, 30 November 1640, pp. 278–79.

[9] *C.S.P., Venetian*, 25:138.

went aboard a ship appropriately named *Hope*. He was in a melancholy mood, sharply aware of England's deepening troubles. While waiting aboard his ship for a favorable wind he observed that there was not one vessel in the harbor that was fully manned and ready to sail. This he attributed to the fact that no man would serve the king unless he were forced into the royal service. He went on to say that if things did not improve in England he would rather die with honor than outlive the peace and honor of his homeland.[10] These were the thoughts that occupied the mind of an Elizabethan Englishman as the lights of Gravesend dropped into the sea on 11 May 1641 — the eve of the earl of Strafford's execution day.

As had been the case in his mission to the North, Roe was again instructed to call upon the authorities at The Hague before proceeding on his mission. He arrived there late in May and reported that he had been "received with the customary ceremonies and treated with the greatest honour."[11] During his brief stay in the Netherlands he had several audiences with the States General. At the first meeting he described to them the nature and objectives of his mission. Subsequently he presented some complaints from English merchants about Dutch violations of commercial treaties and entered into discussion about controversies between the two East India Companies. He was disturbed to find at The Hague what he called "deeply rooted misunderstandings" between the Prince Elector and the prince of Orange, but hoped that he had successfully dissolved them.[12]

Sir Thomas stayed only a few days in the Dutch capital, but, according to the reports that reached the Venetian secretary, he left an impression of great ability.[13] Secretary Vane assured him of the king's "liking and approbation" of his dealings at

---

[10] *C.S.P., Dom., 1640–1641*, Roe to Secretary Vane, 11 May 1641, pp. 573–74.

[11] *C.S.P., Venetian*, 25:158.

[12] *C.S.P., Dom., 1640–1641*, Roe to [Secretary Vane?], 28 May 1641, p. 589.

[13] *C.S.P., Venetian*, 25:162.

The Hague, while the States General wanted to give him a gift of a fine gold chain. This Sir Thomas declined, asking that it might be saved for his return, by which time he hoped to have done something to deserve it.[14]

From The Hague the ambassador and his party made their way eastward to Arnhem so that Roe could pay his respects to Queen Elizabeth at her summer residence at nearby Rhenen on the Rhine. Next the road led to Brussels in the Spanish Netherlands. There Sir Thomas had some difficulty in getting a pass, but some judicious bribery speeded the wheels of Spanish officialdom,[15] and the party was free to make its way to Frankfurt and, finally, early in July, to arrive in Regensburg. The journey had not been a pleasant one and Sir Thomas must have been glad that his wife had not accompanied him, for en route they had suffered the indignity of being robbed by a band of soldiers.[16] This was far from being an unusual occurrence in Germany in those troubled times. Indeed, just a short while before, the very carefully guarded mission of the earl of Arundel had been attacked on its way to Vienna, and two of the ambassador's party had been killed by the bandits.[17]

When Roe arrived in Regensburg the Diet had been in session for about nine months, and many things had happened to affect in one way or another the conditions under which his negotiations would be conducted. At first an unusual measure of harmony had reigned among the delegates. The emperor's appeal for peace and understanding had been well received; and it had even been agreed that, because of the approach of a Swedish force, the emperor might quarter troops in and around the city. At any time in the previous fifty years this suggestion would have been angrily rejected as an attempt to

[14] *C.S.P., Dom., 1641–1643,* Secretary Vane to Roe, 18 June 1641, p. 16; *C.S.P., Venetian,* 25:162.
[15] *C.S.P., Dom., 1641–1643,* Secretary Vane to Roe, 18 June 1641, p. 16.
[16] Ibid., Vane to Rowe [*sic*], 6 August 1641, p. 75; ibid., Sir Richard Cave to Roe, 8 October 1641, p. 134; *C.S.P., Venetian,* 25:176; *C.S.P., Venetian,* 26:179.
[17] David Ogg, *Europe in the Seventeenth Century* (London, 1956), p. 48.

overawe the meeting.[18] At the end of December the Diet had agreed to consider terms for a general peace settlement based on the Peace of Prague, and even offered a safe conduct to Elizabeth of Bohemia and her daughters should they wish to request of the Diet the pension and dowries suitable to the widow and children of a German prince.[19]

The emperor's influence had reached unusual heights. Since the invasion of Germany by the French and the desertion of the Swedes by their German allies, the war had been transformed from a civil to an external conflict. Some national feeling of resentment had developed against the foreign invaders, and opposition to the emperor by a German prince now smacked of treason. There existed in Germany a unity and solidarity that had been unknown for generations.

Under these conditions the task of Sir Thomas Roe would have been greatly simplified. It would have been much easier to deal with a united empire than with an indefinite number of semisovereign principalities fiercely at odds with each other. But unfortunately these favorable conditions had ceased to exist by the time Roe arrived in Regensburg.

The new, ambitious, and forceful elector of Brandenburg, young Frederick William, negotiated a separate peace with Sweden, and this successful unilateral action seemed to demonstrate to many of the princes at the Diet the foolishness of trying to negotiate a general peace through the lumbering machinery of an imperial Diet. The ancient particularism of the German states was almost instantly revived. Was the emperor keeping the war alive as a means of furthering his own political objectives and subverting the rights of the individual princes? The ease with which Brandenburg had negotiated an advantageous peace seemed at least to suggest that he was. Brandenburg's action "had transformed Ferdinand's Diet from a demonstration of imperial unity to a revelation of imperial weakness."[20] Suspicions and animosities that had lurked be-

---

[18] Wedgwood, *The Thirty Years War*, p. 421.
[19] Ibid., pp. 421–22.
[20] Ibid., p. 423.

neath the surface since the Treaty of Prague were once again
abroad in full daylight and Roe's task was made immeasurably
more complex. Under these circumstances, how was he to
achieve any kind of consensus in favor of his proposals?

In the light of these conditions Roe's instructions seemed
unrealistically ambitious. The English government had felt that
it could not properly ask for less than the full reinstatement of
the Prince Palatine to all the lands that his father had once
owned and to the full dignity and privileges of an elector. A
lesser demand would have amounted to a tacit admission of the
Diet's power to deprive Charles Louis of his inheritance. In
practice, however, it had been recognized by officials in London that there was almost no possibility that the Diet would
grant such concessions, so a set of less ambitious objectives had
been decided upon. If, as was expected, the initial demand met
with a firm refusal, Roe was to abandon his efforts to regain
the Upper Palatinate and the electoral vote with the idea of
resuming them at some future and more opportune time. He
was, however, to insist with all his might upon the restoration
of the Lower Palatinate. But initially he was to do everything
in his power to win the full prize and was to fall back upon his
lesser goal only upon instructions from home.[21]

As he approached his task the ambassador himself saw little
cause for optimism. The Diet had fallen into bickering dissension after the announcement of the peace between Sweden and
Brandenburg, and Roe soon came to believe that a number of
the more influential delegates were actually opposed to a settlement and wanted nothing so much as to make the negotiations
drag on all winter.[22] He knew that the duke of Bavaria—the
man now in possession of the lands and titles Roe had come to
reclaim—would be his most determined opponent, and soon
after his arrival he observed that many of the representatives
were governed by Maximilian who, in turn, was governed by

[21] Roe's instructions are described at some length in the report of the
Venetian ambassador; *C.S.P., Venetian,* 25:144.

[22] Mowat, p. 267; citing *State Papers, Germany,* Roe to Sir Henry
Vane, 15 October 1641.

his own selfish interests.[23] He wrote home to express the hope that the king would not expect too much from the negotiations.[24]

Roe was also made aware that the course of his negotiations was affected in a direct way by happenings in England. It was widely recognized at the Diet that the internal troubles of England made it improbable that she would make any strong move to aid the Palatinate. The Spanish and Bavarian representatives even suggested that Roe's authority from the king was no longer sufficient for one who claimed to represent England. They told him that two more men should have been sent to represent the views of the English and Scottish parliaments.[25] This suggestion infuriated Roe, but it seemed to have been answered effectively when the English parliament expressed its strong support of the Palatine cause and when the Scottish parliament declared its intention of sending 10,000 troops to Germany for the Prince Elector's service.[26] These declarations caused Roe's hopes to soar, but the Germans were still skeptical, for they felt that the declarations would add great authority and weight to Roe's demands.[27] But then, in October, the Irish Rebellion occurred and immediately demanded the full

[23] *C.S.P., Dom., 1641–1643*, Roe to Sir Henry Vane, 3 August 1641, p. 71.

[24] Ibid.

[25] *C.S.P., Venetian*, 25:262–63; *A Catalogue of the Harleian Manuscripts in the British Museum* ([London], 1808–1812). The manuscript that is numbered 1901 in this collection is "A paperbook in fol . . . . being a second tome belonging to a former, designed to be a complete Register of the severall Acts, Negotiations, & Letters relating to Sir Thomas Roes Ambassage in Germany for bringing about the Restoration of the Palatine-Family . . . ." Much of the account was written by Roe himself and it will be referred to frequently in what follows. The manuscript will be cited as Harl. MSS 1901, and the page, or folio number will be given, thus: Harl. MSS 1901, f. 5.

[26] *Commons' Journal*, 2:201; *C.S.P., Dom., 1641–1643*, "Declaration of the Parliament of Scotland on Behalf of the Prince Elector Palatine," 12 November 1641, p. 165; ibid., queen of Bohemia to Roe, 11 September 1641, p. 121.

[27] Sir William Boswell, the ambassador at The Hague, believed that the declarations would "give wings to your negotiation and weight to the uttermost of your demands"; ibid., Sir William Boswell to Roe, 13 December 1641, p. 198.

attention of both parliaments. Interest in the Regensburg negotiations evaporated and Elizabeth, in bitter frustration, could only believe that the Irish business was a wicked scheme provoked from Vienna and Madrid for the purpose of preventing her brother, the English king, from extending aid to the Palatine house.[28]

Roe found himself neglected and seemingly forgotten by the authorities in England. His situation provides an interesting commentary on England's stature in world affairs during the autumn of 1641. This ambassador, this personal representative of the king of England, was desperately short of money but was told that even his modest requests were more than the king could afford to pay. He was advised to borrow some money privately.[29] He repeatedly wrote home for instructions, but time and again he received a reply that contained a sentence like this one: "His Majesty being overtaken with one weighty occasion on the neck of another has not yet leisure to give you further directions."[30] It is not surprising that he became despondent and gave himself over to the melancholy belief that seems always to have haunted him—the fear that he had been consigned to the political wilderness and cut off from the approbation of his king.[31]

It would have been unrealistic for Roe to believe that he could wield much influence under these circumstances. He strove to uphold the prestige of his country by speaking with authority and occasional indignation,[32] but the Diet continued

[28] Ibid., queen of Bohemia to Roe, 22 November 1641, p. 172.

[29] Mowat, p. 268; citing *State Papers, Germany*, 10 October 1641. Roe was obliged to borrow some money from Sir Paul Pindar, a man who had already made some very substantial loans to the Crown (ibid., pp. 268–73).

[30] *C.S.P., Dom., 1641–1643*, Secretary Nicholas to Roe, 10 March 1642, p. 295.

[31] Mowat, pp. 267–68; quoting *State Papers, Germany*, Roe to Sir Henry Vane, 15 October 1641.

[32] Harl. MSS 1901, f. 5 (Roe's "Relation of a Conference between the Mediatours & me"); ibid., f. 12b (Letter from Roe to Count Trautsmandorff); ibid., f. 25b (Roe's "Relation of a conference between Sir Thomas, the Danish and the Mentz Ambassadors, May 27, 1642"); *C.S.P., Venetian*, 25:259.

to bog down in dissension and delay so that few people can have been sorry or surprised when, on 10 November, the emperor dissolved it and withdrew in disgust to Vienna, leaving those delegates who wished to do so to follow him there at their leisure. Even before the dissolution of the Diet, Roe had recognized the absolute futility of the negotiations and had turned his efforts to another objective that he could more realistically hope to achieve and which would, at the same time, be of real help and comfort to the Palatine house.

In 1638 Prince Rupert, the third son of the queen of Bohemia, had been taken prisoner while engaged with his older brother in the invasion of Westphalia. He was imprisoned at Linz, the capital of Upper Austria, and, needless to say, his captivity was the cause of much grief to his mother who seemed to have a special affection for her adventurous and headstrong young son.[33] Convinced that no headway could be made in the negotiations that were his primary concern, Roe applied himself wholeheartedly to the task of bringing about the release of the young prince. Elizabeth was not the least bit optimistic about the chances of success,[34] for it seemed rather obvious that the emperor would want to keep Rupert, if for no other reason than to use him as a pawn in the main negotiations.[35] But Roe was apparently undeterred by such possibilities, so he pressed forward and by mid-October, after less than two months of bargaining, he was successful. The only condition imposed by the prince's imperial captors was that he should promise never again to take up arms against the emperor.[36] This promise was readily given by Rupert, who perhaps was already anticipating plenty of exciting employment in the armies of his uncle. The prince wrote an enthusiastic

[33] A. W. Ward, "Elizabeth, Queen of Bohemia" in *D.N.B.*, 6:656.
[34] *C.S.P., Dom., 1641–1643*, queen of Bohemia to Roe, 11 September 1641, pp. 120–21; ibid., Lady Elizabeth Palatine to Roe, 16 August 1641, pp. 91–92.
[35] Ibid., Charles Louis, Elector Palatine to Roe, 18 October 1641, p. 141.
[36] *C.S.P., Venetian*, 25:237.

letter to Roe, thanking him for his service and entrusting his immediate future to the hands of his English friend.[37] The two men arranged a meetingplace, then traveled together to Vienna where they arrived early in November. Sir Thomas quickly became fond of Rupert. His admiration of the vigorous young man was tinged perhaps with a slight envy of Rupert's youthful enthusiasm and impatient energy. Conscious of his own advancing age, and increasingly bothered with the gout, Roe saw the prince as "a young eagle new on his wings . . . longing to take flight,"[38] and saw no reason to retract an earlier statement in which he had characterized Rupert as being "full of spirit and action" and too virile to be wasted in the softness and the entanglements of pleasure.[39] These last words had been written in 1636, but they were surely appropriate to describe the man who would later build such a romantic reputation in the military and naval service of the Royalist cause.

Rupert did not stay long with Roe in Vienna. By 10 December he had rejoined his mother at The Hague, and soon after that he made his way to England to thank Charles I for procuring his freedom.[40] His mother and his elder brother, meanwhile, were expressing their appreciation to Roe, Rupert's more immediate liberator. Elizabeth said that she could not sufficiently express her gratitude to Sir Thomas for securing her son's release, nor did her present circumstances permit her adequately to demonstrate her appreciation. She had, however, petitioned her brother to make Roe the treasurer of England. If he did not do so she would insist on believing that "the honester the man, the worse the luck."[41] The Prince Elector

[37] *C.S.P., Dom., 1641–1643,* Prince Rupert to Roe, 4 October 1641, p. 131.

[38] Mowat, p. 267; quoting *State Papers, Germany,* Roe to Sir Henry Vane, 25 October 1641.

[39] *C.S.P., Dom., 1636–1637,* Roe to the queen of Bohemia, 1 May 1636, p. 402.

[40] C. H. Firth, "Rupert, Count Palatine of the Rhine and Duke of Bavaria," in *D.N.B.,* 17:406.

[41] *C.S.P., Dom., 1641–1643,* queen of Bohemia to Roe, 13 December 1641, p. 198; ibid., same to same, 6 December 1641, p. 191.

called Roe's successful negotiation a "masterpiece," and said that he was trying to persuade the king to appoint Roe to the position of secretary of state made vacant by the dismissal of Sir Henry Vane.[42] Roe did not get either of these positions. Elizabeth, who professed keen disappointment, commiserated with Roe, but then added philosophically that perhaps it was just as well, after all, that he had not received a royal appointment, "for if the King yield to the Parliament's request all will be cashiered that are now in place or office."[43]

With the successful conclusion of his efforts on behalf of Rupert, Roe turned his attention once again to the principal objective of his mission—the reinstatement of the Prince Palatine to the lands and dignity of his father. A series of negotiations was begun in Vienna among Roe and the representatives of the empire, Spain, and Bavaria. The ambassadors of Denmark and Mainz served as the "directors" of the mediation attempts.[44]

Roe believed that the emperor sincerely wanted a settlement. He was in favor now of a general peace, but that was unlikely so long as Maximilian's legalized retention of the Palatinate reminded the other German princes of their own insecurity. Maximilian's earlier disregard for the Germanic Liberties was coming back to haunt him now. He found himself under mounting pressure to disgorge at least some of the land he had taken. But he had no intention of doing so, and in his refusal he had the full backing of Spain.

Under these circumstances no progress was possible in the negotiations. Roe continued to believe that the emperor wanted a settlement, and he blamed the impasse wholly on the other two states who were, he thought, deliberately procras-

---

[42] Ibid., Charles Louis, Elector Palatine, to Roe, 18 October 1641, p. 141; ibid., same to same, 17 December 1641, p. 204.

[43] Ibid., queen of Bohemia to Roe, 7 March 1642, p. 294.

[44] Harl. MSS 1901, f. 5 (Roe's "Relation of a conference between the Mediatours & me"). Although Sir Thomas writes of the ambassador of "Mentz," it is clear that "Mainz" is intended. He speaks of the ambassador as having been sent by the elector.

tinating in the belief that deepening troubles in England and Ireland would undermine the English position still further.[45] With a conviction he can hardly have felt, Roe warned them that they made a grave mistake. In an effort to speed up the lagging negotiations he announced on more than one occasion that he would return to England unless some satisfactory arrangements were not soon concluded.[46] This attempted coercion had no noticeable result and by the end of February it was known in London that the ambassador had requested permission to return home.[47] Queen Elizabeth and Charles Louis reluctantly agreed that this seemed to be the wisest course. Elizabeth felt that it would be detrimental to the honor of the king of England for his ambassador to stay longer and suffer the continued abuse of the rival negotiators.[48] The prince assured Sir Thomas that no one blamed him for his readiness to leave a hopelessly deadlocked conference and expressed his complete satisfaction with the efforts Roe had made on his behalf.[49]

Despite the fact that in March, after five months of frustrated effort, Roe had not achieved a single one of his objectives, he was not granted permission to return home. It was evidently felt in London that England should not withdraw from the negotiations and thus lay herself open to the charge of having wrecked them. In taking this stand the government of Charles I was displaying an unusual measure of tenacity and, late in March, it reaped a modest reward. First, the mediators decided upon the form that any treaty should take; and then,

[45] *C.S.P., Venetian*, 25:259; Harl. MSS f. 34b (Letter from Roe to the Prince Elector.) He says that his opponents feel the prince will soon be "so desperate by the troubles of England that he will at last accept of anything and be forced to quitt all clayme to the Vpper Palitinate [*sic*] & Dignity."

[46] *C.S.P., Venetian*, 25:242. Similar threats to return to England are referred to on pages 253, 270, and 287.

[47] Ibid., p. 298.

[48] *C.S.P., Dom., 1641–1643*, queen of Bohemia to Roe, 7 February 1642, p. 276.

[49] Ibid., Charles Louis, Elector Palatine, to Roe, 23 February 1642, p. 289.

word came from London that Roe was to fall back upon his second, and less ambitious, set of objectives—the restoration of only the Lower Palatinate and the postponement of the dispute over the other lands and the electoral privileges until some later time.[50] These demands were much more realistic and there was now at least room to hope for some progress.

In Vienna the negotiators soon agreed that their efforts would fall into two principal parts: first, the emperor would request of Spain and Bavaria that their holdings in the Palatinate be turned over to him; then, when this had been done, he would make known to Roe his price for transferring the land to Charles Louis.[51]

This was progress of a kind. The method of approach at least had been agreed upon. The first step was up to the emperor: what would he give the duke of Bavaria for the lands in the Lower Palatinate? Maximilian professed to be eager to hear the imperial offer. He declared himself ready to give up some of the land he had seized in the Palatinate and willing to enter upon a treaty the day after the emperor's terms were known.[52] Roe was not convinced. He suspected collusion among his opponents and still believed that it was their purpose "to weary us out, sprung from our own distempers."[53]

His caution was well founded, for the fundamental difficulty of the negotiations remained: no progress could be made without the consent of Maximilian who, in having the actual possession of the disputed lands, held an unbeatable trump. Even with the best will in the world the emperor could not come to an agreement with Roe until he had first accommodated Maximilian.

For almost a month the English ambassador awaited some news from the emperor. When none came it obviously meant that the emperor was finding it impossible himself to reach

---

[50] Ibid., Secretary Nicholas to Roe, 27 March 1642, pp. 301–302; ibid., Charles Louis, Elector Palatine, to Roe, 26 March 1642, p. 301.

[51] Harl. MSS 1901, f. 8b (Letter from Roe to the earl of Arundel).

[52] Ibid., f. 10 (Letter from Roe to Mr. Secretary Nicholas).

[53] Ibid.

agreement with Bavaria. This agreement Sir Thomas regarded as crucial to the success of his own efforts. If Maximilian and Ferdinand could find some mutually acceptable terms then Roe himself would be able to move ahead into his talks with the imperial representative. If not, he would have to negotiate with Bavaria and the empire separately, and he feared that would prove "uery knotty."[54]

At last, on 20 April Roe learned that the emperor's declaration concerning the Lower Palatinate was ready, but that it was being held up until some of the leading German princes could be given a chance to express their views about it.[55] Roe interpreted this as being quite contrary to the procedure that had been agreed upon, and he angrily protested to the mediators and sought to give weight to his words by asserting his readiness to return home.[56] But this threat was now hopelessly ineffective and it was contemptuously said that if the English ambassador wished to return to his country, no one in Vienna would stand in his way.[57] A protesting letter to the imperial representative, Count Trautmansdorff, was scarcely more successful; it simply drew the calm assurance that the ambassador would soon have the emperor's proposals on the question of the restitution.[58]

Finally, at the end of April, the mediators presented Roe with four papers that contained the terms proposed by the emperor and the other "interested parties."[59] One glance was sufficient to indicate to Roe that the proposed terms were (in his words) "absurd, unjust, dishonourable . . . impossible," and deserving of no answer.[60] He reported to the secretary of

[54] Ibid., f. 11b (Letter from Roe to Sir Arthur Hopton).
[55] Ibid., f. 12 (Letter from Roe to Mr. Secretary Nicholas).
[56] Ibid., f. 12b (Letter from Roe to Count Trautmansdorff).
[57] Ibid., f. 22b (Letter from Roe to Mr. Secretary Nicholas). Sir Thomas was reporting a comment made by "an important councillor" to an English priest in Vienna.
[58] Ibid., f. 14 (Letter from Roe to Mr. Secretary Nicholas).
[59] Ibid., f. 15b ("Relation of a Conference betweene the Ambassadors Mediator & Sir Thomas, upon their presentation of the long expected Declaration").
[60] Ibid., f. 18 (Letter from Roe to the queen of Bohemia).

state that he could not even think of them without indignation and "breaking out into Passion."[61] So firmly did he express his indignation to the mediators that they expressed the hope that more moderate and tolerable conditions would be proposed. Roe calmed himself sufficiently to indicate that he would gladly listen to any further proposals.[62]

When his indignation had cooled, Roe attempted to give his superiors in England a more dispassionate appraisal of the negotiations. He was inclined to excuse the emperor by pointing out that he had never needed the support and friendship of Bavaria more than he did at that moment. The satisfaction of Bavaria was a cardinal principle of imperial diplomacy. It was this fact that was causing the emperor's demands upon England to be exorbitant; Bavaria's demands upon him were high. The proposals presented to Roe had stipulated that the Lower Palatinate would be restored in return for England's maintaining 10,000 troops for the imperial armies. The price for the Upper Palatinate would be the payment to Bavaria of a great sum of money. (Sir Thomas was secretly informed that £900,000 was the figure Maximilian had in mind.) The price for the restoration of the electoral dignity was not specified, but Roe suspected that it would amount to some arrangement that would "weaken the whole frame of the Reformed Religion in the Empire."[63] Roe professed to see the hand of Bavaria behind all these excessive demands. He was still confident that the emperor wanted to settle the matter and that the real barrier to the conclusion of an agreement was the "Covetousness and Selfe-Loue" of the Bavarian duke.[64]

There was no possibility that England would meet the demands put forward in the papers presented to Roe in Vienna, but the ambassador did not, on that account, wish to break off the negotiations completely. Having noted Bavaria's insistence on some monetary payment, Sir Thomas offered six hundred

[61] Ibid., f. 16b (Letter from Roe to Mr. Secretary Nicholas).
[62] Ibid., f. 18 (Letter from Roe to Sir William Boswell).
[63] Ibid., f. 19 (Letter from Roe to Mr. Secretary Nicholas).
[64] Ibid., f. 20 (Letter from Roe to Sir Arthur Hopton).

thousand dollars paid over a reasonable period of time. But even as he did so he pointed out that he had no authority from home to make such an offer and that his proposal was therefore to be regarded as being dependent upon subsequent ratification from England. The mediators pressed him to increase the amount of his offer, but he flatly refused.[65]

In this wrangling over money it was possible to detect a subtle moral victory for the English side. Perhaps it was not an important one, but the wresting of even a slight advantage from such adverse conditions was a substantial achievement on Roe's part and may be thought worthy of mention. The ambassador recognized that his opponents, by demanding cash as their price for the Upper Palatinate and by failing to reject his claims on principle, had implied their recognition of the validity of the Palatine cause. They had made it clear that, for them, the obstacle to peace was not a principle but a sum of money and that the war was being prolonged, at least in part, by their greed.[66]

It seemed that Roe at last had a slight advantage, and we can surely suspect that the offer to pay a sum of money to Bavaria was intended as the first step in its exploitation. Sir Thomas knew that there was not the slightest possibility that the king would approve his proposal to pay Bavaria six hundred thousand dollars. But the offer was worth making as a means of further advertising the Bavarian demands, of underscoring the avarice of the duke, of branding him as the main obstacle to peace, and thus undermining his position and influence in a land that was mortally tired of war.

For the first time since his departure from England Roe could feel that he was making some headway toward the achievement of his primary goal. But this happy conviction proved to be short-lived, and the cause of its demise came from an unexpected quarter.

[65] Ibid., f. 23 (Roe's notes on the negotiations from 18–24 May 1642); ibid., f. 25b (Roe's "Relation of a conference between Sir Thomas, the Danish and the Mentz ambassadors, May 27, 1642").
[66] Roe made this point in several dispatches, ibid., ff. 34b, 42, 52, 63.

On 11 May 1642 the two Houses of the English parliament listened to charges that were directed by the French minister in London against Sir Thomas Roe.[67] The French minister asserted that the ambassador, on instructions from home, had promised that England would join the emperor in an offensive and defensive alliance in return for the restoration of the Palatinate.[68] From the French point of view the accusation represented a shrewd stroke. In normal times it would probably have been scoffed at; but now, with the atmosphere in England charged with tension and distrust, there was an inclination on the part of many to believe that the king had, in fact, tried to obtain a treaty for the Prince Elector by means that parliament would not have approved.[69]

It was rather clear that the French aim was to drive still deeper the wedge between Charles I and his people. To do this they had cunningly used a device that would revive in England the old fears against a papist alliance and, at the same time, renew the disputed issue of the Crown's power to conclude treaties—an issue that had been debated recently in the House of Commons.[70] Different people placed different interpretations upon the French motives but Clarendon in his history seems to have voiced the official view accurately when he dismissed the incident by stating flatly that "there was not the least ground or pretence for [the charge], sir Thomas Roe having never made such offer, or anything like it."[71] The government made its stand known when it instructed the English representative in Paris, Richard Browne, to complain to the French king about the charges against Roe and to demand that they be disavowed.[72]

[67] *Commons' Journal*, 2:571; *C.S.P., Dom., 1641–1643*, Philip Burlamachi to Roe, 13 May 1642, p. 320.
[68] Ibid.
[69] Ibid.
[70] Ibid., queen of Bohemia to Roe, 2 June 1642, p. 330.
[71] Clarendon, Edward Hyde, earl of, *History of the Rebellion and Civil Wars in England begun in the year 1641* (Oxford, 1888), 6:179.
[72] *C.S.P., Dom., 1641–1643*, Secretary Nicholas to Roe, 25 May 1642, p. 331.

It is highly probable that all these events had taken place before Roe ever learned that his name was at the center of a controversy in England. As soon as he did learn of the accusation that had been brought against him he wrote vigorous letters of protest and denial to the earl of Holland (who had presented the French complaint in the House of Lords) and to Edmund Waller, who was a member of the House of Commons. To each man he sent a "Protestation for the Vindication of His Honesty and Reputation," and this was read on 8 July to a conference of committees of both houses of parliament that had been convened to consider Roe's reply to the French charges. The "Protestation" was entered in the Journal of the House of Commons, and copies were sent to the king and to the French ambassador. King Charles professed himself to be well pleased with Roe's declaration, and the ambassador stated that he, too, was satisfied with it.[73]

But the damage had already been done. The charges brought against him had come to the attention of the Court of Vienna and Roe felt that they had impaired his effectiveness as a negotiator.[74] It was rumored around the city that, during the discussion in parliament, one of the members had said that the Commons had no desire to oblige, or to be obliged to, the House of Austria and no wish to help the Prince Elector Palatine. This talk had deepened the suspicion in Vienna that parliament might refuse to honor any commitments made by Roe. His stature and authority were seriously impaired and he saw no prospect now of carrying his negotiations to any successful conclusion.

In London, the charges served to demonstrate that Roe's mission was potentially dangerous—that it could be used by England's enemies to create more troubles at home than it was likely to win advantages abroad. The government decided that

[73] Harl. MSS 1901, f. 28b (Letter from Roe to the earl of Holland); ibid., f. 29 (Letter from Roe to Edmund Waller); *Commons' Journal*, 2:663–64, 669–70; C.S.P., *Dom.*, *1641–1643*, Sir Edward Nicholas to Roe, 6 July 1642, p. 351. Roe's protestation of innocence is printed in *Commons' Journal*, 2:663–64.

[74] Harl. MSS 1901, f. 29b (Letter from Roe to Sir William Boswell).

it would be wise to recall its ambassador and by 13 June it was known in Vienna that he had received permission from London to return home and was preparing to leave for England within two weeks.[75] When the mediators heard of his intentions they tried to delay his departure by raising new hopes of a settlement. Roe saw the futility of such hopes, but at the same time did not want to leave Vienna so hastily as to run the risk of incurring the blame for breaking off the negotiations.[76]

He had no doubt as to where that responsibility belonged. He firmly believed that it was the unrealistic demands of the duke of Bavaria stiffened by Spain that had constituted the real stumbling block in the way of peace. He continued to believe that the emperor (whom Roe characterized as a "most benigne and sweete Prince"[77]) sincerely desired a settlement and that Maximilian was the "rock whereon the Peace doth shiprack."[78]

During the last days of his mission Roe sought to achieve two objectives. One of these was to make sure that the breakdown of negotiations could not be blamed upon England. This was fairly clear from the nature of things, but some definite, dramatic evidence would make the point doubly sure. Roe was singularly successful in finding it. He had suspected all along that Spain had been playing an important role in preventing any tangible progress. Her influence had been exerted for the most part behind the scenes, giving support to the duke of Bavaria who had been the more obvious obstacle. But Roe considered that Spanish policy was devoted to maintaining the status quo and keeping her hold on the parts of the Palatinate she occupied. He further suspected that, as a means of making sure that the negotiations would be unproductive the Spanish representatives had actually come to Vienna without plenipo-

[75] Ibid., f. 30 (Letter from Roe to Mr. Secretary Nicholas); ibid., f. 31 (Letter from Roe to Sir Arthur Hopton); C. V. Wedgwood, *The Great Rebellion: The King's War, 1641–1647* (New York, 1959), p. 98.
[76] Ibid., f. 32 (Letter from Roe to the queen of England).
[77] Ibid., f. 31 (Letter from Roe to Sir Arthur Hopton); ibid., f. 27 (Letter from Roe to Lord Faulkland).
[78] Ibid., f. 31 (Letter from Roe to Sir Arthur Hopton).

tentiary powers. He wrote home: "I have discovered and found the foxe in his burrow; but cannot yet absolutely unkennel him. I shall this weeke fire him out, all upon a necessitye to make the Spaniards speak or confesse their tongues are tyed . . . then . . . the envy shall not lye singly upon me, if the treaty brake."[79] He was successful in "firing out the foxe," and the Spaniards were forced to "profes pleynly they cannot treate without new plenipotences." It was clear where the blame lay.

His second objective in the closing days of his stay in Vienna was to prepare the ground for possible later negotiations by securing some statement to the effect that in theory and in principle the Palatine prince was "restorable"—that his satisfaction did "not depend upon the meritts of the Cause, but upon Conditions; and those of a Summe of money."[80] Roe successfully achieved this goal too. He was able to secure a general admission that the Prince Elector would have to be accommodated if the general peace were to be made secure. The representatives also acknowledged that the Prince Elector's cause was "treatable," and Roe took this to mean that they admitted its validity. Finally, Sir Thomas won from the duke of Bavaria a promise that he would negotiate at some future date not only about the Lower Palatinate but also about the Upper Palatinate and the electoral title.[81]

In these agreements Roe found ample cause for optimism. He was confident that he was leaving the cause in much better condition than he had found it and that his negotiations had at least laid the groundwork for future success.[82] He believed that, once the "Bavarian obstruction" was removed, they would be "able to make a good end of bad busines."[83] In this connection he pointed out that the duke was already in his

---

[79] Mowat, p. 272, quoting *State Papers, Germany*, 24 November 1641.
[80] Ibid., f. 42 (Letter from Roe to the earl of Arundel); ibid., f. 34b (Letter from Roe to the Prince Elector).
[81] Ibid.
[82] Ibid., f. 18 (Letter from Roe to the queen of Bohemia).
[83] Ibid., f. 36 (Letter from Roe to Mr. Secretary Nicholas).

seventies and that when he died the restoration of the Palatinate and the dignities that went with it should be easy to achieve. "If the general good inclination be dexterously preserved," he was confident that better terms could be won at some later conference than were possible at that one.[84]

At the last conference he had with the emperor, Roe sought to ensure that the modest advantages he had won would not be allowed to lapse. He obtained an agreement that the negotiations would be kept alive by means of correspondence among England, the empire, and Denmark; and he pointed out in specific terms two minimum conditions that would have to be met before serious conferences could be resumed. First, the sum of money demanded by the duke of Bavaria for the restoration of the Upper Palatinate would have to be reduced to a reasonable sum; and second, the duke would have to declare explicitly his willingness to negotiate about the succession of his electoral title. Sir Thomas asserted that "until his Majesty our King may have some assurance in these poynts, there is little hope either to renew the Treaty, or to perfect it."[85]

The conference with the emperor was one of the last activities in which Roe engaged before leaving Vienna. On 28 June he had written to some of the other negotiators to take his leave of them, and on 12 July he started on the long journey home.[86] He left behind him some favorable impressions. The emperor, who had had plenty of opportunity to see Roe at work, was heard to say on several occasions: "I have met with many gallant persons of many nations, but I scarce ever met with an ambassador till now."[87] As a token of his esteem he presented the departing Englishman with "a cabinet with various pretty devices in silver gilt, worth about 1,000 thalers."[88]

[84] Ibid., f. 34b (Letter from Roe to the Prince Elector).

[85] Ibid., f. 43; ibid., f. 46 (Letter from Roe to Count Lesley).

[86] Ibid., f. 37b (Letters from Roe to Dr. Richel, chancellor of Bavaria, and to the bishop of Wurtzburgh); *C.S.P., Venetian,* 1642–1643, p. 98.

[87] Anthony A. Wood, *Athenae Oxonienses,* ed. and continued by Philip Bliss (London, 1813–1820), 3:114.

[88] *C.S.P., Venetian,* 25:98–99.

Roe's homeward journey seems to have been uneventful. He was in Cologne by the beginning of August and soon after that he arrived at The Hague.[89] Once again, he made a report to the States General, telling them about his negotiations and, at the same time, presenting some grievances from English merchants. He reported that he "received a cold answere, as if they were not dispossessed of some Jealousye," but, despite this indication of discontent, the States General insisted upon giving Sir Thomas the gold chain that had been offered to him earlier.[90]

Although Roe's mission had kept him away from England for more than a year, he had little wish to return, for the breach between King Charles and the parliament had now become a chasm. In June parliament had submitted to the king the "Nineteen Propositions," a series of demands that Charles had called a "mockery and a scorn" and which he had contemptuously rejected. In July parliament had appointed a committee of public safety and put the earl of Essex in charge of the parliamentary army. In August, while Roe was at The Hague, the final step in the descent to war had been taken, for on 22 August, Charles raised the royal standard at Nottingham and thus initiated the military phase of the "Great Rebellion."

[89] G. H. Turnbull, *Hartlib, Dury and Comenius: Gleanings from Hartlib's Papers* (Liverpool, 1947), p. 230. Turnbull cites a letter from Dury to Hartlib, dated 10 August (O.S.), and written at The Hague, in which it is stated that Roe had arrived the previous day.

[90] Harl. MSS 1901, f. 41 (Letter from Roe to Mr. Secretary Nicholas).

CHAPTER *11*

An Unhappy Ending

ROE left The Hague with a heavy heart. He usually looked forward to getting home, but this time it was different. His loyalties in the conflict now beginning were terribly divided, and he saw that the mere act of going home would put him in the position of having to make a choice between the two sides. His friend the elector joined his daughter in trying to persuade him to stay in Holland, but he refused.[1] He felt that he should go to England and try to put himself between the forces of king and parliament, praying God to heal the nation's wounds, or else to take his life so he would not have to feel them.[2]

The ambiguity of his position was demonstrated when he arrived in London in September. An unfriendly mob jeered him as a royalist and, at the same time, he was forbidden by the king to join the cavaliers at York.[3] He was distrusted by both sides; and, in a sense, this was the natural fruit of his life's work. His deep affection for some members of the royal family was well known. Most of his life had been spent in the service of the Crown. He had been a courtier and retained friendships with men who were closely associated with the formulation and direction of royal policies. On the other hand, he had been a persistent critic of many of these policies and had spoken against them in the House of Commons and in an endless stream of letters to people in and out of government. His religious orthodoxy was suspect, and, in any case, his advanced age and failing health made it doubtful that he could have rendered any important service. He dreamed of playing the role of mediator, and time and again he offered his services.[4] But advocates of compromise must have sufficient strength or reputation to command the respect of both sides. Roe did not have these things, and his dream never material- ized. Instead of being a mediator he was merely a man in the middle; attracted to both sides, distrusted for his neutrality, and welcome in neither camp.

With Roe himself taking a neutral position it is difficult now to estimate what his inner thoughts and private loyalties might have been. Some things suggest that he leaned, if anything, toward the parliamentary side. He was active in the Long Parliament as late as April 1641 and was, on the whole, in favor of the reforms which that body contemplated. Until the time of his departure for the Continent it seemed that he was willing to go along with the parliament. The letters that he wrote from Ratisbon and Vienna were entirely noncommital. They reveal nothing of his personal feelings about events in England. Indeed, they suggest that he was interested in English affairs only insofar as they had some bearing on his negotia- tions. However, his reports were directed to the king or to a secretary of state, and it could be argued that his reluctance to write in them about English affairs suggests a certain cir- cumspection. It is difficult to believe that he would not have made some reference to the great events in England if his opinions had been in line with those of the people with whom he corresponded. The implication is that Roe withheld com- ment because his views were at odds with those of the king. This may or may not have been the case, but we do know that, while Roe was at The Hague, the Venetian ambassador there gathered the impression that he had "a strong leaning to the party opposed to his sovereign."[5]

Upon returning to England Roe sought permission to go

---

[1] *C.S.P., Dom., 1644,* Charles Louis to Roe, 7 March 1644, p. 36.
[2] *C.S.P., Venetian,* 26:139.
[3] *C.S.P., Dom., 1641–1643,* Charles Louis to Roe, 6 October 1642, p. 398; ibid., queen of Bohemia to Roe, 28 October, 1642, p. 403.
[4] Harl. MSS 1901, f. 84b, Roe to the Prince Elector, 18 October 1642; ibid., f. 49, Roe to the queen of Bohemia, 19 October 1642; see also ibid., ff. 120b, 74, 80, 81, 110b; *C.S.P., Dom., 1641–1643,* Secretary Nicholas to Roe, 6 December 1643, p. 503.
[5] *C.S.P., Venetian,* 26:151.

before the king to report on his embassy.[6] Otherwise he tried to adopt the neutral posture that would qualify him for the mediator's role he sought. During this period he was careful not to break his connection with either side. He continued to write to the king, while still regarding himself as a member of the House of Commons.[7] Tirelessly he expounded the virtues of moderation and compromise; pointedly he complained that there was no mediator working to bring the two sides together.[8]

Not for the first time in his career, Roe was out of step with his age. In 1642 moderation did not have a chance in England. Both sides were distrustful of neutrality and regarded as enemies all who were not supporters. This was a time for commitment; and it was ironic that a man who had always held so firmly to principle was now, in all honesty, unable to choose. His natural inclination was royalist, but now he believed the king was in the wrong.[9] His strongest affection was for Queen Elizabeth, but how could he serve her without compromising his neutrality? In an age of hot passions he deplored extremism and his hope was not for victory, but for a workable compromise.

This was a difficult and unattractive position that Roe had chosen for himself. The moderate is loved by neither side. Yet there is a sense in which moderation requires the strongest convictions of all. It is hard to hold to the middle way, when all others are taking sides. It takes more courage to stay out of the battle than to join in; more strength to counsel restraint than to call for war. Everything we know about Roe warns us against assuming that he played the moderate because he lacked either conviction or courage. He was neither a moral nor a physical coward, and he tried to stand in the middle

---

[6] Harl. MSS 1901, f. 51, Roe to Secretary Nicholas, 21 December 1642.
[7] *Commons' Journal*, 3 July 1644.
[8] Harl. MSS 1901, f. 84b, Roe to the Prince Elector, 18 October 1642.
[9] J. A. R. Marriott, *The Life and Times of Lucius Cary, Viscount Falkland* (New York, 1907), pp. 292–93, quoting Roe to Falkland, 6 April 1643.

because that is where he thought he ought to be. As an experienced and rather old man of the world he hoped that his most valuable service might be that of helping to heal his country's wounds and restoring that unity which alone could be the springboard of great actions.

He dreamed his dream for several months; and, when at last he saw that he could not persuade the two sides to negotiate, he tried to stir up sentiment in favor of accepting Dutch arbitration.[10] But this, too, proved futile, and he was finally forced to recognize that there was nothing more he could do to help bring the two sides together.

This threw him back upon the project that had engaged his attention for so long, but which by now must have seemed, to everyone but him, a trifling irrelevance. He prepared to resume his labors for the restoration of the Palatinate. This necessitated his drawing closer to the royalist side, but he was apparently willing to do this. He sought permission to go to the king, but at first he was refused, possibly out of consideration for his welfare, but more probably because of some suspicion about his loyalty.[11] However, in January 1643 he was given permission to join the king at Oxford. He went there promptly and, during his audience, was instructed to take charge of royal correspondence relating to German affairs and to keep alive the negotiations with the Palatinate.[12]

Roe was pleased to be given this responsibility and applied himself with characteristic dedication to his task. He did not stay at Oxford, but worked at his home in London and at the one in Woodford. There were obvious inconveniences in this arrangement, and even some danger, for he was occupying a

[10] Harl. MSS 1901, f. 81, Roe to Mr. Burlemachy (the king's financial agent) 23 May 1643; ibid., f. 80, Roe to the Princess Elizabeth, 12 May 1643; ibid., f. 78b, Roe to Sir Dudley Carleton, 11 May 1643.

[11] Ibid., f. 51, Roe to Mr. Secretary Nicholas, 21 December 1642.

[12] Ibid., f. 52, Roe to M. Curtius, 8 February 1643; ibid., f. 57b, Roe to the Prince Elector, 17 February 1643. The group of letters contained in ff. 48–126 was titled by Roe: "Letters written after my coming home; being commanded by His Majesty to continew the Negotiation of the Cause-Palatin, & to correspond with his Ministers beyond Seas."

strange middle ground in which he acted partly as a member of parliament and partly as a minister of the king.[13]

This does not seem to have troubled him, and he threw himself wholeheartedly into his work. He was sufficiently realistic to recognize that England's voice in foreign affairs was now little more than a whisper and that, under those circumstances, the restoration of the Palatinate was unlikely to be achieved. His purpose was simply to keep the issue alive and to prevent it from dropping out of sight. The most effective way of doing this, it appeared, was to make it clear that the restitution of the Palatinate was inextricably involved with the question of a general peace in Germany and that it must, therefore, be an issue in any talk of an overall settlement.

This was an entirely realistic appraisal, and it held out some hope of success, because on the Continent the desire for a general peace was growing stronger every day. The Diet of Ratisbon had been dissolved in November 1641, but before disbanding the delegates had arranged for the following spring a meeting of the "Deputationstag" to discuss certain domestic German problems that needed to be settled before any general peace negotiations were begun with the other powers. It was toward this assembly that Roe's efforts were now directed. He sent his instructions to a certain M. Curtius, a man who had previously served the queen of Bohemia, and who now acted in the capacity of an agent for Roe.

Curtius's role was simply to try to influence the delegates and make them kindly disposed toward the Palatine family. He must have done his work effectively, for real progress was made at the early sessions of the assembly. In April Roe was delighted to learn that the delegates had decided that the

---

[13] Ibid., f. 50, Roe to the Princess Elizabeth, December 1642; ibid., f. 74: "I am guilty of no offense to the Parliament, but in my absence and disability to serve them, wherein I am as guilty toward [His] Matie." See also ibid., f. 87: "I lye at a continuall guard, to protect me from suspition, but I shall preserve my selfe from any guilt: for all my endeavours shall have no end, nor no other can be wholesome for the kingdom, but accommodation."

exclusion of the Palatine family was one of the major obstacles to European peace and that the problem should be taken under consideration. Roe felt that, to this point, he had attained everything he could possibly hope for and that the best course was to sit back and leave matters to the deliberations of the assembly.[14] His hopes received a further boost when a representative of the emperor actually visited Oxford to assure King Charles that the question of the Palatinate would be considered at the general peace conferences which were even then being prepared for the cities of Munster and Osnabruck.[15] Roe spoke of "these fayre and positive" indications[16] and allowed himself to believe that the "Worke [was] almost halfe done."[17] To bring it to a successful conclusion it would obviously be useful to have the English and Palatine view forcefully expressed at the conference. Accordingly, he wrote to the king urging that an ambassador be sent at once. But Charles was either unable or unwilling to press the apparent advantage, and Roe was dismayed when he was told that, "for some domestic respects," the sending of an ambassador was out of the question.[18]

To us, who seek to review these events objectively, it seems altogether reasonable that a king hard pressed by civil war would give scant regard to the fortunes of a distant nephew. But to Roe it must have seemed that, after years of frustrating toil, the whole complex issue had been brought to the brink of satisfactory solution, only to be jeopardized by the king's refusal to send a representative.

He found it most difficult to conceal his disappointment, but he did not give up the work. On the king's command he drew up detailed instructions for the royal ministers abroad, telling them how they might best advance the Palatine cause from their various posts. These instructions were submitted to the

[14] Ibid., ff. 64b, 65, 66, 66b, 67b.
[15] Ibid., f. 101b, Roe to Mr. Brown, 9 August 1643.
[16] Ibid.
[17] Ibid.
[18] *C.S.P., Dom., 1641–1643*, Secretary Nicholas to Roe, 19 May 1643, p. 461.

king at Oxford and then sent on to the ambassadors.[19] He drafted letters to a number of kings and princes who would be represented at the forthcoming conferences; and these letters, which asked the dignitaries to respect the interests of the Palatine family, were also forwarded over the royal signature.[20] Privately, Sir Thomas wrote to English representatives in many lands and urged them to do everything possible to win support and persuade the governments of those countries to regard the restoration of the Palatinate as a necessary part of any European peace.

But even while these efforts were being made, events in Germany were condemning his hopes to disappointment. The duke of Bavaria (who, Sir Thomas was convinced, now controlled the emperor) was working hard to keep the question of the Palatinate off the agenda of the peace conferences. He clearly hoped to settle the matter in his favor at the meeting of the German princes (many of whom he could influence) rather than have it discussed at Munster and Osnabruck by the European powers who would be less susceptible to his persuasions.[21] By late September it was known that France and Sweden shared the English point of view and favored negotiating the problem at the general conference. But there was also evidence that at Frankfurt, where the German princes were still meeting, Bavaria was winning the upper hand and convincing more and more of the princes of the rightness of its cause.

And then on 24 November 1643 the imperialist forces defeated the French at Tuttlingen. Roe foresaw that this would have important repercussions on the conferences and that in particular it would weaken the hopes of the Elector Palatine. "The Austrians, after this blast," he wrote, "will swell beyond measure, and will give the Law in Germany."[22] He was

---

[19] Ibid.

[20] Harl. MSS 1901, ff. 1b, 2, 2b, 3, 3b, 4, 5.

[21] Ibid., f. 108, Roe to Secretary Nicholas, 23 September 1643.

[22] Ibid., f. 117, same to same, 19 December 1643.

quickly confirmed in his fears. Just two days later he reported to the Prince Elector that the Austrians and the Bavarians were so confident since their victory that they were saying openly that they no longer cared where the Palatine cause was debated, because they felt that under any circumstances they were the masters of the situation.[23] The most powerful voice in favor of restitution was now singing a different tune.

These developments made it clear that no decision about the Palatinate would be reached until the general conferences got under way at Munster and Osnabruck and that even then the decision was unlikely to be a favorable one. The opening of those conferences had been arranged for March 1642, but two years later ambassadors were still arriving and no business had been transacted. During this long period of inactivity Roe's fortunes declined drastically and by January 1644 he had become engulfed in a deep pessimism that led him at last to abandon all hope of influencing the future of the Palatinate.[24] England, alone of all the western powers, was sending no delegate to the peace conferences, and he himself was being excluded from the modest favors of an embattled court.[25] There was nothing he could do, and it was with a sigh for labors lost that he commended the cause to God and "hanged [it] . . . vpon the Hookes of Hope, untill [His] will [should] be revealed."[26]

He was confined to his bed for increasingly long periods now and was still at a loss to understand the king's attitude toward him. To Prince Rupert he complained that, although many men were being preferred and favored, he who had served faithfully and long was neglected. He wished that the king would let him know his faults and tell him how he had been defective in duty or obedience.[27]

---

[23] Ibid., f. 117b, Roe to the Prince Elector, 21 December 1643.
[24] Ibid., f. 118, Roe to Mr. Avery, 17 January 1644.
[25] Ibid., f. 116b, Roe to Prince Rupert, 14 December 1643; ibid., f. 114, Roe to Secretary Nicholas, 11 November 1643.
[26] Ibid., f. 118, Roe to Mr. Avery, 17 January 1644.
[27] Ibid., f. 116b, 14 December 1643.

As his health and his political influence deteriorated, financial difficulties began once more to press upon him. The rents that constituted his main source of income either proved impossible to collect or were taken from him by the parliament, which had come to regard him with active hostility.[28] In February 1644 he was notified that the parliamentary Committee for the Advance of Money had levied on him an assessment of £600.[29] The committee's purpose was to raise money for the parliamentary armies, but it is significant to note that members of parliament were normally assessed by the House to which they belonged and were exempt from the committee's scrutiny. In being assessed by both the House of Commons and the committee, Roe was evidently being subjected to unusually severe treatment.[30]

These parliamentary levies placed Roe in an awkward situation and made the tenure of his neutral position even more difficult. If he failed to pay the money demanded of him, his remaining resources were likely to be confiscated. On the other hand, his submission to parliament on this score would make him suspect in the eyes of the court. Any action carried its penalty, but he had little choice in the matter and, complaining bitterly, he paid the sum demanded of him.

[28] Ibid., f. 72, Roe to Secretary Nicholas, 4 May 1643.
[29] *Calendar of the Proceedings of the Committee for Advance of Money, 1642–1656,* 1:302.
[30] Initially Roe must have refused to pay the sum demanded of him, for his goods were seized and his estates sequestered. However, on 3 June he was told that these restrictions would be "taken off" if, within ten days, he would pay £150 and strike a tally in the exchequer for a like amount or authorize the committee to receive that sum from his rents in Gloucestershire. He paid these assessments (*Calendar of the Proceedings of the Committee for Advance of Money, 1642–1656,* 1:302). The ratio used by the committee in making its assessment was one-twentieth of the real property and one-fifth of the personal estate. If this formula was applied in Roe's case, he must have been worth an absolute minimum of £12,000. However, the committee's estimates of a man's worth were often notoriously high, and this might have been the reason for Roe's initial refusal to pay. But it is also true that Lady Roe owned some property, and it seems that she made no payment to the committee for it. The combined assets of the Roes must therefore have been quite considerable (ibid.).

These financial demands were but one form of the pressure he had to endure. In April 1643 the House of Commons issued a general call for the return of absent members to their seats. The purpose was clearly to expose those members who had deserted parliament for the king. Sir Thomas did not respond to the summons, and the sergeant-at-arms sent a messenger to his house. Roe, however, was too ill to leave home, and although some of the members "harangued against" him, his excuses were accepted.[31] A year later his ill health once again made it possible for him to avert a summons from the contending parties. When Charles I called to Oxford the assembly that came to be known as the "Anti-Parliament," the House of Commons had a special meeting to count those members who had deserted to the king.[32] Roe was specifically summoned to attend the king, but, even if he had wanted to align himself with either side, he was by now too ill to respond. He sent his regrets to Oxford, but was probably rather relieved to have so plausible an excuse for inaction.[33]

Throughout the winter months his health continued to decline, and in those twilight days he reluctantly accepted the aged invalid's passive role. He was no longer consulted by either side, and he ceased to receive instructions from the king about the conduct of his foreign correspondence. When a French representative visited Oxford to talk, among other things, about the Palatinate, Roe was not even invited to attend. This hurt his pride, and he commented to Queen Elizabeth that the money spent to entertain the Frenchman would have been more than enough to keep him for the rest of his life.[34]

Although he was now totally excluded from any active role, Roe continued to comment on the passing scene. In his last

[31] Harl. MSS 1901, f. 74, Roe to Lord Falkland, May 1643; *Commons' Journal*, 3:38, 45.

[32] Rex, *University Representation*, p. 163.

[33] Harl. MSS 1901, f. 118, Roe to Mr. Secretary Nicholas, 17 January 1644.

[34] Ibid., f. 119, Roe to the queen of Bohemia, 20 February 1644.

days he became increasingly critical of royal policy. He felt that the king was being too intransigent and that much more could have been gained by judicious compromise. The parliament, he felt, was at least willing to discuss the possibility of a settlement, and the king, by refusing their advances, had made himself appear an enemy of peace.[35] For his part, he came to believe that the only way to achieve peace was the "Parliamentary way"—"the meeting of the King, and his subjects in Parliament wherein all disputes, and breaches may be reconciled, and bound up by votes and lawes, which are the only, and publique security."[36] This view was a long way from the opinion of Charles I and the majority of the Cavaliers, but it seems fairly to indicate the political philosophy that Sir Thomas Roe came to hold at the end.[37] In a sense it had been his theme all along: the need for cooperation, compromise, and unity; the virtues of reasonableness and moderation, and the call for a patriotism that looked beyond faction to long-term national interests.

There was time for thought as winter gave way again to spring. His illness had long since entered its chronic phase, and gout's sharp arthritic pains kept him bedridden and made him declare that merely to be lame would now be pure happiness.[38] Queen Elizabeth tried to persuade him to go to see a famous Polish doctor, but Roe replied that he was too ill to travel and that, in any case, he was prepared to die.[39] In the graceful hyperbole of his time he professed himself weary of the world and ready to take his leave of it. Elizabeth tried to rally him. "I see many reasons in your last letter," she wrote, "why you should be weary of the world, and willing to leave it, but there are none that show you useless unto it or the same fit to want

[35] Marriott, *The Life and Times of Lucius Cary, Viscount Falkland,* pp. 292–93; quoting Roe to Falkland, 6 April 1643; Harl. MSS 1901, f. 122, Roe to Mr. Avery, 20 June 1644.

[36] Ibid., f. 74, Roe to Lord Falkland, May 1643.

[37] Rex, *University Representation,* p. 162.

[38] Harl. MSS 1901, f. 122b, Roe to the queen of Bohemia, 20 June 1644.

[39] *C.S.P., Dom., 1644,* queen of Bohemia to Roe, 16 June 1644, pp. 209–10.

you." If honor obliges men to risk their lives for their country, there must be a stricter law that requires them to preserve their lives for the same cause.[40] It was a fine sentiment, and it was with such expressions that Elizabeth tried to convince her old friend that he still had a part to play. But Sir Thomas would not be consoled. In what appears to have been his last letter to the lady he had always regarded as a queen, he gave free rein to his melancholy: "All things tend to ruin," and his only desire is now to be buried face down so he would not see the universal disorders that were wrecking his country.[41]

His thoughts must surely have ranged far beyond the mere contemplation of his own sad condition. Few men of his time had a richer store of varied memories, and it is pleasant to think that they must have afforded him some diversion and some measure of relief. Perhaps from his bedroom his mind flew back to the torpid heat of Guiana and pondered the fate of the men he had tried to establish there. Surely the glittering court at Ajmere and the obstinate officials at Surat must have had a place in his memories. The years spent at Constantinople had left their mark, too; and recollections of his work there must have brought some satisfaction to dreary days of pain. Men reunited with their families, prisoners released, wars ended —notable accomplishments, to be but part of a lifetime's work. And then, there was stubborn John Dury, still trudging Europe in endless search of his goal, proclaiming an idea too pure for the worldly men whose help he sought. Roe must have thought of him, and thinking, wished him well. For excitement he could remember the engagement with the Maltese galleys or the German robber band that had waylaid him in more recent years. As mementos of work well done he could look at the medal presented by his king, or the gold chain that represented the esteem of the Dutch States General, or the cabinet that spoke of his association with the Holy Roman Emperor. And must there not have been a twinge of

40 Ibid.
41 Harl. MSS 1901, f. 122b, Roe to the queen of Bohemia, 20 June 1644.

remorse, that service faithfully done had not prevented tragedy, but had led to a lonely sickroom and reaped only the frustration of his fondest hopes—England divided, Europe at war, Elizabeth still dispossessed, the Protestant alliance unrealized, and the political ambitions of a lifetime unfulfilled. Would not the paths he had advocated for so long have led to happier results? But that was idle speculation, and the recognition perhaps jerked him back to his bed and his pain.

He maintained his status as a parliamentary representative of Oxford University to the last, and parliament never deprived him of it. On 3 July 1644 he applied to the Speaker for a safe-conduct to go to Bath in search of some relief from his painful disease.[42] Permission was granted and the journey was made. But then, in the moving words of Anthony A. Wood, "this worthy person, Sir Thomas Roe, did after all his voyages and ramblings take a little breath; but soon after, seeing how untowardly things went between the King and his parliament, did willingly surrender it to Him that first gave it, on the 6th day of November in 1644, and two days after that his body was buried privately in the church at Woodford, near to Wansted in Essex."[43]

Although Roe's widow survived him by more than twenty years, and was very comfortably provided for, no monument was ever erected to him and the epitaph that was written remained unused.[44] The church at Woodford was rebuilt and enlarged in 1815–1816, so that now even the spot where he lies is unknown.

---

[42] *Commons' Journal,* 3:549. Stanley Lane-Poole, "Sir Thomas Roe," in *D.N.B.,* 17:89, gives the date as 2 July 1643, but this certainly is an error.

[43] Anthony à Wood, *Athenae Oxonienses,* ed. and continued by Philip Bliss (London, 1813–1820), 3:114.

[44] An epitaph was written by Dr. Gerard Langbaine, the keeper of the Oxford University archives. Lady Roe lived on at Woodford and died in 1670. Her will is in the Essex County Record Office (ref. E.R.O. D/DMe F1/1). There is one intriguing reference to her in the local records. It is reported how "Dame Ellen Rowe of Woodford, wid., 6 June, 1658, being the Lord's Day, about 11 A.M. in the parish church there, assaulted Joan, wife of Dan. Holdenby" (*Calendar of Essex Assize Files in the Public Record Office, 1646–1659,* vol. 3, File 35/99/T: 26 July, 1658 #34). Nothing more is known about the incident.

In more recent times, however, efforts have been made to memorialize him in some suitable fashion. In 1911 a simple ceremony took place in the central reading room of the library at Leyton. On that occasion there was unveiled a crayon portrait of Sir Thomas Roe. It had been copied from the Van Miereveldt portrait in the National Portrait Gallery and was presented to the borough by the Ratepayers' Association. The original plan had been to identify the place of Roe's birth with an appropriate plaque, but no one was able to discover the house or its site, so the portrait was decided upon instead. At the ceremony Sir William Foster spoke of the chief incidents of Roe's life, and Mr. A. P. Wire told the history of the portrait.[45]

The ceremony at Leyton represented the modest tribute of townspeople proclaiming the memory of a native son. In 1927 a more august assembly paid its tribute. The scene was St. Stephen's Hall, one of the great shrines of English freedom, and the site of all the major events in parliamentary history from the time of Edward VI to that of William IV. There the prime minister (Stanley Baldwin) unveiled the eight panels that now decorate the walls of the ancient place. They illustrate great events from England's past, and one of them depicts "Sir Thomas Roe, Envoy from King James the First of England to the Moghul Emperor, [who] succeeds by his courtesy and firmness at the Court of Ajmir in laying the foundation of British influence in India, 1614."[46] So he is remembered in the place where he served, on three separate occasions, as a member of parliament; and it is somehow fitting that the only contemporaries depicted in the other panels are Queen Elizabeth and Sir Walter Raleigh—three people of like spirit who shared a common vision of England's destiny.

A less conspicuous kind of memorial to Roe is to be found in the Bodleian Library, which was founded during his lifetime. From the beginning he had been one of its benefactors and was

[45] "Notes of the Quarter," *Essex Review* 20 (1911): 45–46.
[46] Sir Bryan H. Fell, *The Houses of Parliament: A Short Guide to the Palace of Westminster*, rev. K. R. Mackenzie (London, 1950), p. 19.

constantly on the lookout for some rare treasure to send there. From Contsantinople he had sent the documents now catalogued as the "Roe MSS., A.D. 1629."[47] Mainly in Greek, and dealing with theological subjects, they comprised one of the first collections given to the library.[48] In later years Roe added to this initial gift by sending more manuscripts and a large collection of coins, all of which were gratefully received.[49] Some of the donations were sent through Archbishop Laud, who was greatly interested in the development of the library. Roe might have been trying to curry favor with Laud through these gifts, but since some were given after Laud's fall, it seems likely that Sir Thomas had been sincere when he had said he made the gifts "in gratitudinis suae erga Matrem Academiam perpetuum testimonium."[50]

The most endurable memorial of all is sometimes created by the historian, but in this respect Roe has not received the attention he deserves. From time to time someone has become interested in a specific part of his career, but no attempt has been made to study the story of his life with any degree of thoroughness. It is easy to see, moreover, why Roe's life and work have not been carefully studied in their entirety; for, while he was a most attractive individual and worthy of the respect of any biographer, there is something both elusive and frustrating in his story. His experiences were so varied and ranged over such a wide area, that Roe's biographer must presume to say something about any number of matters that lie in the fringe areas of conventional English history: trade with India, Persia, Turkey, and the Baltic; diplomatic relations with Germany, Poland, Sweden, and the Ottoman Porte; foreign policy, at a time when all eyes were upon domestic events.

[47] F. Madan and H. H. E. Craster, *A Summary Catalogue of Western Manuscripts in the Bodleian Library at Oxford* (Oxford, 1922), p. 10.
[48] Ibid.
[49] Ibid.; Charles E. Mallet, *A History of the University of Oxford* (London, 1924), 2:223; *C.S.P., Dom., 1629–1631*, William Strode, "public orator of the University of Oxford," to Roe, 7 March 1631, p. 530.
[50] Madan and Craster, *A Summary Catalogue of Western Manuscripts in the Bodleian Library at Oxford*, p. 10.

This great variety results in a certain lack of focus and penetration, and this undoubtedly helps to explain Roe's relative obscurity.

Ultimately Roe failed in the things which, to him, mattered most. His age somehow contrived to pass him by, and this imparted to his designs an irritating irrelevance. H. R. Trevor-Roper's figure of the ghost lingering after sunrise comes to mind; and if we dismiss it, we do so only because it seems too severe and not because it is basically mistaken. Roe's pleas were neglected and his advice was scorned; and the probability that he was correct in most of his opinions does not alter the fact that he was without power to change the course of events. He was an Elizabethan, and the Elizabethan Age was dead.

Despite these limitations, Roe's story deserves more attention than it has received. For one thing, it invites us into areas that need to be explored further by English historians who have, perhaps, been too provincial in concentrating their attention so heavily upon the domestic events of the century in which Roe lived. Roe was one of the leading letterwriters of his time. There is enjoyment and vast instruction to be gained from the heavy correspondence he carried on with some of the leading figures of the time. His acquaintances ran the gamut from Raleigh to Laud and from Pym to Prince Henry, but there is always the feeling that Roe held up his head, even in such a distinguished company. Occasionally we are angered by the sugary phrases in which he asked for advancement, but we also recognize that, in office or out, he never surrendered his right to make an independent judgment or advocate an unpopular policy.

He seems to have been a thoroughly upright man. He was fair and just in his dealings with those of inferior station; and, so far as we can tell, he never took improper advantage of the many opportunities he had in India and Turkey to line his own pockets. He was charitable,[51] kindly, and brave. Men enjoyed

[51] He sent a boy through university at his own expense and paid his tithe to the church regularly and willingly (*C.S.P., Dom., 1633–1634*, Roe

his company, for he was a good conversationalist, witty and cultured.[52] He was constant in his affections, patriotic to the core, and religious in a tolerant and enlightened way that was in refreshing contrast to the ideas of most of his contemporaries.[53]

Indeed, the discovery of some minor moral blemish would come almost as a relief to his biographer, apprehensive of being accused of viewing his subject too charitably. But the evidence suggests nothing more serious than his exaggerated whining about financial difficulty and his servile pleas for advancement. But if these were vices, they were common ones, and greater men than Roe have been charged with them.

It is a pity that so little is known of Roe's personal life, but only scattered pieces of evidence remain. His marriage was evidently a happy one, although references to Lady Roe are few and far between. The Roes had no children of their own, but became very attached to the two girls they adopted.

---

to Henry, earl of Manchester, 9 January 1634, p. 404; Lane-Poole, "Sir Thomas Roe," in *D.N.B.*, 17:90). At Cirencester, which he had represented in the parliament of 1621, he provided charitable gifts in memory of his mother. A sermon was to be preached on the anniversary of her death each year and a sum of money was set aside for apprenticing poor children (Welbore St. Clair Baddeley, *A History of Cirencester* [Cirencester, 1924], p. 243*n*; W. R. Williams, *The Parliamentary History of the County of Gloucester, including the Cities of Bristol and Gloucester, and the Boroughs of Cheltenham, Cirencester, Stroud and Tewkesbury, from the earliest times to the present day, 1213-1898, with biographical and genealogical notices of the members* [Hereford, 1898], p. 155).

[52] John Dury, who spent a good deal of time with Roe and must have known him well, said that he was usually "free spoken and full of mirth and wit" (G. H. Turnbull, *Hartlib, Dury and Comenius: Gleanings from Hartlib's Papers* [Liverpool, 1947], Dury to Hartlib, 26 May 1640, p. 207).

[53] W. K. Jordan, *The Development of Religious Toleration in England from the Accession of James I to the Convention of the Long Parliament (1603-1640)* (Cambridge, Mass., 1936), p. 365, says that Roe was "vigorously opposed to the sharp doctrinal orthodoxy" then prevalent in England and on the Continent. He was certainly esteemed by the advocates of church unity. In 1641, Thomas Hayne dedicated his book *The Life and Death of Dr. Martin Luther* . . . to Roe (Gunnar Westin, "Negotiations about Church Unity, 1628-1634," in *Uppsala Universitets Arsskrift, 1932* [Uppsala, 1932], p. 183).

Actually, the "adoption" seems to have been only a temporary arrangement. The girls kept their family name of Rupa and, after some five years in England, returned to the Continent, one to Queen Elizabeth's court at Rhenen and the other to the court of Brandenburg. Sir Thomas often inquired about them, and letters to and from Elizabeth contained many affectionate references and accounts of their exploits and, later, their loves. One of the girls, named Jane, married shortly before Roe's death, but what became of the other is unknown.[54]

Contemporaries and later writers alike have said only good things of Sir Thomas Roe, and perhaps it would not be inappropriate to conclude this study with some of the comments that have been made about him from time to time.

In March 1737 the historian Thomas Carte, having read through many of Roe's papers, wrote of him:

> I cannot sufficiently admire his Rare Abilities, judgment and Integrity, his Extraordinary Sagacity in discovering the views and designs of those with whom he treated, and his admirable dexterity in guarding against their Measures and bringing them over to his purpose. Wise, Experienced, penetrating and knowing, he was never to be surprized or deceived, and though no Minister ever had greater difficulties to struggle with or was employed by a Court that had less power to Support him, yet he Supported all his Employments with dignity and came out of them with Reputation and honour. In all the honest Arts of Negotiation he had few Equalls, (I dare say) no Superiors.[55]

About three years after Carte had written these words, the great volume of *The Negotiations of Sir Thomas Roe . . . to the Ottoman Porte* was published by the Society for the Encouragement of Learning. The preface to this large volume is unsigned, but it was probably written by the same Thomas Carte. If such is the case, it is worthy of note that, even after the detailed study which the publication of the book necessitated, Carte still retained his high regard for Roe's ability. The

[54] There are several scattered references to the girls in *C.S.P., Dom.*, between September 1635 and February 1641.
[55] British Museum, Add'l. MS, 6190, f. 34, quoted in William Foster, *Embassy*, p. lviii.

following passage illustrates the point: "For the practical knowledge of the trade and commerce of England, we are not afraid to say, that he had no equal in his own time, nor hardly in any other. For he had not only a genius and inclination fitted to promote the natural advantages of his native country in that way; but such opportunities of cultivating both, that hardly any other man ever had."[56]

These statements deal with Roe's professional abilities, but his personal integrity was equally impressive. Anthony Wood made this evaluation of him:

> In all . . . employments, whether domestic or foreign, he did manifestly shew what eminence there was treasur'd up in him, and what admirable parts he was endowed with. The truth is, those that knew him well have said, that there was nothing wanting in him toward the accomplishment of a scholar, gentleman or courtier; that also, as he was learned, so was he a great encourager and promoter of learning and learned men. His spirit was generous and public, and his heart faithful to his prince. He was a great statesman, as good a commonwealth's man, and as sound a Christian as our nation hath had in many ages.[57]

These views were written long ago, in the generous phrases of a courtly age. But more recent historians, among them such eminent names as S. R. Gardiner, G. M. Trevelyan, and Sir William Foster have added their endorsement to the sentiments expressed in that earlier day. In our own day, other careful students have found no reason to disagree.[58]

[56] *Negotiations*, p. x.
[57] Anthony à Wood, *Athenae Oxonienses*, 3:113.
[58] H. R. Trevor-Roper, G. E. Aylmer, A. L. Rowse, C. V. Wedgwood, and David Mathew are among the contemporary historians who have spoken generously of Roe and his work.

BIBLIOGRAPHY

Primary Sources

Acts of the Privy Council of England, vols. 39, 40, 44. London: His Majesty's Stationery Office, 1933–1958.

Acts of the Privy Council of England, Colonial Series, vol. 1. London: His Majesty's Stationery Office, 1908.

Baker, L. M., comp. *The Letters of Elizabeth Queen of Bohemia*, with an introduction by C. V. Wedgwood. London: The Bodley Head, 1953.

Bernier, F., *Travels in the Mogul Empire, 1656–1668*. Edited by A. Constable and V. A. Smith. Oxford, 1914.

Calendar of Essex Assize Files in the Public Record Office, 1646–1659. (Essex Record Office, Chelmsford.)

Calendar of the Patent Rolls Preserved in the Public Record Office, Elizabeth, Volume 1, 1558–1560. London: His Majesty's Stationery Office, 1939.

Calendar of the Proceedings of the Committee for Advance of Money, 1642–1656, preserved in the State Paper Department of Her Majesty's Public Record Office. London: Her Majesty's Stationery Office, 1888.

Calendar of the Proceedings of the Committee for Compounding etc., [sic] *1643–1660, preserved in the State Paper Department of Her Majesty's Public Record Office*. London: Her Majesty's Stationery Office, 1891.

Calendar of State Papers and Manuscripts, Relating to English Affairs Existing in the Archives and Collections of Venice, and in other libraries in Northern Italy. Edited by Allen B. Hinds. London: His Majesty's Stationery Office, 1925.

Calendar of State Papers, Colonial Series, 1574–1660, Preserved in the State Paper Department of Her Majesty's Public Record Office. London: Longman, Green, Longman and Roberts, 1860.

Calendar of State Papers, Colonial Series, East Indies, China and Japan, 1513–1616, preserved in Her Majesty's Public Record Office and Elsewhere. London: Longman, Green, Longman and Roberts, 1862.

Calendar of State Papers, Colonial Series, East Indies, China and Japan, 1617–1624. London: Longman and Co., 1870.

Calendar of State Papers, Colonial Series, East Indies and Persia, 1630–1634, Preserved in the Public Record Office and the India Office. London: Her Majesty's Stationery Office, 1892.

Calendar of State Papers, Domestic Series, James I, 1603–1625. London: Her Majesty's Stationery Office, 1857–1872.

Calendar of State Papers, Domestic Series, Charles I, 1625–1643. London: Her Majesty's Stationery Office, 1858–1897.

Calendar of State Papers, Domestic Series, Charles II, 1660–1661, preserved in the State Paper Department of Her Majesty's Public Record Office. London: Longman, Green, Longman and Roberts, 1860.

Calendar of Wills proved and enrolled in the Court of Husting, London, 1258–1688, preserved among the Archives of the Corporation of the City of London at the Guildhall. London, 1890.

[Carte, Thomas (?)], editor, *The Negotiations of Sir Thomas Roe, in his Embassy to the Ottoman Porte, from the Year 1621 to 1628 Inclusive: Containing A Great Variety of Curious and Important Matters, relating not only to the Affairs of the Turkish Empire, but also to those of the Other States of Europe in that Period: His correspondences with the most illustrious persons for Dignity or Character; as with the Queen of Bohemia, Bethlem Gabor Prince of Transylvania, and other Potentates of Different Nations, And c. And many useful and instructive Particulars, as well in relation to Trade and Commerce, as to Subjects of Literature; as Antient Manuscripts Coins, Inscriptions, and other Antiquities.* London: Printed by Samuel Richardson at the Expence of the Society for the Encouragement of Learning, 1740.

Catalogue of the Harleian Manuscripts, in the British Museum [London] 1808–1812.

Collection de Documents Inédits sur l'histoire de France: Lettres, Instructions Diplomatiques et Papiers d'État du Cardinal de Richelieu, 8 volumes. Edited by M. Avenel. Paris: Imprimerie Nationale, 1853–1877.

Essex Session Rolls, volumes 21, 23. (Essex Record Office, Chelmsford.)

Foster, William, ed., *The Embassy of Sir Thomas Roe to the Court of the Great Mogul, 1615–1619, as narrated in his journal and correspondence.* London: Printed for Hakluyt Society, 1899.

———, *The English Factories in India, 1618–1621: A Calendar of Documents in the India Office, British Museum and Public Records Office.* Oxford: The Clarendon Press, 1906.

———, ed., *The Voyage of Nicholas Downton to the East Indies, 1614–15, As Recorded in Contemporary Narratives and Letters.* London: The Hakluyt Society, 1939.

Gardiner, Samuel Rawson, ed., *The Fortescue Papers; consisting chiefly of Letters Relating to State Affairs, Collected by John Packer, Secretary to George Villiers, Duke of Buckingham.* Westminster: Printed for the Camden Society, 1871.

————, ed., *Letters relating to the mission of Sir Thomas Roe to Gustavus Adolphus 1629–30.* Westminster: Printed for the Camden Society, 1875.

Great Britain, Historical Manuscripts Commission, *Fourth Report: Papers relating to John Durye's mission to the Continent with the object of effecting a reconciliation between the Lutherans and Calvinists.* London, 1874.

————, *Report on the Manuscripts of Alan George Finch, Esq., of Burley-on-the-Hill, Rutland.* London: His Majesty's Stationery Office, 1913.

Great Britain, Parliament, House of Commons, *Journals of the House of Commons.* London, n.d.

The Harleian Miscellany: A Collection of Scarce, Curious, and Entertaining Pamphlets and Tracts, as well in Manuscript as in print. London: Printed for White and Co., and John Murray, and John Harding, 1809.

Harlow, V. T., *Ralegh's Last Voyage, Being an account drawn out of contemporary letters and relations, both Spanish and English, of which the most part are now for the first time made public, concerning the voyage of Sir Walter Raleigh, knight, to Guiana in the year 1617 and the fatal consequences of the same.* London: The Argonaut Press, 1932.

Jacobs, Joseph, ed., *Epistolae Ho-Elianae. The Familiar Letters of James Howell.* London: David Nutt, 1892.

A Journal of all the Courts, Actes, Contracts, Sentences, Ends of Controversies and other Business concerning the English Nation in the tyme of the Right Honorable Sʳ. Thomas Roe, Embassadour resident from his Maᵗᵗᵉ of great Brittayne at the Port of Constantinople, begunne the First of January 1621. London: Public Record Office.

Kingsbury, Susan M., ed., *The Records of the Virginia Company of London.* Washington, D.C.: Government Printing Office, 1906.

McLean, John, ed., *Letters from George Lord Carew to Sir Thomas Roe, Ambassador to the Court of the Great Mogul 1615–1617.* London: Printed for the Camden Society, 1860.

Macray, William Dunn, *Annals of the Bodleian library, Oxford, with a notice of the earlier library of the University . . . 2d ed. enl., and continued from 1868 to 1880.* Oxford: The Clarendon Press, 1890.

Madan, Falconer and Craster, H. H. E., *A Summary Catalogue of Western Manuscripts in the Bodleian Library at Oxford.* Oxford: The Clarendon Press, 1922.

Markham, Clements R., ed., *The Voyages of Sir James Lancaster K'. to the East Indies, with abstracts of Journals of Voyages to the East Indies, during the seventeenth century, preserved in the India Office. And the voyage of Captain John Knight (1606), to seek the north-west passage.* London: The Hakluyt Society, 1877.

The Noble Collection, "Sir Thomas Rowe." (Guildhall Library, London.)

Notestein, Wallace, ed., *The Journal of Sir Simonds D'Ewes from the beginning of the Long Parliament to the opening of the trial of the Earl of Strafford.* New Haven: Yale University Press, 1923.

———; Relf, Frances Helen; and Simpson, Hartley, eds., *Commons Debates 1621.* New Haven: Yale University Press, 1935.

Purchas, Samuel, *Hakluytus Posthumus or Purchas His Pilgrimes.* Glasgow: James MacLehose and Sons, 1905.

Roe, Lady Eleanor, Lady Roe's Will. (Essex Record Office, Chelmsford.)

Roe, Sir Thomas, *Sir T. Roe's Speech at the Council Table about the alteration of the Coyn, in July, 1640; with some observations thereon.* London, 1695.

———, "Sir Thomas Roe's Speech in Parliament. Wherin he sheweth the Cause of the Decay of Coin and Trade in this Land, especially of Merchants Trade: And also propoundeth a Way to the House, how they may be increased," in *The Harleian Miscellany.* London: Printed for White and Co., and John Murray, and John Harding, 1809.

Sainsbury, Ethel Bruce, *A Calendar of the Court Minutes etc. of the East India Company, 1635–1639.* Oxford: The Clarendon Press, 1907.

State Papers Foreign, Levant Company. (Public Record Office, London.)

State Papers Foreign, Turkey. (Public Record Office, London.)

Stock, Leo Frances, ed., *Proceedings and Debates of the British Parliaments respecting North America,* vol. 1, 1542–1648. Washington, D.C.: Carnegie Institution of Washington, 1924.

Yonge, Walter, *Diary of Walter Yonge, esq., justice of the peace, and M.P. for Honiton, written at Colyton and Axminster, co. Devon, from 1604–1628.* Edited by George Roberts. London: Camden Society, 1848.

Secondary Sources

Ahnlund, Nils, *Gustav Adolf the Great,* translated from the Swedish by Michael Roberts. Princeton: Princeton University Press; American-Scandinavian Foundation, New York, 1940.

Andrews, Charles M., *The Colonial Period of American History, vol. 4, England's Commercial and Colonial Policy.* New Haven: Yale University Press, 1938.

Aylmer, G. E., *The King's Servants: The Civil Service of Charles I, 1625–1642.* New York: Columbia University Press, 1961.

Baddeley, Welbore St. Clair, *A History of Cirencester.* Cirencester, 1924.

Barck, Oscar T., Jr., and Lefler, Hugh T. *Colonial America.* New York: The Macmillan Co., 1968.

Batten, Joseph Minton, *John Dury, Advocate of Christian Reunion.* Chicago: The University of Chicago Press, 1944.

Beaven, Rev. Alfred B., *The Aldermen of the City of London with notes on the Parliamentary Representation of the City, the Aldermen and the Livery Companies, the Aldermanic Veto, Aldermanic Baronets and Knights, etc.* London: E. Fisher and Company Limited, 1908–13.

Bessé, Alfred de, *The Turkish Empire: its historical, statistical, and religious condition; also its manners, customs, etc.* Translated, revised and enlarged (from the fourth German edition) . . . by Edward Joy Morris. Philadelphia: Lindsay and Blakiston, 1854.

Bougeant, Le Pere, *Histoire des Guerres et des Négociations qui précédèrent le traité de Westphalie, sous le Règne de Louis XIII et le Ministere des Cardinaux Richelieu et Mazarin* (3 vols.). Paris: Musier Fils, 1767.

Bowen, Catherine Drinker, *Francis Bacon, the Temper of a Man.* Boston: Little, Brown and Company, 1963.

———, *The Lion and the Throne: The Life and Times of Sir Edward Coke, 1552–1634.* London: Hamish Hamilton, 1957.

Brown, Alexander, *English Politics in Early Virginia History.* Boston: Houghton Mifflin and Company, 1901.

———, *The Genesis of the United States.* Boston: Houghton Mifflin and Company, 1891.

Brett-James, Norman G., *The Growth of Stuart London.* London: George Allen and Unwin Ltd., 1935.

Brunton, D., and Pennington, D. H., *Members of the Long Parliament.* Cambridge, Mass.: Harvard University Press, 1954.

Burghclerc, Lady, *Strafford.* London: MacMillan and Co., Ltd., 1931.

The Cambridge History of India: Volume 4 The Mughul Period, edited by Sir Richard Burn. New York: The MacMillan Co., 1937.

Clarendon, Edward Hyde, Earl of, *History of the Rebellion and Civil Wars in England begun in the year 1641.* Oxford: The Clarendon Press, 1888.

Cobbett, William, *The Parliamentary History of England from the earliest period to the year 1803.* London: Printed by T. C. Hansard (etc.), 1806–1820.

Craven, Wesley Frank, *Dissolution of the Virginia Company: The*

Failure of a Colonial Experiment. New York: Oxford University Press, 1932.

———, *The Southern Colonies in the Seventeenth Century, 1607–1689*. Volume 1 of W. H. Stephenson and E. M. Coulter, eds., *A History of the South*. Baton Rouge: Louisiana State University Press, 1949.

Danvers, Frederick Charles, *The Portuguese in India Being a History of the Rise and Decline of their Eastern Empire*. London: W. H. Allen and Co., Ltd., 1894.

Davies, Godfrey, *The Early Stuarts, 1603–1660*. Oxford: The Clarendon Press, 1937.

Davis, Ralph, "England and the Mediterranean, 1570–1670," in F. J. Fisher, ed., *Essays in the Economic and Social History of Tudor and Stuart England, in Honour of R. H. Tawney*. Cambridge: University Press, 1961.

Doyle, J. A., *English Colonies in America, Virginia, Maryland and the Carolinas*. New York: Henry Holt and Company, 1882.

Dunbar, Sir George, *India and the Passing of Empire*. New York: Philosophical Library, 1952.

Edmundson, G. C., "The Relations of Great Britain with Guiana," in *Transactions of the Royal Historical Society*, Fourth Series, vol. 6. London: Royal Historical Society, 1923.

Epstein, M., *The Early History of the Levant Company*. London: G. Routledge and Sons, 1908.

Evans, Florence M. Greir (Mrs. C. S. S. Higham), *The Principal Secretary of State*. Manchester: The University Press, 1923.

Fagniez, Gustave, *Le Père Joseph et Richelieu (1577–1638)*. Paris: Librairie Hachette et Cⁱᵉ, 1894.

Fell, Sir Bryan H., *The Houses of Parliament: A Short Guide to the Palace of Westminster*. Revised by K. R. Mackenzie. London: Eyre and Spottiswoode, 1950.

Foster, Joseph, *Alumni Oxonienses: The Members of the University of Oxford, 1500–1714: Their parentage, birthplace, and year of birth, with a record of their degrees*. Oxford: Parker and Co., 1892.

Foster, Sir William, "The East India Company, 1600–1740," in *British India, 1497–1858*, vol. 4 of H. H. Dodwell, ed., *The Cambridge History of the British Empire*. Cambridge: The University Press, 1929.

———, "The East India Company's Hospital at Poplar," in *The Home Counties Magazine*, vol. 12, 1910.

———, *England's Quest of Eastern Trade*. London: A. & C. Black, Ltd., 1933.

Gardiner, Samuel Rawson, *History of England from the accession of James I to the outbreak of the civil war 1603–1642*. London: Longmans, Green, and Co., 1883–1884.

———, *History of the Great Civil War, 1642–1649*. London: Longmans, Green, and Co., 1893.

Gater, Sir George, and Godfrey, Walter H., eds., *Trafalgar Square and Neighbourhood (The Parish of St. Martin-in-the-fields, Part 3)*, vol. 20 of *London County Council Survey of London*. London: The London County Council, 1940.

Gokhale, B. G., "Indians and the British: A Study in Attitudes," *History Today* 13 (April 1963): 230–38.

Gosse, Edmund, *The Life and Letters of John Donne, Dean of Saint Paul's*. New York: Dodd, Mead and Co., 1899.

Green, Mary Anne Everett, *Elizabeth, Electress Palatine and Queen of Bohemia*, rev. S. C. Lomas. London: Methuen and Co., 1909.

Hadjiantoniou, George A., *Protestant Patriarch: The Life of Cyril Lucaris (1572–1638) Patriarch of Constantinople*. Richmond, Va.: John Knox Press, 1961.

Halecki, Oscar, *Borderlands of Western Civilization: A History of East Central Europe*. New York: The Ronald Press Co., 1952.

Harlow, V. T., ed., *Colonizing Expeditions to the West Indies and Guiana, 1623–1667*. London: Printed for the Hakluyt Society, 1925.

Herbert, William, *The History of the Twelve Great Livery Companies of London, principally compiled from their grants and records*. London: Published by the author, 1836.

Herford, C. H., and Simpson, Percy, eds., *Ben Jonson*. Oxford, 1925.

Hinton, R. W. K., *The Eastland Trade and the Common Weal*. Cambridge: Cambridge University Press, 1959.

Hodgkin, R. H., "Elizabeth of Bohemia, Daughter of James I and VI," in Robert S. Rait, ed., *Five Stuart Princesses*. New York: E. P. Dutton and Co., 1902.

Holme, Rev. C., *A History of the Midland Counties*. Rugby, 1891.

Hunter, Sir William Wilson, *A Brief History of the Indian Peoples*. Oxford: The Clarendon Press, 1907.

Innes, A. D., *The Maritime and Colonial Expansion of England under the Stuarts 1603–1714*. London: Sampson, Low, Marston and Co., Ltd. (n.d.).

Jameson, J. Franklin, "William Usselinx, Founder of the Dutch and Swedish West India Companies," *Papers of the American Historical Association*, vol. 2, no. 3. New York, 1887.

Jones, J. R., *Britain and Europe in the Seventeenth Century*. New York: W. W. Norton and Co., Inc., 1966.

Jordan, W. K., *The Development of Religious Toleration in England from the Accession of James I to the Convention of the Long Parliament (1603–1640)*. Cambridge, Mass.: Harvard University Press, 1936.

Kempson, G. A. E., "Rendcomb," in W. P. W. Phillimore, ed., *Gloucester Notes and Queries*, vol. 6, 1894–1895. London, 1896.

Kenyon, Sir Frederic, *Our Bible and the Ancient Manuscripts*, rev. A. W. Adams. New York: Harper and Brothers, 1958.

Kershaw, R. N., "The Elections for the Long Parliament, 1640," *The English Historical Review,* vol. 38, 1923, pp. 496–508.

Kincaid, Dennis, *British Social Life in India 1608–1937.* London: George Routledge & Sons, Ltd., 1938.

Kingsbury, Susan M., "A Comparison of the Virginia Company with the Other English Trading Companies of the Sixteenth and Seventeenth Centuries," in *Annual Report of the American Historical Association for the Year 1906.* Washington, D.C.: Government Printing Office, 1908.

Knolles, Richard, *The generall historie of the Turkes, from The first beginning of that Nation to the rising of the Othoman Familie: with all the notable expeditions of the Christian Princes against them. Together with The Lives and Conquests of the Othoman Kings and Emperours. With a New Continuation from ye yeare of our Lord 1629 unto the yeare 1638 faithfully collected,* 5th ed. London: Printed by Adam Islip, 1638.

Lane-Poole, Stanley, "An Ambassador to the Sultan," *Cornhill Magazine,* n.s. no. 3, vol. 7, pp. 468–81.

―――, *Medieval India from the Mohammedan Conquest to the Reign of Akbar the Great.* Vol. 4 of A. V. Williams Jackson, ed., *History of India.* London: The Grolier Society, 1906.

Lee, Maurice, Jr., "The Jacobean Diplomatic Service," *American Historical Review* 72 (July 1967): 1264–82.

Lewis, Samuel, *A Topographical Dictionary of England.* London: S. Lewis and Co., 1848.

Lipson, E., *The Age of Mercantilism.* Vol. 3 of *The Economic History of England.* London: A. & C. Black, Ltd., 1961.

Lyall, Sir Alfred, *The Rise and Expansion of the British Dominion in India.* London: John Murray, 1914.

McGarry, Patrick S., F.S.C., "Ambassador Abroad: The Career and Correspondence of Sir Thomas Roe at the Courts of the Mogul and Ottoman Empires 1614–1628: A Chapter in Jacobean Diplomacy." Ph.D. Diss., Columbia University, 1963.

Mallet, Charles Edward, *A History of the University of Oxford.* 3 vols. London: Methuen & Co., Ltd., 1924.

Mariéjol, J. H., *Henri IV et Louis XIII (1598–1643).* Volume 6, part 2, of Ernst Lavisse, ed., *Histoire de France Illustrée depuis les Origines Jusqu'à la Revolution.* Paris: Librairie Hachette, 1911.

Marriott, J. A. R., *The Life and Times of Lucius Cary, Viscount Falkland.* New York: G. P. Putnam's Sons, 1907.

Masselman, George, *The Cradle of Colonialism.* New Haven: Yale University Press, 1963.

Mathew, David, *The Age of Charles I.* London: Eyre and Spottiswoode, 1951.

―――, *The Jacobean Age.* London: Longmans, Green and Co., 1938.

——, *The Social Structure in Caroline England*. Oxford: The Clarendon Press, 1948.

Mattingly, Garrett, *Renaissance Diplomacy*. London: Jonathan Cape, 1955.

Mee, Arthur, ed., *Northamptonshire: County of Spires and Stately Homes*. London: Hodder and Stoughton, Ltd., 1945.

Michard, M. M., ed., *Memoires du Cardinal de Richelieu*. Vol. 8 of *Nouvelle Collection des Mémoires pour servir a l'histoire de France, depuis le XIIIᵉ siècle jusqu'à la fin du XVIIIᵉ*. Paris: L'Editeur du Commentaire Analytique du Code Civil, 1838.

Mitchell, W. M., *The Rise of the Revolutionary Party in the English House of Commons, 1603–1629*. New York: Columbia University Press, 1957.

Moir, Thomas L., *The Addled Parliament of 1614*. Oxford: The Clarendon Press, 1958.

Morant, Philip, *History and Antiquities of Essex*. 2 vols. 1768.

Mores, Edward Rowe, The History and Antiquities of Tunstall in Kent in *Bibliotheca Topographica Britannica*. London: Printed by and for J. Nichols, 1790.

Mottram, R. H., *Traders' Dream*. New York: D. Appleton-Century Co., 1939.

Mowat, R. B., "The Mission of Sir Thomas Roe to Vienna, 1641–2." *English Historical Review* 25 (1910): 264–75.

Nichols, John, *The Progresses, Processions and Magnificent Festivities of King James I*. . . . London, 1828.

Notestein, Wallace, "The Winning of the Initiative by the House of Commons: The Raleigh Lecture on History," *Proceedings of the British Academy*. London, 1924.

Ogg, David, *Europe in the Seventeenth Century*. London: Adam and Charles Black, 1956.

Oswald, Arthur, "Stamford Hall, Leicestershire, II and III." *Country Life*, December 11 and 18, 1958.

Page, William, ed., *The Victoria History of the County of Buckingham*. London: The St. Catherine Press, n.d.—1928.

——, and Doubleday, H. Arthur, eds., *The Victoria History of the County of Bedford*. Westminster: Archibald Constable and Co., Ltd., 1904–1918.

Pagès, G., *La Guerre de Trente Ans, 1618–1648*. Paris: Payot, 1949.

Panikkar, K. M., *Malabar and the Portuguese, Being a History of the Relations of the Portuguese with Malabar from 1500 to 1663*. Bombay: D. B. Taraporevala Sons & Co., 1929.

Preclin, Edmond, and Tapié, Victor-L., *Le XVIIᵉ Siècle Monarchies Centralisées (1610–1715)*. Paris: Presses Universitaires de France, 1949.

Prestwich, Menna, *Cranfield Politics and Profits under the Early Stuarts: The Career of Lionel Cranfield, Earl of Middlesex*. Oxford: The Clarendon Press, 1966.

Pugh, R. B., *The Victoria History of the County of Cambridge and the Isle of Ely*. London: The Oxford University Press, 1938–1960.

Rex, Millicent Barton, *University Representation in England, 1604–1690*. (Volume 15 of Études présentées à la Commission internationale pour l'Histoire des Assemblées d'états.) London: George Allen and Unwin, Ltd., 1954.

Roberts, Michael, *Gustavus Adolphus: A History of Sweden, 1611–1632*. London: Longmans, Green and Co., 1958.

Rowse, Alfred Leslie, *The England of Elizabeth: The Structure of Society*. London: The Macmillan Company, 1950.

————, *Shakespeare's Southampton, Patron of Virginia*. London: The Macmillan Company, 1965.

————, *Sir Walter Ralegh: His Family and Private Life*. New York: Harper and Brothers, 1962.

Sinor, Denis, *History of Hungary*. London: George Allen and Unwin, Ltd., 1959.

"Sir Thomas Rowe of Leyton," *Leyton Public Library Magazine*, vol. 1, no. 4, 1899.

Smith, Vincent A., *The Oxford History of India*, third edition **rev. and ed. by Percival Spear**. Oxford: The Clarendon Press, 1958.

Smyth, John (of Nibley), *The Berkeley Manuscripts: The Lives of the Berkeleys, Lords of the Honour, Castle and Manor of Berkeley in the County of Gloucester from 1066 to 1618 with a description of the Hundred of Berkeley and of its inhabitants*, ed. Sir John MacLean. Gloucester: 1883.

Spear, Thomas George Percival, *India: A Modern History*. Ann Arbor: The University of Michigan Press, 1961.

Stephen, Sir Leslie and Lee, Sir Sidney, eds., *The Dictionary of National Biography*. London: Oxford University Press, 1949–1950.

Stow, John, *A Survey of London*, ed. Charles L. Kingsford. Oxford: The Clarendon Press, 1962.

Strachan, Michael, *The Life and Adventures of Thomas Coryate*. London: Oxford University Press, 1962.

————, "Sampson's Fight with Maltese Galleys, 1628," *The Mariner's Mirror*, 55, no. 3 (1969): 281–89.

Thompson, Edward, *Sir Walter Raleigh, Last of the Elizabethans*. New Haven: Yale University Press, 1936.

————, and Garratt, G. T. *The Rise and Fulfillment of British Rule in India*. London: Macmillan and Co., 1934.

Torne, P. O. von, "Poland and the Baltic in the first half of the Seventeenth Century," in W. F. Reddaway and others, eds., *The Cambridge History of Poland from the Origins to Sobieski*. Cambridge: The Cambridge University Press, 1950.

Trevelyan, George M., *Illustrated English Social History*, vol.

2, *The Age of Shakespeare and the Stuart Period.* New York: Longmans, Green and Co., 1942.

Trevor-Roper, Hugh Redwald, "Historical Revision No. CVII, Archbishop Laud." *History* 30 (1945): 181–90.

——, *Archbishop Laud, 1573–1645.* Hamden, Conn.: Archon Press, 1962.

"A True Relation, without all Exception, of strange and admirable Accidents, which lately happened in the Kingdom of the great Magor, or Mogul, who is the greatest Monarch of the East Indies . . . Written and certified by Persons of good Import, who were Eye-witnesses of what is here reported." London: Printed by J. D. for Thomas Archer, 1622. In *Harleian Miscellany,* London: White and Co., and John Murray, and John Harding, 1809.

Turnbull, G. H., *Hartlib, Dury and Comenius: Gleanings from Hartlib's Papers.* Liverpool: University Press of Liverpool, 1947.

Turner, Edward Raymond, *The Privy Council of England in the Seventeenth and Eighteenth Centuries 1663–1784.* Baltimore: The Johns Hopkins Press, 1927.

Wallace, Willard M., *Sir Walter Raleigh.* Princeton, N.J.: Princeton University Press, 1959.

Ward, Sir A. W.; Prothero, Sir G. W.; and Leathes, Sir Stanley, eds., *The Cambridge Modern History:* vol. 4, *The Thirty Years War.* Cambridge: The University Press, 1934.

Wedgwood, Cicely Veronica, *The Great Rebellion: The King's Peace, 1637–1641.* New York: The Macmillan Co., 1956.

——, *The Great Rebellion: The King's War, 1641–1647.* New York: The Macmillan Co., 1959.

——, *The Thirty Years War.* New York: Doubleday and Co., Inc., 1961.

Weibull, Lauritz, "Gustave-Adolphe et Richelieu," *Revue Historique,* no. 174 (Juillet-Décembre, 1934).

Welsby, Paul A., *George Abbot the Unwanted Archbishop, 1562–1633.* London: S.P.C.K., 1962.

Westin, Gunnar, "Negotiations about Church Unity, 1628–1634," in *Uppsala Universitets Arsskrift, 1932.* Uppsala: A. B. Lundequistska Bokhandeln, 1932.

Whalley, Peter, *The History and Antiquities of Northamptonshire, compiled from the Manuscript Collections of the late learned Antiquary John Bridges, Esq.* Oxford, 1791.

Wilbur, Marguerite Ever, *The East India Company and the British Empire in the Far East.* New York: Richard R. Smith, 1945.

Willcox, William Bradford, *Gloucestershire, A Study in Local Government, 1590–1640:* vol. 39 of *Yale Historical Publications.* New Haven: Yale University Press, 1940.

Williams, W. R., *The Parliamentary History of the County of Gloucester, Including the Cities of Bristol and Gloucester, and the Boroughs of Cheltenham, Cirencester, Stroud and Tewkes-bury, from the earliest times to the present day, 1213–1898, with biographical and genealogical notices of the members.* Hereford, 1898.

Williamson, Hugh Ross, *Sir Walter Raleigh.* London: Faber and Faber, Ltd., 1951.

Williamson, James A., *English Colonies in Guiana and on the Amazon, 1604–1668.* Oxford: The Clarendon Press, 1923.

Willson, David Harris, *King James VI and I.* London: Jonathan Cape, 1956.

———, *The Privy Councillors in the House of Commons, 1604–1629.* Minneapolis: The University of Minnesota Press, 1940.

Wire, A. P., "An Essex Worthy: Sir Thomas Roe," *Essex Review* 20 (1911): 135.

Wood, Alfred C., *A History of the Levant Company.* London: Oxford University Press, 1935.

Wood, Anthony à, *Athenae Oxonienses. An exact history of all the writers and bishops who have had their education in the University of Oxford. To which are added the Fasti, or Annals of the said University.* A new edition with additions and a continuation by Philip Bliss . . . . London: Printed for F. C. and J. Rivington, 1813–1820.

Woodruff, Philip, *The Men Who Ruled India: The Founders of Modern India.* New York: St. Martin's Press, 1954.

Wright, Thomas, *The History and Topography of the County of Essex.* London, 1836.

INDEX

Abbot, George, archbishop of Canterbury, 154, 156, 157, 201, 202

Abbot, Sir Maurice, 110–11, 111n

Acheen, 25

Aetna, Mount. *See* Etna, Mount

Afghanistan, 49

Agra, 26, 51, 53

Ahmadabad: East India Company factory at, 77, 79; mentioned, 61, 95, 97

Ajmere: East India Company factory at, 77; mentioned, 45–47, 62, 80, 88, 121, 271

Akbar the Great, 49, 50, 52

Aldworth, Thomas, 30–31

Aleppo, 47, 121, 155

Alexandria, 21, 22, 121

Algiers, pirates of, 119, 122–23, 125, 139, 142; mentioned, 140–41, 164

Altmark, treaty of, 178, 181

Amazon, river: Roe's exploration of, 14, 15; colony near, 17, 18; mentioned, 10

Amsterdam, 175

Anne, East India Company's ship, 98, 99

Anne, Queen, 8

Anstruther, Sir Robert, 193–207

Anti-parliament, 269

Arabian Sea, 38

Armada, Spanish. *See* Spanish Armada

Arnhem, 241

Arundel and Surrey, Thomas Howard, earl of: and art treasures, 154, 155; and West

Indies Company, 197; mission to Vienna, 212, 241; mentioned, 239

Asaph Khan: personal qualities, 58; opposes English interests, 58; court connections of, 58–59; rise to power, 59; and Roe's interpreter, 62, 63; asserts friendship toward the English, 65; Roe's treaty turned over to, 65; delays Roe's proposals, 65–66, 68, 70; Roe complains to, 67; to deal with foreign ambassadors, 69, 70; tells Roe to stay away from court, 69; influence of, 72; rejects proposals, 72; alienated from Khurram, 93; won over to Roe's side, 93, 93n; mentioned, 72, 87, 88

Austria, 125, 168, 172

Aylmer, G. E., 278n

Bailie, Mr., 31

Baldwin, Stanley, 273

Baltic Sea, 167, 169, 174

Bantam, 25

Barbary, 142

Barbary pirates: prisoners of, 123, 138–42, 164, 271; mentioned, 119, 122, 123, 125, 138

Barwalde, treaty of, 183, 184

Bath, 272

Bavaria, 176, 183, 211, 248, 250–53 passim

Bavaria, duke of. *See* Maximilian, duke of Bavaria

Bedford, Lucy Russell, countess of, 154